HUMAN RIGHTS
Theory and Practice

HUMAN RIGHTS

Theory and Practice

Geetanjali

CENTRUM PRESS
NEW DELHI-110002 (INDIA)

CENTRUM PRESS
H.O.: 4360/4, Ansari Road, Daryaganj,
New Delhi-110002 (India)
Tel: 23278000, 23261597, 23255577, 23286875
B.O.: No. 1015, Ist Main Road, BSK IIIrd Stage,
IIIrd Phase, IIIrd Block, Bangalore-560085 (INDIA)
Tel: 080-41723429
Email: centrumpress@gmail.com
Visit us at: www.centrumpress.com

Human Rights: Theory and Practice

First Edition, 2011

ISBN 978-93-80921-65-5

PRINTED IN INDIA

Printed at Tarun Offset Printers, Delhi-110053

Contents

Preface *vii*

1. Introduction to the System of Human Rights 1
2. History of Human Rights 34
3. Human Security in Theory and Practice 92
4. International Human Rights Law 113
5. Regional Systems of Protection and Promotion 125
6. Freedom from Poverty 138
7. Human Rights by Issue 150
8. Passing Legislation for Human Rights 277

Bibliography 283

Index 286

Preface

Human rights are rights and freedoms to which all humans are entitled. Proponents of the concept usually assert that everyone is endowed with certain entitlements merely by reason of being human. Human rights are thus conceived in a universalist and egalitarian fashion. Such entitlements can exist as shared norms of actual human moralities, as justified moral norms or natural rights supported by strong reasons, or as legal rights either at a national level or within international law. However, there is no consensus as to the precise nature of what in particular should or should not be regarded as a human right in any of the preceding senses, and the abstract concept of human rights has been a subject of intense philosophical debate and criticism. The human rights movement emerged in the 1970s, especially from former socialists in eastern and Western Europe, with major contributions also from the United States and Latin America.

The movement quickly jelled as social activism and political rhetoric in many nations put it high on the world agenda. By the 21st century, the human rights movement expanded beyond its original anti-totalitarianism to include numerous causes involving humanitarianism and social and economic development in the Third World. The objective of this book is to provide the whole knowledge about the Human rights by which user can learn about all the concepts of this book. We hope that the concepts written in this book will help the reader to understand and learnt about the "Human Rights Theory and Practice" in a most comprehensive way.

Author

1

Introduction to the System of Human Rights

As the Universal Declaration of Human Rights states, "freedom, justice and peace in the world" are founded on the basis of "the inherent dignity and the equal and inalienable rights of all members of the human family." At the same time, every man, woman and child has the right to peace and the absence of violence.

The violation of human rights and armed conflict are often inextricably linked; systematic abuse of the human rights of particular sectors, communities or groups can result in conflict, and violent conflict in turn results in further violations of human rights. In other words, human rights are inextricably linked to issues of conflict, peace and security.

There can be no form of good governance, justice, rule of law or security without respect for human rights. Yet too often, states forego basic human rights-particularly civil and political rights-in the name of security. It can be a difficult balancing act. Since the "war on terror" was launched, for example, the civil rights of sectors of the United States population have been threatened in the name of security for the majority.

In many other countries, including Afghanistan, Colombia, Iraq and Russia, the fundamental human rights of many communities have been violated. Upholding human rights can be a challenging goal, particularly in societies with a history of violence or oppression. In such societies, violence, fear and impunity must be replaced by peace, freedom and accountability. This involves transforming the way the government interacts with citizens. Human rights must be integrated into every facet of reconstruction and institution building. This requires a commitment by the government, civil society and the international community to support, implement and enforce human rights standards. This stage provides an overview of human rights and related law in the context of conflict. It highlights the impact of human rights violations on women and provides examples of efforts to prevent, document and redress human rights violations.

WHAT ARE HUMAN RIGHTS

Human rights can be defined as the rights of all individuals regardless of sex, race, colour, language, national origin, age, class or religious or political beliefs to certain fundamental freedoms. Human rights are universal, inalienable, indivisible and interrelated. Every state has the obligation to promote universal respect for all human rights without discrimination, regardless of cultural or other differences. Every person not only has rights, but also has the responsibility of respecting the rights of others. Although modern human rights laws were formulated in the wake of World War II, they have ancient and global origins. The great religious traditions-Buddhism, Christianity, Confucianism, Hinduism, Judaism and Islam-include such universal human rights tenets as the responsibility of human beings towards others and respect for human dignity.

Philosophies around the world have long explored the nature of relations between individuals and the moral responsibilities of individuals within society. This prevalence of human rights principles in moral and religious traditions across the world makes a strong case against those who claim that human rights are a "western concept." The first recorded version of a human rights declaration dates back to 570 BC and Cyrus the Great of Persia. His Charter of Freedom of Humankind recognised the right to liberty, security, freedom of movement and residence, right of property, freedom of religion, right to work and the prohibition of slavery. Throughout the centuries, other documents established the rights and responsibilities of citizens of countries, including the Treaty of Westphalia, the Bill of Rights in Britain, the French Declaration of the Rights of Man and Citizens and the US Bill of Rights.

The founding documents for modern international human rights are called The International Bill of Human Rights and consists of the United Nations Charter, the Universal Declaration of Human Rights, the International Covenant on Civil and Political Rights and the International Covenant on Economic, Social and Cultural Rights. The UN Charter establishes the legal and conceptual framework for contemporary international human rights law. Article 1 of the UN Charter recognises that one of the UN's purposes is to promote and encourage respect for human rights and fundamental freedoms. Article 55(c) states that the United Nations shall promote "universal respect for, and observance of, human rights and fundamental freedoms for all without distinction as to race, sex, language or religion."

The Universal Declaration of Human Rights recognises the universality of human rights; the preamble states that the UDHR is a "common standard of achievement for all peoples and all nations." Although the UDHR is not a treaty, it has become a source of customary international law, meaning that states have a sense of legal obligation to observe norms and these norms are reflected in the general practice of states. The UDHR has gained widespread acceptance among states and is considered to be an authoritative interpretation of human rights in the UN Charter. The UDHR articulates political and civil rights as well as economic and social rights and has served as a basis for more than 20 international human rights treaties.

The human rights and fundamental freedoms in the UDHR include:

- Right to non-discrimination;
- Right to life, liberty and security;
- Prohibition of slavery;
- Prohibition of torture and cruel, inhuman or
- Degrading treatment or punishment;
- Right to equality before the law;

- Prohibition of arbitrary arrest, detention or exile;
- Right to a fair and public hearing;
- Right to privacy;
- Freedom of movement and residence;
- Right to nationality and citizenship;
- Right to marriage and family;
- Right to own property;
- Freedom of thought, conscience and religion;
- Freedom of opinion and expression;
- Freedom to peaceful assembly and association;
- Right to representative government;
- Right to social security;
- Right to work;
- Right to adequate standard of living;
- Right to education; and
- Right to participate in cultural life.

The ICCPR and the ICESCR treaties are legally binding. By ratifying them, states are bound to abide by their provisions. These two conventions include more detailed explanations of the rights and freedoms enumerated in the UDHR. The ICCPR covers civil and political rights, sometimes referred to as "first generation" rights. The ICESCR specifies social, economic and cultural rights, also referred to as "second generation" rights. Although the UN has reaffirmed that all human rights are equal in importance, civil and political rights have received more attention in implementation and enforcement.

Implementation of each of these conventions is monitored by a UN committee: the ICCPR by the UN Human Rights Committee and the ICESCR by the UN Committee on Economic, Social and Cultural Rights. The ICCPR has two optional protocols. A protocol supplements a treaty and adds additional procedures or provisions or interprets existing provisions in another treaty. The purpose of the first Optional Protocol to the ICCPR is to establish enforcement mechanisms by allowing individual victims of human rights abuses to communicate directly with the Committee on Human Rights. The ICESCR does not have a similar protocol for enforcement.

Numerous international documents—treaties, declarations, resolutions, recommendations, decisions and actions—have been developed in the years since the International Bill of Rights was created, addressing such human rights topics as non-discrimination, self-determination, women's rights, children's rights, prohibitions against slavery and forced labour, transitional justice and rule of law, humanitarian law and other rights and freedoms.

For example, the UN Convention Against Torture and Other Cruel, Inhuman or Degrading Treatment or Punishment came into force in 1987. Specialised international agencies of the UN, the International Labour Organization and other multilateral institutions have contributed to the recognition and respect for human rights. Regional institutions have created their own instruments to guarantee human rights, including the African Charter of Human and People's Rights, Asian Human Rights Charter, European Convention on Human Rights and the American Convention on Human Rights.

Individual governments have responded to international human rights obligations and to pressure from multilateral organisations, other governments and non-governmental organisations by formulating legislation, regulations, court decisions and pronouncements addressing human rights. All of these documents and actions have helped define, explain and expand the scope of international human rights standards.

WHAT ARE WOMEN'S HUMAN RIGHTS

Women's experiences of human rights violations are heavily coloured by their sex, gender roles and status in society. For example, they more often experience cruel, inhuman or degrading treatment through gender-based violence. They are denied economic human rights by the disproportionate impact of economic policies. They are targets of discrimination in laws pertaining to citizenship, family and property. They are denied social rights in the form of restrictive reproductive laws and policies. To elaborate on the International Bill of Human Rights instruments, in 1979 the

Convention on the Elimination of All Forms of Discrimination against Women was drafted. It came into force in 1981. In 1999 the CEDAW Optional Protocol came into force. This provides two mechanisms for enforcing the convention.

The Protocol permits women to submit claims of discrimination directly to the committee that oversees CEDAW compliance. It allows the committee to initiate its own investigations into violations of women's rights in countries that are signatories to the Protocol. CEDAW has been a touchstone for women's rights activists worldwide. It inspired numerous related declarations, policies and programmes. The 1995 Beijing Platform for Action that emerged from the Fourth World Conference on Women, is another critical and even more comprehensive document.

This and other policy documents are not legally binding, but they do supplement existing human rights instruments and set new standards in terms of governments' and the international community's commitments to women's human rights.

VIOLATIONS AGAINST WOMEN: KEY ISSUES

Human rights violations against women are often rooted in discrimination. Because of their unequal status in many societies, economic and social development, health conditions and criminal activities often have a disproportionate impact on women. Violence against women: "Any act of gender-based violence that results in, or is likely to result in, physical, sexual or psychological harm or suffering to women, including threats of such acts, coercion, or arbitrary deprivation of liberty, whether occurring in public or in private life."

Violence against women is a widespread human rights abuse around the world. Women experience violence during peace and conflict, in the home and in the workplace. Often, governments fail to prevent such violence, crimes are treated as less seriously than other types of violence, and perpetrators are not punished. Women endure mistreatment and discrimination in the law enforcement and judicial systems. Types of violence that affect women disproportionately include domestic violence, sexual assault and harassment, honour killings, harmful traditional practices such as female genital mutilation and gender-based crimes during armed conflict, specifically sexual assault and rape. Women are also particularly vulnerable to trafficking for forced labour and other illicit purposes.

Data published in 2004 reveals that 80 per cent of the victims trafficked across international borders are girls and women, and 70 per cent of those girls and women are trafficked for sexual exploitation. The disproportionate effects of this type of crime on women are often exacerbated by corruption in the government—officials who facilitate trafficking rings. Often governments react to trafficking problems by instituting laws and policies that punish trafficking victims rather than the criminals who are involved. Women political prisoners also experience gendered forms of violence and humiliation. Often sexual torture is used. Pregnant women are often threatened with beatings or having their children taken away from them. Even in cases of relatively minor actions, such as public protests, in many instances, women who are arrested can be subjected to virginity tests and penalised for so-called immoral behaviour.

Health and Reproductive Rights: Malnutrition, pregnancy complications, inadequate health access and care and increasingly, HIV/AIDS, are all problems that affect women in high numbers around the world. Violence against women, the spread of diseases, including HIV/AIDS, gender discrimination and lack of access to information and health care all make women particularly susceptible to illness and death.

Women's health rights are intertwined with various other human rights found in the Universal Declaration on Human Rights and other instruments, including the right to non-discrimination, the right to liberty and security of person, the right to life and survival, the right to be free from inhuman and degrading treatment, the right to privacy, the right to marriage and family and the right to education. Educational Rights: Girls are denied equal access to education in many countries. Of all children worldwide who receive less than four years of education, twothirds are girls. Of the 60 per cent of children worldwide who are not in school, girls are 60 per cent. Illiteracy affects girls and women disproportionately— 70 per cent of the world's illiterate are women, and more than half of the world's women over the age of 15 cannot read or write. Women's lack of education limits their political and economic opportunities. Women's education rights are linked to other fundamental human rights, including the right to equality, the right to work, the right to an adequate standard of living and freedom of thought, conscience, religion and belief.

Economic and Labour Rights: Women are 70 per cent of the world's poor and own only one per cent of the world's wealth. Overall, women have less control than men over resources, including cash, credit, property, land and wealth in societies around the world. Women in many countries around the world are denied legal rights to own, inherit or transfer property, land and wealth. These disparities affect women's full enjoyment of other human rights. In the workplace, women have fewer job opportunities than men, they are paid less and they work longer hours. Women perform unpaid domestic labour and are relegated to lower-paid sectors of the economy. Women encounter discriminatory laws and practices in the workplace. In addition, they experience a high incidence of sexual harassment and workplace violence.

Women in specific sectors, such as migrant work and domestic service, are particularly vulnerable to abuse. Women often face a double burden of domestic responsibilities in the home combined with employment outside the home. In post conflict situations, this is compounded because women are often the sole breadwinners and heads of households, and may also be faced with the effects of displacement, destruction and lack of family labour. In addition, as widows, in many societies women are discriminated against and have limited rights to inheritance, property ownership or even custody of their children. Parental and Marital Rights: Lack of equality in marriage, including limited rights to divorce and child custody, not only results in a violation of women's rights, but can also result in violence against women in the home. Civic and Political Rights: In many countries, women are denied opportunities for civic and political participation through discriminatory laws, practices and views. In addition, women are faced with poverty, lack of education, endemic violence and other constraints that prevent them from becoming involved in public life. As a result, women are under represented in political organisations and parties, elected office and formal government structures. Women face specific challenges in the areas of voter registration and voting, campaigning for political office and representation in legislatures.

ADDRESSING HUMAN RIGHTS DURING CONFLICT: WHAT LAWS EXIST

Over the centuries and across the world, attempts have been made to limit wartime behaviour and codify military conduct. The concept of war crimes is noted in Hindu codes dating back to 200 BC, while in 1625 the notion of "humanitarian treatment of civilians" was suggested. However, significant development and change can be attributed to Henri Dunant, founder of the International Committee of the Red Cross, who played a critical role in drafting the first Geneva Convention to protect the sick and wounded in wartime.

This convention, signed in 1864, was followed by a number of treaties between 1899 and 1925 relating to the use of poisonous gas and the practice of biological warfare.In the following decades, other conventions emerged, addressing issues ranging from the treatment of prisoners of war in 1929 to four conventions on the protection of civilians and shipwreck victims in 1949.

In 1977, two additional protocols to the 1949 conventions extended protection to civilians in civil war as well. Together this body of legislation is known as International Humanitarian Law. The basic protection and prohibitions stated in the four 1949 Conventions and Additional Protocols of 1977 include the following.

1. *Distinctions between soldiers and civilians*: Combatants must be clearly distinguished from civilians by wearing uniforms and carrying weapons openly. Exceptions are made for medical and religious personnel, who may wear uniforms. Medical personnel may also carry small arms to use in self-defence against illegal attacks.
   - Mercenaries are combatants who are not nationals of any party to the conflict, are often paid more than soldiers and are not protected by the conventions.
   - A civilian shooting a soldier is liable for prosecution, but a soldier shooting another soldier is not.
   - A soldier that violates the rules of separation with civilians and endangers the life of civilians is no longer protected by the conventions.
2. *Prisoners of War*: Prisoners of war must be treated humanely. Specifically they must not be subjected to torture, medical or scientific experiments of any kind. Violence towards or intimidation and public displays of POWs are illegal. POWs must not be used as human shields. They should not be exposed to danger. POWS cannot be punished for acts committed during fighting-unless the opposing side would punish its own soldiers for the same act.
3. *Treatment of journalists*: In the first three conventions, journalists were considered civilian members of the military and were protected as combatants. For example, they did not have to respond to interrogation. Their status changed in the 1977 Protocols, which explicitly recognised them as civilians. As a result, journalists cannot be deliberately targeted, detained, questioned or mistreated any more than other civilians. But it also means that journalists must not wear military uniform or carry weapons.
4. *Treatment of civilians*: The four 1949 Geneva

Conventions and the 1977 additional protocols protect civilians in wartime. Specifically:

- "Civilians are not to be attacked—either directly or indiscriminately in areas where they are present;
- There is no destruction of property unless justified by military necessity;
- Individuals and groups must not be deported, regardless of motive;
- Civilians must not be taken hostages;
- Civilians must not be subject to outrages on their dignity, and they must not be tortured, enslaved or raped;
- Civilians must not be subject to collective punishment or reprisals;
- Civilians must not receive differential treatment based on race, religion, nationality or political allegiance; and
- Warring parties must not use or develop biological or chemical weapons, and must not allow children under 15 to participate or be recruited into the armed forces."

Since the 1977 protocols, efforts have been made to raise the minimum legal age to 18 for participation in hostilities and armed forces. This is recommended in the Optional Protocol to the Convention on the Rights of the Child on the Involvement of Children in Armed Conflict. Despite resistance on the part of many states, with the changes in the nature and conduct of war and in response to advocacy efforts of the human rights community, the international legal framework is evolving.

In addition, the statutes of the International Criminal Court and indictments emerging from the international tribunals for Rwanda and the former Yugoslavia have broken new ground in the field of international law as it relates to war and the use of sexual violence. For example, as a result of rulings in cases against key commanders in the Bosnian conflict, notions of liability for rape have expanded so that individuals can be held responsible not only for committing the act, but also for planning, abetting or ordering it. They can also be held responsible for knowing that rape is taking place, but failing to stop it.

WOMEN'S HUMAN RIGHTS IN WAR AND CONFLICT

The onslaught of violence and war affects the security and human rights of men and women in society. In most instances, the basic social, economic or political rights of men and women are violated, as schools close, health care services diminish, the economy weakens and jobs are lost and militias and armed forces take over. In addition for men, enforced conscription into fighting forces, imprisonment and death are immediate dangers. Often there are greater restrictions placed on men than women in terms of travel or movement, for example. For women, the circumstances vary. While they may not be in immediate danger of conscription, they are more vulnerable to attack within their homes and communities—from security forces or criminal gangs and looters.

In Iraq, girls and working women in particular have been affected as violence on the streets and fear of kidnapping have increased. Women and girls are often deliberately targeted for sexual abuse as a means of "dishonouring" their community or "demoralising" their male cohorts in liberation or ideological struggles. In Nepal, women from areas controlled by Maoists are often targets of abuse by state security forces. In Iran, in the immediate years after the 1979 revolution, young women with "leftist" tendencies were raped in jail prior to execution, as it was said that "virgins" go to heaven. Reports of rape and even the deliberate spread of HIV/AIDS as strategies of war have been commonplace in the Democratic Republic of the Congo and elsewhere in Africa. But the emphasis on sexual violence against women and the depiction of women in conflict situations as passive, vulnerable victims detracts attention from other violations and challenges facing them. For example, in Bosnia, in the 1990s, many women did not want to draw attention to their own experiences of rape; instead they wanted to focus on the mass killings of their male relatives and the needs of the children and elderly. The focus on women as rape victims has the danger of stripping away their dignity and sense of agency. Similarly, in Afghanistan, while internationally the "burkha" was highlighted as the symbol of women's subjugation, it was not a priority for Afghan women themselves.

They were more concerned about addressing fundamental issues of survival such as access to health care, education, food and ensuring security in the streets. By definition, refugees and internally displaced women have had their most basic rights to security violated and continue to face a range of other abuses on a daily basis. In peace negotiations, women remain marginalised, and their concerns are often ignored or traded off. Post conflict—a time when there is an opportunity to redress discrimination and initiate programmes and policies that would uphold women's rights—they remain either invisible or are addressed in token projects.

DEFENDING AND UPHOLDING HUMAN RIGHTS IN CONFLICT: WHAT IS BEING DONE

Despite the existence of international laws and conventions codifying war, in reality, human rights violations take place regularly, and civilians have been increasingly caught in the crossfire. In World War I, civilian casualties accounted for an estimated 1.5 per cent of casualties. In World War II they represented 65 per cent, largely as a result of the bombing raids over cities. By the 1990s, civilians made up between 80 to 90 per cent of casualties.

Violent conflict brings such devastation that survival and the protection of life become the key goals for those who are caught in the violence and for those who choose to help. In Bosnia and Rwanda, there were countless tales of neighbours hiding neighbours from security forces or mothers shielding their children from massacre. In Central America and elsewhere, the church as an institution was critical in protecting civilians. In South Africa, the leadership of the liberation movement played a critical role in not only promoting respect for the human rights of all, but also curbing the potential violence and violations that could have occurred. On a global scale, governmental and nongovernmental humanitarian organisations and agencies are at the front lines, providing food, shelter, medical care and some security away from the violence.

The International Committee of the Red Cross was a pioneer in this field, and remains one of the world's leading movements committed to protecting the lives and dignity of victims of war and internal conflict and giving assistance. In addition, as mandated in the Geneva Conventions, the ICRC is permitted to visit prisoners of war and civilian internees, monitor their treatment in accordance with international humanitarian laws, facilitate communication with their families and have confidential dialogues about their status with the authorities holding them.

In recent years, new initiatives have emerged. For example, Peace Brigades International sends teams of volunteers into areas suffering from conflict and repression to accompany human rights activists and others threatened by political violence. Given that perpetrators of violence—particularly states—are sensitive to witnesses, PBI's presence can help stem the violations. Similarly the Non-violent Peaceforce, composed of organisations and individual members, is dedicated to establishing a trained, civilian, non-violent peace force that is sent to areas of conflict to prevent human rights violations, death and destruction and to promote a space for non-violent interaction.

In 2002, some 130 peace force delegates from 47 countries went to Sri Lanka to launch their first project. But the protection of social, economic, cultural or political human rights becomes either a secondary goal or impossible in times of conflict for the victims and for international actors. For example, despite the outcry against the humanitarian crisis in Darfur, Sudan, in 2004, the international community has not been able to stem the flow of people being forced out of their homes and villages. In the Palestinian territories, despite the Geneva Conventions stating that the destruction of property is illegal, thousands of homes and olive groves have been razed to the ground by occupying Israeli forces. In the face of such overwhelming obstacles, activists often resort to documenting the abuses they witness and reporting on them. As international organisations such as Amnesty International or Human Rights Watch state, they "investigate, and expose human rights violations and hold abusers accountable." By shedding light on the abusive practices of governments or those in power, they seek to hold them accountable to the international policy community and the public. This continuous monitoring and public reporting can be effective. For example, in 2004, reports by international organisations including the ICRC and HRW about abuses by US military personnel against civilians in detention in Afghanistan and Iraq, prompted public enquiries, punishment for some of the perpetrators and changes in practice towards other prisoners.

Journalists and the media also play a critical role. For example, reports from a United Kingdom -based newspaper prompted investigations into allegations of abuse against local women and young girls by UN peacekeepers in the DRC. In 1994, a New York–based newspaper was the first to report on the "rape camps" in Bosnia. These reports played a significant role in persuading the UN system to establish war crimes tribunals. Local groups including NGOs are also key actors. Often they have access to areas in conflict and through their networks and ties with communities are able to gather information without putting their contacts in danger.

They are also often trusted more locally and are thus able to elicit more information. In South Asia, for example, the South Asia Forum for Human Rights brings together human rights and peace activists in public dialogues. The organisation works with local media to build their capacities in reporting on the war and issues of human rights abuse. They also conduct "peace audits" to monitor governments' commitments to peace processes. A different approach was taken by the women of Las Madres de la Plaza de Mayo in Argentina. Throughout the worst years of the military dictatorship in the 1970s and 1980s, they held vigils and peaceful protests, carrying poster-size portraits of their missing children and relatives, which exposed the rampant human rights abuses of the regime. Many groups advocate for justice, redress and an end to impunity for crimes committed during war. Lawyers often form associations to advocate for human rights legislation. They also can become champions of human rights in court, taking on critical cases. For example, the 2003 Nobel Laureate, Shirin Ebadi, is renowned for not only fighting for women's and children's legal rights, but also seeking to frame these rights in the context of Islamic law.

The documentation of abuses serves as the basis for their claims. In addition, in Bosnia, for example, local women's organisations provided counselling to victims and assisted their preparations for appearances as witnesses at the international tribunal. In many instances, organisations also develop human rights training programmes targeting key governmental security and legal personnel. This has a dual purpose. On the one hand they raise awareness and understanding of human rights law among entities that are often accused of abusing rights. On the other hand, training sessions can provide a venue for interactions that lead to increased governmental/civil society cooperation on the development of policies, legislation and increased support for human rights principles.

ADDRESSING CLAIMS AND ENFORCING LAWS: WHAT MECHANISMS EXIST?

INTERNATIONAL LEVEL

Internationally, and within the UN system, a number of mechanisms exist through which NGOs and other groups or individuals can report human rights violations.

Key institutions at the international level include:

- *UN Commission on Human Rights*: This commission consists of 53 member states elected by the UN Economic and Social Council. It conducts fact-finding studies and discussions about human rights issues in countries that come to its attention, without requiring the approval of the related government.

Under a specific procedure created by ECOSOC, the Commission can consider cases of massive violations of human rights that are brought to attention by individuals or groups. If the Commission decides to consider the case, the accused government is invited to participate in the proceedings. The proceedings are otherwise confidential, and there is no communication with the author of the complaint.

- *UN Human Rights Committee*: This committee of 18 independent experts was established to monitor implementation of the ICCPR. The Committee examines progress reports from states, considers state complaints against other states and addresses individual complaints by victims. The Committee can consider individual complaints against states that have ratified the ICCPR and the first Protocol to the ICCPR. The Committee makes factual and legal findings and produces non-binding recommendations.
- *UN Committee on Economic, Social and Cultural Rights*: This Committee receives formal NGO submissions and oral statements and organises discussions with experts relating to human rights embodied in the ICESCR. The Committee does not accept individual complaints.
- *UN Commission on the Status of Women*: The purpose of this Commission is to promote implementation of the principle of equal rights. The Commission prepares recommendations and reports to ECOSOC on promoting women's rights in political, economic, civil, social and educational fields.
- *UN Committee on the Elimination of All Forms of Discrimination Against Women*: This UN Committee reports on and monitors the implementation of CEDAW. Signatory governments are required to submit reports on their progress. NGOs can communicate with the Committee and can submit "shadow reports" on countries' compliance with CEDAW. Under the CEDAW Optional Protocol, the

Committee can accept individual complaints, but enforcement is weak.

- *UN Committee Against Torture*: This UN Committee accepts individual complaints and communications under certain circumstances. It issues general comments on themes relating to the right to be free from torture and cruel, inhuman and degrading treatment and punishment.

REGIONAL LEVEL

Regional mechanisms for reporting human rights violations include:

- *The Inter-American Commission on Human Rights*: The Commission is part of the Organization of American States and was created by the American Convention on Human Rights. It receives individual, group and NGO petitions, observes human rights situations, publishes reports, conducts on-site visits, organises conferences and meetings and recommends various measures to governments. The procedure for submitting an individual complaint is as follows: the state that is the subject of the complaint must be a member of the OAS. The petitioner must have exhausted all domestic remedies. The petitioner must submit the complaint within six months after the final decision in the country. The Commission issues a report with conclusions and recommendations and has the option of referring the case to the Inter-American Court of Human Rights.
- *The Inter-American Commission of Women*: This commission is the advisory body to the OAS in all matters relevant to women in the Western Hemisphere and reports to the governments and offers recommendations. Cases can be submitted directly to the CIM.
- *The African Commission on Human and People's Rights*: The Commission considers complaints by individuals and groups against states as well as complaints by

one state against another. The Commission can only issue recommendations to governments, not binding decisions.

- *The European Court of Human Rights*: The process for submitting a complaint is as follows: an individual can file a case, the Court determines if it is admissible, the Court seeks a settlement; if no settlement is reached, the Court makes a decision on the merits of the case. The Court allows human rights advocates to initiate cases, inform the Court and play a role in settlements.
- *The European Committee for the Prevention of Torture*: Any citizen of the Council of Europe can invoke the Convention on Torture. Recent justice mechanisms established in post conflict situations including the International Criminal Tribunal for the former Yugoslavia and the International Criminal Tribunal for Rwanda- and the mixed international and national mechanisms created in places such as East Timor, Sierra Leone, Cambodia and Iraq-have been important in bringing accountability to major perpetrators of war crimes, crimes against humanity and genocide. The International Criminal Court which came into effect in 2002 as a permanent international judicial mechanism for addressing these types of crimes committed by individuals, is also a milestone. But these mechanisms cannot and do not provide redress for all victims. Nor do they appear to prevent other atrocities.

As a 2004 Human Rights Watch World Report notes, there is still a lack of political will and systematic follow up to hold violators accountable. Consequently, there remains "an extraordinary and awful gap between existing international legal standards and practice."

PROMOTING OF HUMAN RIGHTS FOR CULTURE AND CONFLICT SOCIETIES

In societies where the abuse of human rights—be it political persecution or general oppression of the public or particular sectors—has been normal practice, change takes time. In many instances, there is no understanding or acceptance that certain practices are abusive. This is particularly true when it relates to violations against women—whether domestic violence or public harassment. Creating change and building the foundations of understanding and respect for human rights is a long and multifaceted process.

It requires political leadership, strong legislation and effective enforcement mechanisms, together with extensive education and public awareness-raising in community and religious institutions, schools, the workplace, as well as through the media. While the challenges are great, in the aftermath of war and conflict, societies and political leaders often have the opportunity not only to reflect on the devastation caused by war and human rights violations, but may be committed to pursuing policies and values that would prevent the resurgence of atrocities.

Civil society groups too are often mobilised and committed to righting past wrongs. International attention and financial and technical support are also available to initiate changes ranging from the adoption of new policies, legislation and programmes that promote human rights ideals to the establishment of mechanisms to monitor adherence. At the national level, state institutions with the mandates, capabilities and willingness to ensure respect for human rights can be created.

Legislative and judicial systems can be designed and given the task of protecting human rights and women's rights. A fundamental requirement for the protection of human rights is judicial independence. The judiciary must be mandated and equipped to provide legal redress for victims of women's human rights abuses. Judicial mechanisms can be used to enforce women's human rights. For example, international human rights standards can be brought into the courts through individual cases—litigation is a valuable tool to force changes to the legal system. In addition, civil society can advocate for the establishment of human rights commissions or offices to monitor implementation of human rights and women's rights.

Training programmes can be developed to ensure that staff understand and accept human rights and women's rights principles. In addition, other mechanisms can be established to monitor human rights and provide redress for victims of violations. In some countries, human rights commissions are addressing the issues. They can be given a broad mandate to review law and practice, educate people about the importance of human rights, advise governments, litigate human rights issues by supporting individual applicants, take cases to court and intervene in cases. In South Africa, a Human Rights Commission was established in accordance with the 1996 constitution.

Its objectives include awareness-raising and providing human rights education, making recommendations to the state regarding the implementation of human rights laws, undertaking studies regarding human rights issues and violations for parliament and investigating complaints and seeking redress in cases where human rights have been violated. Such mechanisms must come together with not only extensive public understanding of basic human rights, but also changes in social and cultural attitudes.

One of the greatest challenges is to nurture and establish a culture of governmental and state accountability regarding respect for human rights NGOs and other civil society organisations, such as trade unions or professional associations, play a key role in advocating for, and monitoring adherence to, international human rights standards and women's rights. For example, Amnesty International has run human rights awareness training programmes in Somaliland and elsewhere for civil society and government representatives. The aim was to build knowledge of general human rights issues—from political and civil rights to cultural and developmentrelated rights—in different fields and activities. The Institute of War and Peace Reporting focuses on intensive trainings for journalists in conflict-affected societies to raise standards of journalism as well as awareness of human rights. In the South and North Caucuses, IWPR has worked with journalists, not only building their capacities, but also improving communication across a region that is rife with misunderstanding and distrust. In Central Asia, Freedom House—an international NGO promoting political and economic freedom—is supporting and strengthening the work of human rights defenders in Uzbekistan, Tajikistan, Kyrgyzstan and Kazakhstan. In Algeria, the organisation is supporting human rights groups working on issues relating to people still missing and "disappeared" in the aftermath of Algeria's bloody civil war. Human rights education is another means of gradually building understanding and support for human rights. The Human Rights Education Association operates internationally, training activists, assisting in the development of curricula and teaching materials, supporting institutional development and strengthening networks of human rights activists. For example in Croatia, HREA helped develop human rights teaching materials aimed at elementary and secondary schools.

Human rights education can also be integrated into cultural events, theatre and media. For example, in 2004 in the UK and US, the "documentary theatre" piece "Guantanamo, Honour Bound to Defend Freedom" was performed, drawing on spoken evidence from the US base where hundreds of detainees in the "war on terror" are kept. It is a powerful means of bringing wider public attention to the experiences of individuals caught in the system.

Across Africa, particularly in war-torn countries, local and traditional theatre is used to convey messages of human rights. In South Africa, for example, a travelling theatre company performs short plays in secondary schools depicting social pressures that force teenagers into having unsafe sex. Through interaction with students the performance conveys messages of HIV prevention, as well as self-dignity and notions of reproductive rights.

FOCUSING ON WOMEN'S HUMAN RIGHTS

Human rights advocates use constitutional guarantees and international laws, norms and mechanisms to hold governments accountable for respecting human rights, to broaden the conception of human rights and to improve monitoring and enforcement of human rights standards. Women's human rights advocacy uses similar strategies to improve respect for women's human rights. Advocacy may focus on laws and policies that affect women, on national, regional and international institutions that are involved in enforcing human rights and on prevalent attitudes in society.

Women's rights advocacy involves a number of steps:

- Identifying the issues through research, fact finding and consultation;
- Addressing the rights and needs through practical programmes and projects;
- Gaining acceptance of the right in the law through political action, awareness-raising and education; and
- Enforcing rights through monitoring and litigation.

The global Women's Initiative for Gender Justice operates through a network of groups and individuals committed to strengthening women's human rights and building capacities among women and institutions to use international mechanisms ranging from the ICC to CEDAW and others. Founded in 1997, the group has also been effective at raising awareness and support for women's human rights among mainstream human rights organisations, government and UN personnel. Other international women's NGOs such as Madre, which are active in conflict-affected areas, address human rights issues through support of grassroots organisations and the implementation of practical programmes.

Madre addresses "sustainable development; community improvement and women's health; violence and war; discrimination and racism; self determination and collective rights; women's leadership development; and human rights education." Similarly the UK-based NGO Womankind Worldwide educates women on human rights issues through practical programmes within their "four literacies" model:

- Body literacy—building women's knowledge of their physical and mental health needs, addressing taboos and making decisions based on facts not fears;
- Civil literacy—deepening understanding and

knowledge of political and civil rights and promoting participation in decision-making;

- Word literacy—supporting women's education, encouraging reading, writing and creativity; and
- Money literacy—building numeric skills and understanding of basic economics and encouraging entrepreneurship.

Women's Learning Partnership for Rights, Development and Peace also works globally and in partnership with local organisations. Its primary focus is to build women's leadership capacities and to bridge the digital divide by providing women with alternative means of communication and interaction. Across Asia, Africa and the Middle East, WLP has worked with national partners to promote understanding of women's human rights and develop strategies to overcome discrimination and address gender-based violence.

At the national level, too, women's rights advocates focus on legislative, policy and programmatic issues. In South Africa, for example, during the transition from apartheid to democracy, over 90 organisations from across the political spectrum came together to form the Women's National Coalition. Over two years, they consulted some three million women and emerged with a twelve-point Women's Charter. By virtue of being extensive, the process proved that women's rights advocates had a strong national constituency whose demands had to be addressed.

The Charter was drawn on during the drafting of the constitution. In Afghanistan, in spite of the security risks, the Afghan Women's Network mobilised support across ethnic lines and among rural and urban communities in 2003 to draft a 16-point Women's Bill of Rights. The bill addresses a wide range of issues affecting women from their lack of political participation to their demands for equal rights in inheritance and the right to seek divorce. While attaining all of these rights may be a long-term goal and ideal, articulating and presenting them as the result of an extensive consultation helps to raise awareness and discussion about the issues and to have at least some key points incorporated into legislation. This in turn provides a legal framework upon which future advocacy efforts can be built. Often in grassroots communities, women are unaware of their human rights and do not understand how human rights are directly relevant to their lives. NGOs can combine practical assistance with human rights training and awareness. For example in Colombia, the NGO Limpal assists internally displaced women by running income-generating projects, providing education on women's constitutional rights and advocating on behalf of the internally displaced.

In Rwanda, women's groups such as Benimpuhwe have built homes for female-headed households, launched projects to provide communities with accessible potable water and initiated training programmes in agriculture for women. Through these practical efforts the organisation has reached grassroots groups and raised awareness about a range of human rights issues, including health, nutrition and reproductive rights.

Effective advocacy for women's human rights at the local level also requires an understanding of local laws and practices as they affect women, so that context-specific approaches can be developed. For example, NGOs in Egypt found that it was more effective to educate local communities about the harmful effects of FGM than to teach the International Bill on Human Rights in the abstract. Elsewhere, NGOs have targeted community members who perform FGM, informed them of the long-term damage that is caused, and enlisted them in advocacy efforts.

The struggle to attain equal rights at the risk of cultural and political backlash is a common challenge for women's rights advocates worldwide. Groups have taken different approaches. For example, across the Arab world, with support from the United Nations Development Fund for Women, women's groups have engaged religious leaders in the debate on CEDAW and its compatibility with Islamic Sharia law. The goal of such efforts is to gain acceptance of the principles enshrined in CEDAW within the local cultural and political arena. In this way resistance to its ratification is limited, and at the point of implementation, advocates can draw on a wider base for support. Ultimately, the struggle for women's human rights cannot be undertaken either in a vacuum, removed from society at large or merely at the margins. Raising awareness among and mobilising women is one important step. Building support among men and leaders is another.

TAKING STRATEGIC ACTION: WHAT CAN WOMEN PEACE BUILDERS DO

- Design and initiate training and education programmes in human rights and gender equality for all branches of government and ministries, departments and offices, including members of the military establishment, the security forces, the police and the judiciary.
  - Expand education and training on women's human rights into other sectors where women experience discrimination.
  - Teach women's human rights to civil society organisations and to community and religious leaders.
- Build support among local leaders, parliamentarians and government officials to integrate human rights protections for women into all policies and legislation.
- Advocate for the ratification of regional and international human rights instruments, including CEDAW.
- Press for investigations and prosecutions in cases of human rights abuses.
  - Engage in dialogue with government representatives about specific human rights issues and cases.
  - Form alliances with human rights organisations and other civil society groups at the international, regional and national levels to pool resources and reach a wider audience with your message.
- Propose new laws or amendments to existing laws to eliminate discrimination against women.

- Support judicial independence and legal authority to consider human rights violations against women.
- Use the domestic court system, regional and international commissions and courts and other available mechanisms to adjudicate individual cases of human rights violations against women.

- Analyse government actions regarding women's human rights and highlight areas where improvement is needed.
  - Track human rights practices over time.
  - Gather evidence of gross violations of human rights.
- Provide information to human rights commissions or offices in your country and to regional and international bodies about government progress in supporting women's human rights.
- Utilise various forms of media—print, radio and television—to inform the public in your country about women's human rights issues and cases.
- Initiate letter-writing campaigns and circulate petitions.

A SELECTED LIST OF HUMAN RIGHTS

The following human rights are protected under international law:

- *Life, liberty and physical integrity of the person*: This includes the right to be treated with humanity and dignity and with due process of law, and prohibitions on arbitrary killing and detention, torture and other cruel treatment.
- *Civic freedoms*: Basic freedoms protected include freedom of thought, opinion and expression, freedom of religious belief and practice, of movement within a state, and the right to peaceful assembly and association. Other civil rights include the protection of privacy and family life, and the right to equality before the law.

- *Political rights*: In addition to freedom of speech and association, international law protects rights to participate in public affairs, and to vote in free and fair elections.
- *Employees' rights*: International law protects workers' rights to associate, to organise and bargain collectively, and to a safe and healthy work environment and provides guarantees for a living wage and reasonable working hours. Discrimination in employment and in the workplace is prohibited.
- *Economic and social rights*: International law guarantees the right to education, to work, to the highest attainable standard of physical and mental health, and to an adequate standard of living, including food and housing.
- *Right to a clean and healthy environment*: This right is protected especially in situations where environmental hazards harm other rights, including to life, health or privacy
- *Children's rights*: In addition to the general protection of human rights law, children enjoy particular rights including the right to have decisions made in their best interests. International law also prohibits child labour, employment that might endanger their health or safety, and the exploitation of children.
- *Access to information*: This includes the right to receive information held by public or private bodies where key public interests are at stake or where it is essential to protect other human rights.
- *Rights of special groups*: International law protects the rights of indigenous peoples, linguistic, religious or racial minorities, the disabled and the elderly. It prohibits discrimination and exploitation of such groups.
- *Right to justice*: This includes the right to redress for victims of human rights abuses, and punishment for perpetrators. International law also guarantees access

to courts and other procedures, so that further abuses can be prevented.

- *International law prohibits discrimination*: This includes on grounds including race, colour, sex, language, religion, political opinion, national or social origin, birth or other status. It also prohibits forced or bonded labour, and slavery.
- *Scope of human rights protection*: Human rights as protected in international law are not absolute. Most rights are subject to restrictions where public security or the rights of others require it. Many rights can be further restricted in situations of national emergency. With respect to economic, social and cultural rights, it is recognised that states' duties are subject to resource constraints. States are expected to realise these rights progressively.

LINKS BETWEEN DECENTRALISATION AND HUMAN RIGHTS

In what ways does devolution of power influence respect for human rights? What opportunities arise for human rights advocacy in relation to local government? Our point of departure is that impacts may be positive, negative or both. We certainly do not assume that decentralisation necessarily improves respect for human rights.

In many situations, the effect may be negative – and this risk will no doubt be greater where decentralisation is designed and implemented without taking account of human rights. We begin, however, by discussing ways in which decentralisation may have a positive effect on respect for human rights. Later on, we list some of the risks that may occur when powers of local government are increased.

WHEN MIGHT DECENTRALISATION IMPROVE PROTECTION OF HUMAN RIGHTS?

When it Enhances Political Rights

The Universal Declaration of Human Rights protects "the

right to take part in the government of [one's] country" and provides that "[t]he will of the people shall be the basis of the authority of government..." When decentralisation establishes local democracy where none existed before, this will be a definite gain for democratic rights. In India, for example, decentralisation considerably widened "the democratic base of the Indian polity". Every five years some 3.4 million representatives are elected if one includes all the village councils, and district, city and town authorities.

When it Leads to More Effective Government

Decentralisation ought to improve governance and public administration. Where power is devolved and exercised closer to the population served, at least in theory those in authority should be in a better position to act responsibly and accountably than office-holders who operate at a greater distance.

Effective enjoyment of rights requires governments to administer many types of programmes and institutions. Fair trials and due process of law require effective courts. Basic civil rights require the establishment and maintenance of official records.

Freedoms of assembly and association, and rights to privacy and protection from harassment, require effective police forces. The protection of health and provision of education require governments to finance and administer health centres and schools, and provide sanitation and water supplies, veterinary services etc. All these services may be managed more accountably and efficiently at local level. Where this is achieved, devolution of responsibility should lead to improved respect for human rights.

When it Helps Achieve Economic and Social Rights

It is usually claimed that decentralisation will deliver basic services more efficiently. These services normally include housing, education, and health care. International law protects basic economic and social rights. If a rural population has better access to schools and health centres, or safe drinking water, as a result of decentralisation, then decentralisation can be seen to have improved protection of these rights. In the Philippines, survey respondents have consistently said that health services have improved since local governments assumed responsibility for them. Further, "while there is no systematic data yet, anecdotal evidence indicates that the socio-economic benefits from decentralisation appear quite strong".

When it Promotes Accountability

If government becomes more democratic – at regional, district and village level – people are more likely to believe that they can influence decisions that affect them, and to act accordingly. The notion of accountability is one of the core justifications for empowering local government, and accountability is exercised by participation.

Through participation in elections and official meetings, members of the public can ensure that their views are sought and heard. The idea that governments should be accountable, and that any person may properly seek remedies when their rights are abused, is central to human rights. If populations, which have been marginalised or have never exercised political influence, perceive that they can influence decisions through local democracy, they are likely to be more willing to assert their rights.

There is no surer way to retard respect for human rights than spreading the belief that speaking up is pointless. In the Philippines, "Nation wide survey data shows that citizens are more satisfied with their local governments than with the national government and feel they are more able to influence the former than the latter". Similarly, in China, elections have been permitted at village level, where citizens are able to vote for candidates of their choice. Outside observers have detected in this process the "signs of a democratic spirit" which, if developed, could have far reaching implications in the country.

When it Increases Local Autonomy and Empowers Disadvantaged Group

In certain cases, decentralisation and increased autonomy

– for minority linguistic, religious or ethnic groups – may be linked explicitly. District and regional boundaries may be redrawn to ensure that a particular group is in the majority. In Uganda, eleven entirely new districts have been formed in the past five years specifically to give a political and territorial form to ethnic or linguistic groups. Where the population of rural areas is predominantly indigenous, or otherwise distinct from the urban population, establishing local democracy can enhance their autonomy and their control over policies that affect them.

The best planned decentralisation processes widen and deepen democracy. This creates opportunities to bring disadvantaged or marginalised groups into the electoral process. A proportion of seats on local councils may be reserved for women, indigenous groups or lower castes.

- In India, A large number of formerly excluded groups and communities are now included in these decision-making bodies. As the Indian population has 14.3% Scheduled Castes and 8% Scheduled Tribes, about 660,000 elected members, *i.e.*, 22.5% of the total membership in the rural and urban local bodies will be from Scheduled Castes and Tribes.

The right of women to vote may first be recognised at local level. Broadening democracy creates real opportunities to improve protection of women's rights. Where women have been prevented from participating in national politics, their involvement in local elections may be promoted.

In India, for example, one-third of all seats and all chairpersons are reserved for women—so over one million women are elected to 3 tiers of panchayats. Even where affirmative action programmes are not in place, women often participate more actively in local politics. In the Philippines, women make up 25% of elected local government officials. When Bolivia decentralised, it legally recognised local forms of organisation and involved them.

The law on citizen participation affirmed that civil society organisations, including ethnically-based ones, were the principal discussion partners of local government. As a result many indigenous and peasant organisations have participated in the work of local authorities and in managing their affairs. Bolivia's experience has confirmed that, while the process is a long-term one, local actors have been willing to assume responsibility and take care of the institutions and financial resources that decentralisation has made available.

2

History of Human Rights

The history of human rights involves religious, cultural, philosophical and legal developments throughout recorded history. While the modern human rights movement hugely expanded in post-World War II era, the concept can be traced through all major religions, cultures and philosophies.

Ancient Hindu law, Confucianism, the Quran and the Ten Commandments all outline some of the rights now included in the Universal Declaration of Human Rights. The concept of natural law, guaranteeing natural rights despite varying human laws and customs, can be traced back to Ancient Greek philosophers, while Enlightenment philosophers suggest a social contract between the rulers and the ruled.

The world's first Buddhist state in India, known as the Maurya Empire, established the world's first welfare system, including free hospitals and education. The African concept of ubuntu is a cultural view of what it is to be human. Modern human rights thinking is descended from these many traditions of human values and beliefs.

PREMATURE HISTORY OF HUMAN RIGHTS

ANCIENT WORLD

While it is known that the reforms of Urukagina of Lagash, the earliest known legal code, must have addressed the concept of rights to some degree, the actual text of his decrees has not yet been found. The oldest legal codex extant today is the Neo-Sumerian Code of Ur-Nammu. Several other sets of laws were also issued in Mesopotamia, including the Code of Hammurabi one of the most famous examples of this type of document. It shows rules, and punishments if those rules are broken, on a variety of matters, including women's rights, men's rights, children's rights and slave rights. The prefaces of these codes invoked the Mesopotamian gods for divine sanction. Societies have often derived the origins of human rights in religious documents. The Vedas, the Bible, the Qur'an and the Analects of Confucius are also among the early written sources that address questions of people's duties, rights, and responsibilities.

MAURYA EMPIRE

The Maurya Empire of ancient India established unprecedented principles of civil rights in the 3rd century BC under Ashoka the Great. After his brutal conquest of Kalinga in circa 265 BC, he felt remorse for what he had done, and as a result, adopted Buddhism. From then, Ashoka, who had been described as "the cruel Ashoka" eventually came to be known as "the pious Ashoka".

During his reign, he pursued an official policy of nonviolence and the protection of human rights, as his chief concern was the happiness of his subjects. The unnecessary slaughter or mutilation of animals was immediately abolished, such as sport hunting and branding. The first welfare state was established. Ashoka also showed mercy to those imprisoned, allowing them outside one day each year, and offered common citizens free education at universities. He treated his subjects as equals regardless of their religion, politics or caste, and constructed free hospitals for both humans and animals.

Ashoka defined the main principles of nonviolence, tolerance of all sects and opinions, obedience to parents, respect for teachers and priests, being liberal towards friends, humane treatment of servants, and generosity towards all. These reforms are described in the Edicts of Ashoka. In the Maurya Empire, citizens of all religions and ethnic groups also had rights to freedom, tolerance, and equality. The need for tolerance on an egalitarian basis can be found in the Edicts of Ashoka, which emphasize the importance of tolerance in public policy by the government. The slaughter or capture of prisoners of war was also condemned by Ashoka. Some sources claim that slavery was also non-existent in ancient India. Other state, however, that slavery existed in ancient India, where it is recorded in the Sanskrit Laws of Manu of the 1st century BC.

EARLY ISLAMIC CALIPHATE

Many reforms in human rights took place under Islam between 610 and 661, including the period of Muhammad's mission and the rule of the four immediate successors who established the Rashidun Caliphate. Historians generally agree that Muhammad preached against what he saw as the social evils of his day, and that Islamic social reforms in areas such as social security, family structure, slavery, and the rights of women and ethnic minorities improved on what was present in existing Arab society at the time. For example, just as to Bernard Lewis, Islam "from the first denounced aristocratic privilege, rejected hierarchy, and adopted a formula of the career open to the talents."

John Esposito sees Muhammad as a reformer who condemned practices of the pagan Arabs such as female infanticide, exploitation of the poor, usury, murder, false contracts, and theft. Bernard Lewis believes that the egalitarian nature of Islam "represented a very considerable advance on the practice of both the Greco-Roman and the ancient Persian world." Muhammed also incorporated Arabic and Mosaic laws and customs of the time into his divine revelations. The Constitution of Medina, also known as the Charter of Medina, was drafted by Muhammad in 622.

It constituted a formal agreement between Muhammad and all of the significant tribes and families of Yathrib, including Muslims, Jews, and pagans. The document was drawn up with the explicit concern of bringing to an end the bitter inter tribal fighting between the clans of the Aws and Khazraj within Medina. To this effect it instituted a number of rights and responsibilities for the Muslim, Jewish and pagan communities of Medina bringing them within the fold of one community-the Ummah. The Constitution established the security of the community, freedom of religion, the role of Medina as a haram or sacred place, the security of women, stable tribal relations within Medina, a tax system for supporting the community in time of conflict, parametres for exogenous political alliances, a system for granting protection of individuals, a judicial system for resolving disputes, and also regulated the paying of blood-wite.

Muhammad made it the responsibility of the Islamic government to provide food and clothing, on a reasonable basis, to captives, regardless of their religion. If the prisoners were in the custody of a person, then the responsibility was on the individual. Lewis states that Islam brought two major changes to ancient slavery which were to have far-reaching consequences. "One of these was the presumption of freedom; the other, the ban on the enslavement of free persons except in strictly defined circumstances," Lewis continues. The position of the Arabian slave was "enormously improved": the Arabian slave "was now no longer merely a chattel but was also a human being with a certain religious and hence a social status and with certain quasi-legal rights."

Esposito states that reforms in women's rights affected marriage, divorce, and inheritance. Women were not accorded with such legal status in other cultures, including the West, until centuries later. The Oxford Dictionary of Islam states that the general improvement of the status of Arab women included prohibition of female infanticide and recognizing women's full personhood. "The dowry, previously regarded as a bride-price paid to the father, became a nuptial gift retained by the wife as part of her personal property." Under Islamic law, marriage was no longer viewed as a "status" but rather as a "contract", in which the woman's consent was imperative. "Women were given inheritance rights in a patriarchal society that had previously restricted inheritance to male relatives." Annemarie Schimmel states that "compared to the pre-Islamic position of women, Islamic legislation meant an enormous progress; the woman has the right, at least just as to the letter of the law, to administer the wealth she has brought into the family or has earned by her own work." Watt explains: "At the time Islam began, the conditions of women were terrible—they had no right to own property, were supposed to be the property of the man, and if the man died everything went to his sons." Muhammad, however, by "instituting rights of property ownership, inheritance, education and divorce, gave women certain basic safeguards." Haddad and Esposito state that "Muhammad granted women rights and privileges in the sphere of family life, marriage, education, and economic endeavors, rights that help improve women's status in society."

However, other writers have argued that women before Islam were more liberated drawing most often on the first marriage of Muhammad and that of Muhammad's parents, but also on other points such as worship of female idols at Mecca. Sociologist Robert Bellah argues that Islam in its seventh-century origins was, for its time and place, "remarkably modern in the high degree of commitment, involvement, and participation expected from the rank-and-file members of the community." This is because, he argues, that Islam emphasized the equality of all Muslims, where leadership positions were open to all. Dale Eickelman writes that Bellah suggests "the early Islamic community placed a particular value on individuals, as opposed to collective or group responsibility."

MAGNA CARTA

Magna Carta is an English charter originally issued in 1215. Magna Carta was the most significant early influence on the extensive historical process that led to the rule of constitutional law today. Magna Carta influenced the development of the common law and many constitutional documents, such as the United States Constitution and Bill of Rights. Magna Carta was originally written because of disagreements amongst Pope Innocent III, King John and the English barons about the rights of the King. Magna Carta required the King to renounce certain rights, respect certain legal procedures and accept that his will could be bound by the law. It explicitly protected certain rights of the King's subjects, whether free or fettered — most notably the writ of habeas corpus, allowing appeal against unlawful imprisonment. For modern times, the most enduring legacy of Magna Carta is considered the right of habeas corpus. This right arises from what are now known as clauses 36, 38, 39, and 40 of the 1215 Magna Carta.

The Magna Carta also included the right to due process:

- "No Freeman shall be taken or imprisoned, or be disseised of his Freehold, or Liberties, or free Customs, or be outlawed, or exiled, or any other wise destroyed; nor will We not pass upon him, nor condemn him, but by lawful judgment of his Peers, or by the Law of the Land. As suggested, sell to no man, as suggested, not deny or defer to any man either Justice or Right."

MODERN HUMAN RIGHTS MOVEMENT

The conquest of the Americas in the 16th century by the Spanish resulted in vigourous debate about human rights in Spain. The debate from 1550-51 between Las Casas and Juan Ginés de Sepúlveda at Valladolid was probably the first on the topic of human rights in European history. Several 17th and 18th century European philosophers, most notably John Locke, developed the concept of natural rights, the notion that people are naturally free and equal. Though Locke believed natural rights were derived from divinity since humans were creations of God, his ideas were important in the development of the modern notion of rights.

Lockean natural rights did not rely on citizenship nor any law of the state, nor were they necessarily limited to one particular ethnic, cultural or religious group. Two major revolutions occurred that century in the United States and in France. The Virginia Declaration of Rights of 1776 sets up a number of fundamental rights and freedoms. The later United States Declaration of Independence includes concepts of natural rights and famously states "that all men are created equal, that they are endowed by their Creator with certain unalienable rights, that among these are life, liberty and the pursuit of happiness." Similarly, the French Declaration of the Rights of Man and Citizen defines a set of individual and collective rights of the people. These are, in the document, held to be universal - not only to French citizens but to all men without exception.

1800 AD TO WORLD WAR I

Philosophers such as Thomas Paine, John Stuart Mill and Hegel expanded on the theme of universality during the 18th and 19th centuries. In 1831 William Lloyd Garrison wrote in a newspaper called The Liberator that he was trying to enlist his readers in "the great cause of human rights" so the term human rights probably came into use sometime between Paine's The Rights of Man and Garrison's publication.

In 1849 a contemporary, Henry David Thoreau, wrote about human rights in his treatise On the Duty of Civil Disobedience which was later influential on human rights and civil rights thinkers. United States Supreme Court Justice David Davis, in his 1867 opinion for Ex Parte Milligan, wrote "By the protection of the law, human rights are secured; withdraw that protection and they are at the mercy of wicked rulers or the clamor of an excited people." Many groups and movements have managed to achieve profound social changes over the course of the 20th century in the name of human rights. In Western Europe and North America, labour unions brought about laws granting workers the right to strike, establishing minimum work conditions and forbidding or regulating child labour.

The women's rights movement succeeded in gaining for many women the right to vote. National liberation movements in many countries succeeded in driving out colonial powers. One of the most influential was Mahatma Gandhi's movement to free his native India from British rule.

Movements by long-oppressed racial and religious minorities succeeded in many parts of the world, among them the civil rights movement, and more recent diverse identity politics movements, on behalf of women and minorities in the

United States. The foundation of the International Committee of the Red Cross, the 1864 Lieber Code and the first of the Geneva Conventions in 1864 laid the foundations of International humanitarian law, to be further developed follc ving the two World Wars.

BETWEEN WORLD WAR I AND WORLD WAR II

The League of Nations was established in 1919 at the negotiations over the Treaty of Versailles following the end of World War I. The League's goals included disarmament, preventing war through collective security, settling disputes between countries through negotiation, diplomacy and improving global welfare.

Enshrined in its Charter was a mandate to promote many of the rights which were later included in the Universal Declaration of Human Rights. The League of Nations had mandates to support many of the former colonies of the Western European colonial powers during their transition from colony to independent state. Established as an agency of the League of Nations, and now part of United Nations, the International Labour Organization also had a mandate to promote and safeguard certain of the rights later included in the UDHR:

- "The primary goal of the ILO today is to promote opportunities for women and men to obtain decent and productive work, in conditions of freedom, equity, security and human dignity".

AFTER WORLD WAR II

Rights in War and the Geneva Conventions

The Geneva Conventions came into being between 1864 and 1949 as a result of efforts by Henry Dunant, the founder of the International Committee of the Red Cross. The conventions safeguard the human rights of individuals involved in conflict, and follow on from the 1899 and 1907 Hague Conventions, the international community's first attempt to define laws of war. Despite first being framed before

World War II, the conventions were revised as a result of World War II and readopted by the international community in 1949.

The Geneva Conventions are:

- First Geneva Convention "for the Amelioration of the Condition of the Wounded and Sick in Armed Forces in the Field"
- Second Geneva Convention "for the Amelioration of the Condition of Wounded, Sick and Shipwrecked Members of Armed Forces at Sea"
- Third Geneva Convention "relative to the Treatment of Prisoners of War"
- Fourth Geneva Convention "relative to the Protection of Civilian Persons in Time of War"

In addition, there are three additional amendment protocols to the Geneva Convention:

- *Protocol I*: Protocol Additional to the Geneva Conventions of 12 August 1949, and relating to the Protection of Victims of International Armed Conflicts. As of 12 January 2007 it had been ratified by 167 countries.
- *Protocol II*: Protocol Additional to the Geneva Conventions of 12 August 1949, and relating to the Protection of Victims of Non-International Armed Conflicts. As of 12 January 2007 it had been ratified by 163 countries.
- *Protocol III*: Protocol Additional to the Geneva Conventions of 12 August 1949, and relating to the Adoption of an Additional Distinctive Emblem. As of May 20, 2008, it had been ratified by 28 countries and signed but not yet ratified by an additional 59 countries

All four conventions were last revised and ratified in 1949, based on previous revisions and partly on some of the 1907 Hague Conventions. Later conferences have added provisions prohibiting certain methods of warfare and addressing issues of civil wars. Nearly all 200 countries of the world are "signatory" nations, in that they have ratified these conventions. The International Committee of the Red Cross is the controlling body of the Geneva conventions.

Universal Declaration of Human Rights

The Universal Declaration of Human Rights is a non-binding declaration adopted by the United Nations General Assembly in 1948, partly in response to the barbarism of World War II. The UDHR urges member nations to promote a number of human, civil, economic and social rights, asserting these rights are part of the "foundation of freedom, justice and peace in the world". The declaration was the first international legal effort to limit the behaviour of states and press upon them duties to their citizens following the model of the rights-duty duality.

- "...recognition of the inherent dignity and of the equal and inalienable rights of all members of the human family is the foundation of freedom, justice and peace in the world".

The UDHR was framed by members of the Human Rights Commission, with Eleanor Roosevelt as Chair, who began to discuss an International Bill of Rights in 1947. The members of the Commission did not immediately agree on the form of such a bill of rights, and whether, or how, it should be enforced. The Commission proceeded to frame the UDHR and accompanying treaties, but the UDHR quickly became the priority.

Canadian law professor John Humphrey and French lawyer Rene Cassin were responsible for much of the cross-national research and the structure of the document respectively, where the articles of the declaration were interpretative of the general principle of the preamble. The document was structured by Cassin to include the basic principles of dignity, liberty, equality and brotherhood in the first two articles, followed successively by rights pertaining to individuals; rights of individuals in relation to each other and to groups; spiritual, public and political rights; and economic, social and cultural rights. The final three articles place, just as to Cassin, rights in the context of limits, duties and the social and political order in which they are to be realised.. Humphrey and Cassin intended the rights in the UDHR to be legally enforceable through some means, as is reflected in the third clause of the preamble:

- "Whereas it is essential, if man is not to be compelled to have recourse, as a last resort, to rebellion against tyranny and oppression, that human rights should be protected by the rule of law".

Some of the UDHR was researched and written by a committee of international experts on human rights, including representatives from all continents and all major religions, and drawing on consultation with leaders such as Mahatma Gandhi.

The inclusion of both civil and political rights and economic, social and cultural rights was predicated on the assumption that basic human rights are indivisible and that the different types of rights listed are inextricably linked. Though this principle was not opposed by any member states at the time of adoption, this principle was later subject to significant challenges.

BILL OF RIGHTS 1689

The Bill of Rights is an act of the Parliament of England, whose title is An Act Declaring the Rights and Liberties of the Subject and Settling the Succession of the Crown. It is often called the English Bill of Rights. The Bill of Rights was passed by Parliament in December 1689.

It was a re-statement in statutory form of the Declaration of Right presented by the Convention Parliament to William and Mary in March 1689, inviting them to become joint sovereigns of England. It enumerates certain rights to which subjects and permanent residents of a constitutional monarchy were thought to be entitled in the late 17th century, asserting subjects' right to petition the monarch, as well as to have arms in defence.

It also sets out-or, in the view of its drafters, restates-certain constitutional requirements of the Crown to seek the consent of the people, as represented in parliament. Along with the 1701 Act of Settlement the Bill of Rights is still in effect, one of the main constitutional laws governing the succession to the throne of the United Kingdom and-following British colonialism, the resultant doctrine of reception, and independence-to the thrones of those other Commonwealth realms, by willing deference to the act as a British statute or as a patriated part of the particular realm's constitution.

Since the implementation of the Statute of Westminster in each of the Commonwealth realms the Bill of Rights cannot be altered in any realm except by that realm's own parliament, and then, by convention, and as it touches on the succession to the shared throne, only with the consent of all the other realms.

In the United Kingdom, the Bill of Rights is further accompanied by the Magna Carta, Habeas Corpus Act 1679 and Parliament Acts 1911 and 1949 as some of the basic documents of the uncodified British constitution. A separate but similar document, the Claim of Right Act, applies in Scotland. The English Bill of Rights 1689 inspired in large part the United States Bill of Rights.

PROVISIONS OF THE ACT

The Bill of Rights laid out certain basic rights for all Englishmen. These rights continue to apply today, not only in England, but in each of the jurisdictions of the Commonwealth realms as well.

The people, embodied in the parliament, are granted immutable civil and political rights through the act, including:

- Freedom from royal interference with the law. Though the sovereign remains the fount of justice, he or she cannot unilaterally establish new courts or act as a judge.
- Freedom from taxation by Royal Prerogative. The agreement of parliament became necessary for the implementation of any new taxes.
- Freedom to petition the monarch.
- Freedom from the standing army during a time of peace. The agreement of parliament became

necessary before the army could be moved against the populace when not at war.

- Freedom for Protestants to have arms for their own defence, as suitable to their class and as allowed by law.
- Freedom to elect members of parliament without interference from the sovereign.
- Freedom of speech and debates; or proceedings in Parliament ought not to be impeached or questioned in any court or place out of Parliament.

Certain acts of James II were also specifically named and declared illegal by the Bill of Rights, while James' flight from England in the wake of the Glorious Revolution was also declared to be an abdication of the throne.

Also, in a prelude to the Act of Settlement to come twelve years later, the Bill of Rights barred Roman Catholics from the throne of England as "it hath been found by experience that it is inconsistent with the safety and welfare of this Protestant kingdom to be governed by a papist prince"; thus William III and Mary II were named as the successors of James VII and II and that the throne would pass from them first to Mary's heirs, then to her sister, Princess Anne of Denmark and her heirs and, further, to any heirs of William by a later marriage. The monarch was further required to swear a coronation oath to maintain the Protestant religion.

AUGMENTATION AND EFFECT

The Bill of Rights was later supplemented by the Act of Settlement in 1701. Both the Bill of Rights and the Claim of Right contributed a great deal to the establishment of the concept of parliamentary sovereignty and the curtailment of the powers of the monarch.

Leading, ultimately, to the establishment of constitutional monarchy, while also along with the Penal Laws, settle the political and religious turmoil that had convulsed Scotland, England and Ireland in the 17th century. It was a predecessor of the United States Bill of Rights, the Canadian Charter of Rights and Freedoms, the United Nations Universal

Declaration of Human Rights and the European Convention on Human Rights. For example, as with the Bill of Rights, the US constitution requires jury trials and prohibits excessive bail and "cruel and unusual punishments." Similarly, "cruel, inhuman or degrading punishments" are banned under Article 5 of the Universal Declaration of Human Rights and Article 3 of the European Convention on Human Rights.

The bill continues to be cited in legal proceedings in the Commonwealth realms. For instance, on 21 July 1995 a libel case brought by Neil Hamilton against The Guardian was stopped after Justice May ruled that the Bill of Rights' prohibition on the courts' ability to question parliamentary proceedings would prevent The Guardian from obtaining a fair trial. Section 13 of the Defamation Act, 1996, was subsequently enacted to permit an MP to waive his parliamentary privilege.

The Bill of Rights was also invoked in New Zealand in the 1976 case of Fitzgerald v. Muldoon and Others, which centred on the purporting of newly appointed Prime Minister Robert Muldoon that he would advise the Governor-General to abolish a superannuation scheme established by the New Zealand Superannuation Act, 1974, without new legislation. Muldoon felt that the dissolution would be immediate and he would later introduce a bill in parliament to retroactively make the abolition legal.

This claim was challenged in court and the Chief Justice declared that Muldoon's actions were illegal as they had violated Article 1 of the Bill of Rights, which provides "that the pretended power of dispensing with laws or the execution of laws by regal authority is illegal." Two special designs of the British commemorative two pound coins were issued in the United Kingdom in 1989 to celebrate the tercentenary of the Glorious Revolution.

One referred to the Bill of Rights and the other to the Claim of Right. Both depict the Royal Cypher of William and Mary and the mace of the House of Commons; one also shows a representation of the St Edward's Crown and, another, the Crown of Scotland.

CAIRO DECLARATION ON HUMAN RIGHTS IN ISLAM

The Cairo Declaration of Human Rights in Islam is a declaration of the member states of the Organisation of the Islamic Conference adopted in Cairo in 1990, which provides an overview on the Islamic perspective on human rights, and affirms Islamic Shari'ah as its sole source. CDHRI declares its purpose to be "general guidance for Member States [of the OIC] in the Field of human rights".

This declaration is usually seen as an Islamic response to the post-World War II United Nations' Universal Declaration of Human Rights of 1948. Predominantly Muslim countries, such as Sudan, Iran, and Saudi Arabia, frequently criticized the Universal Declaration of Human Rights for its perceived failure to take into account the cultural and religious context of non-Western countries.

In 1981, the post-revolutionary Iranian representative to the United Nations Said Rajaie-Khorassani articulated the position of his country regarding the Universal Declaration of Human Rights, by saying that the UDHR was "a secular understanding of the Judeo-Christian tradition", which could not be implemented by Muslims without trespassing the Islamic law. The CDHRI was adopted on August 5, 1990 by 45 foreign ministers of the Organisation of the Islamic Conference to serve as a guidance for the member states in the matters of human rights.

The Declaration starts by forbidding "any discrimination on the basis of race, colour, language, belief, sex, religion, political affiliation, social status or other considerations". It continues on to proclaim the sanctity of life, and declares the "preservation of human life" as "a duty prescribed by the Shariah". In addition the CDHRI guarantees "non-belligerents such as old men, women and children", "wounded and the sick" and "prisoners of war", the right to be fed, sheltered and access to safety and medical treatment in times of war. The CDHRI gives men and women the "right to marriage" regardless of their race, colour or nationality, but not religion. In addition women are given "equal human dignity", "own rights to enjoy", "duties to perform", "own civil entity", "financial independence", and the "right to retain her name and lineage", though not equal rights in general. The Declaration makes the husband responsible for the social and financial protection of the family.

The Declaration gives both parents the rights over their children, and makes it incumbent upon both of them to protect the child, before and after birth. The Declaration also entitles every family the "right to privacy". It also forbids the demolition, confiscation and eviction of any family from their residence. Furthermore, should the family get separated in times of war, it is the responsibility of the State to "arrange visits or reunions of families".

Article 10 of the Declaration states: "Islam is the religion of unspoiled nature. It is prohibited to exercise any form of compulsion on man or to exploit his poverty or ignorance in order to convert him to another religion or to atheism." The Declaration protects each individual from arbitrary arrest, torture, maltreatment and/or indignity. Furthermore, no individual is to be used for medical or scientific experiments. It also prohibits the taking of hostages of any individual "for any purpose" whatsoever. Moreover, the CDHRI guarantees the presumption of innocence; guilt is only to be proven through a trial in "which he [the defendant] shall be given all the guarantees of defence".

The Declaration also forbids the promulgation of "emergency laws that would provide executive authority for such actions". Art. 19 stipulates that there are no other crimes or punishments than those mentioned in the Sharia, which include corporal punishment and capital punishment. The right to hold public office can only be exercised in accordance with the Sharia, which forbids Muslims to submit to the rule of non-Muslims.

The Declaration also emphasizes the "full right to freedom and self-determination", and its opposition to enslavement, oppression, exploitation and colonialism. The CDHRI declares the rule of law, establishing equality and justice for all. The CDHRI also guarantees all individuals the "right to participate, directly or indirectly in the administration of his country's public affairs". The CDHRI also forbids any abuse of authority 'subject to the Islamic Shari'ah.' Article 22(a) of the Declaration states that "Everyone shall have the right to express his opinion freely in such manner as would not be contrary to the principles of the Shari'ah." 22(b) states that "Everyone shall have the right to advocate what is right, and propagate what is good, and warn against what is wrong and evil just as to the norms of Islamic Shari'ah." 22(c) states: "Information is a vital necessity to society.

It may not be exploited or misused in such a way as may violate sanctities and the dignity of Prophets, undermine moral and ethical values or disintegrate, corrupt or harm society or weaken its faith." 22(d) states "It is not permitted to arouse nationalistic or doctrinal hatred or to do anything that may be an incitement to any form of racial discrimination." The CDHRI concludes in article 24 and 25 that all rights and freedoms mentioned are subject to the Islamic Shariah, which is the declaration's sole source. The CDHRI declares "true religion" to be the "guarantee for enhancing such dignity along the path to human integrity". It also places the responsibility for defending those rights upon the entire Ummah.

CRITICISM

The CDHRI could be criticized for falling short of international human rights standards by distinguishing different fundamental equality of men and women (Art 6) and for permitting killing just as to Sharia law (Art 2A).

Whereas the Universal declaration states:

- 'Everyone is entitled to all the rights and freedoms set forth in this Declaration, without distinction of any kind, such as race, colour, sex, language, religion, political or other opinion, national or social origin, property, birth or other status.'

CDHRI does not guarantee equal rights, but merely equal dignity: Article 6

- Woman is equal to man in human dignity, and has rights to enjoy as well as duties to perform; she has her own civil entity and financial independence, and the right to retain her name and lineage.

- The husband is responsible for the support and welfare of the family.

'All men are equal in terms of basic human dignity and basic obligations and responsibilities, without any discrimination on the basis of race, colour, language, belief, sex, religion, political affiliation, social status or other considerations.' In particular, CDHRI has been criticised for failing to guarantee freedom of religion.

In a joint written statement submitted by the International Humanist and Ethical Union, a non-governmental organization in special consultative status, the Association for World Education and the Association of World Citizens: a number of concerns were raised, that the CDHRI limits Human Rights, Religious Freedom and Freedom of Expression. It concludes: "The Cairo Declaration of Human Rights in Islam is clearly an attempt to limit the rights enshrined in the UDHR and the International Covenants.

It can in no sense be seen as complementary to the Universal Declaration." The Centre for Inquiry in September 2008 in an article to the United Nations writes that the CDHRI: "undermines equality of persons and freedom of expression and religion by imposing restrictions on nearly every human right based on Islamic Sharia law." Article 5 prohibits imposing any restrictions on marriage stemming from "race, colour or nationality." Similarly, CDHRI is criticized as not endorsing equality between men and women; moreover, it is accused of asserting the superiority of men. Adama Dieng, a member of the International Commission of Jurists, criticised the CDHRI.

He argued that the declaration gravely threatens the inter-cultural consensus on which the international human rights instruments are based; that it introduces intolerable discrimination against non-Muslims and women. He further argued that the CDHRI reveals a deliberately restrictive character in regard to certain fundamental rights and freedoms, to the point that certain essential provisions are below the legal standards in effect in a number of Muslim countries; it uses the cover of the "Islamic Shari'a " to justify the legitimacy of practices, such as corporal punishment, which attack the integrity and dignity of the human being.

CHARTER 08

Charter 08 is a manifesto initially signed by over 303 Chinese intellectuals and human rights activists to promote political reform and democratization in the People's Republic of China. It was published on 10 December 2008, the 60th anniversary of the Universal Declaration of Human Rights, named after Charter 77 issued by dissidents in Czechoslovakia. Since its release, more than 8,100 people inside and outside of China have signed the charter.

DEMANDS

Many of the original signatories were prominent citizens inside and outside the government, including lawyers; a Tibetan blogger, Woeser; and Bao Tong, a former senior Communist Party official, who all faced a risk of arrest and jail. The Charter calls for 19 changes to improve human rights in China, including an independent legal system, freedom of association and the elimination of one-party rule.

"All kinds of social conflicts have constantly accumulated and feelings of discontent have risen consistently," it reads. "The current system has become backward to the point that change cannot be avoided." China remains the only large world power to still retain an authoritarian system that so infringes on human rights, it states. "This situation must change! Political democratic reforms cannot be delayed any longer!"

Specific demands are:

1. A federated republic.
2. Amending the Constitution.
3. An independent judiciary.
4. Civic education.
5. Election of public officials.
6. Financial and tax reform.

7. Freedom of assembly.
8. Freedom of association.
9. Freedom of expression.
10. Freedom of religion.
11. Guarantee of human rights.
12. Legislative democracy.
13. Protection of private property.
14. Protection of the environment.
15. Public control of public servants.
16. Rural–urban equality.
17. Separation of powers.
18. Social security.
19. Truth in reconciliation.

The opening paragraph of the charter states:

"This year is the 100th year of China's Constitution, the 60th anniversary of the Universal Declaration of Human Rights, the 30th anniversary of the birth of the Democracy Wall, and the 10th year since China signed the International Covenant on Civil and Political Rights. After experiencing a prolonged period of human rights disasters and a tortuous struggle and resistance, the awakening Chinese citizens are increasingly and more clearly recognizing that freedom, equality, and human rights are universal common values shared by all humankind, and that democracy, a republic, and constitutionalism constitute the basic structural framework of modern governance. A "modernization" bereft of these universal values and this basic political framework is a disastrous process that deprives humans of their rights, corrodes human nature, and destroys human dignity. Where will China head in the 21st century? Continue a "modernization" under this kind of authoritarian rule? Or recognize universal values, assimilate into the mainstream civilization, and build a democratic political system? This is a major decision that cannot be avoided".

RESPONSE

China

The Chinese government has said little publicly on the

Charter. On 8 December 2008, two days before the 60th anniversary of the United Nations General Assembly's adoption of the Universal Declaration of Human Rights, Liu Xiaobo was detained by police, hours before the online release of the Charter. He was detained and later arrested on June 23, 2009, on charges of "suspicion of inciting the subversion of state power." Several Nobel Laureates have written a letter to President Hu Jintao asking for his release. In response, the Chinese government is trying to crush the dissidents: at least 70 of its 303 original signatories have been summoned or interrogated by police while domestic media have been forbidden to interview anyone who has signed the document. Police have also searched for or questioned a journalist, Li Datong, and two lawyers, though none have been arrested. State media has been banned from reporting on the manifesto. A blogging website popular with activists, bullog.cn, which may have had ties to the Charter, has been shut down. On 25 December 2009 Liu Xiaobo was sentenced to 11 years in prison for "inciting subversion of state power" activities by the court.

International Response

A number of foreign governments, including the United States, Germany, and Taiwan have condemned the harassment of supporters of Charter 08 as well as hailed the Charter. International press has generally covered the Charter positively, and international NGOs have supported its message. Other international figures, including the Dalai Lama, have also voiced their support and admiration of the Charter. Artist ShawNshawN depicted a 90 x 30 inch painting of the 19 demands of the Charter.

CYRUS CYLINDER

The Cyrus Cylinder is a Babylonian document of the 6th century BC, discovered in the ruins of Babylon in 1879 and now in the British Museum. It is a clay cylinder, broken into several fragments, on which is written a declaration in Akkadian cuneiform script. The text is in the name of the Achaemenid Persian king Cyrus the Great. The cylinder was created following the Persian conquest of Babylon in 539 BC, when the Persian army under Cyrus invaded the Neo-Babylonian Empire and incorporated it into the Persian Empire. The Babylonian king Nabonidus was defeated in battle by the Persians and was deposed by Cyrus, who replaced him as ruler of Babylonia. The text on the cylinder commemorates the Persian victory and praises Cyrus's kingly virtues, listing his genealogy as a king from a line of kings, in contrast with the low-born Nabonidus. The deposed king is denounced as an impious oppressor of the people of Babylonia. The victorious Cyrus is portrayed as having been chosen by the chief Babylonian god Marduk to restore peace and order to the Babylonians.

The text says that Cyrus was welcomed by the people of Babylon as their new ruler and entered the city in peace. It appeals to Marduk to protect and to help Cyrus and his son Cambyses. It exalts Cyrus's efforts as a benefactor of the citizens of Babylonia who improved their lives, repatriated displaced peoples and restored temples and cult sanctuaries across Mesopotamia. It concludes with a description of the work of Cyrus in repairing the city wall of Babylon, in which he found a similar inscription by an earlier Babylonian king. The Assyro-British archaeologist Hormuzd Rassam discovered the cylinder during an excavation carried out for the British Museum. It had been placed as a foundation deposit in the foundations of the Esagila, the city's main temple. The British Museum, the cylinder reflects a long tradition in Mesopotamia where, from as early as the third millennium BC, kings began their reigns with declarations of reforms.

Cyrus's declaration shows how he sought to obtain the loyalty of his new Babylonian subjects by stressing his legitimacy as king, and showing his respect for the religious and political traditions of Babylonia. It has widely been regarded as an instrument of ancient Mesopotamian propaganda, most likely created by the Babylonian priests of Marduk working at the behest of Cyrus. The tradition of royal propaganda represented by the cylinder was revived in the late 1960s when the last Shah of Iran called it "the world's first charter of human rights". That interpretation has been disputed by many historians and has been characterised as anachronistic and tendentious, reflecting a misunderstanding of the cylinder's status as a generic foundation deposit. Nonetheless it became a key symbol of the Shah's political ideology and has since come to be regarded as part of Iran's cultural identity. The cylinder has also been linked to the repatriation of the Jews following their Babylonian captivity. A passage referring to the restoration of cult sanctuaries and repatriation of deported peoples has been widely interpreted as evidence of a general policy under which the Jews were allowed to return home, although it identifies only Mesopotamian sanctuaries, and makes no mention of Jews, Jerusalem or Judea.

HUMAN RIGHTS

Iranian Governmental View

The Cyrus Cylinder was dubbed the "first declaration of human rights" by the pre-1979 Iranian government, a reading first advanced by its Shah, The White Revolution of Iran. Pahlavi made Cyrus the Great a key figure in government ideology and associated himself personally with the Achaemenids. He wrote that "the history of our empire began with the famous declaration of Cyrus, which, for its advocacy of humane principles, justice and liberty, must be considered one of the most remarkable documents in the history of mankind." The Shah described Cyrus as the first ruler in history to give his subjects "freedom of opinion and other basic rights" - although the text of the cylinder itself says nothing about citizens' rights. In 1968, the Shah opened the first United Nations Conference on Human Rights in Tehran by saying that the Cyrus Cylinder was the precursor to the modern Universal Declaration of Human Rights. In his 1971 Nowruz speech, the Shah declared that 1971 would be Cyrus the Great Year, during which a grand commemoration would be held to celebrate 2,500 years of Persian monarchy. It would serve as a showcase for a modern Iran in which the contributions that Iran had made to world civilization would be recognized. The main theme of the commemoration was the centrality of the monarchy within Iran's political system, identifying the Shah with the famous monarchs of Persia's past, and with Cyrus the Great in particular.

The Shah looked to the Achaemenid period as "a moment from the national past that could best serve as a model and a slogan for the imperial society he hoped to create." The Cyrus Cylinder was adopted as the symbol for the commemoration, and Iranian magazines and journals published numerous articles about ancient Persian history. The British Museum loaned the original cylinder to the Iranian government for the duration of the festivities; it was put on display at the Shahyad Monument in Tehran, where a replica of the cylinder is still on display. The 2,500 year celebrations commenced on October 12, 1971 and culminated a week later with a spectacular parade at the tomb of Cyrus in Pasargadae.

On October 14, the shah's sister, Princess Ashraf Pahlavi, presented the United Nations Secretary General U Thant with a replica of the cylinder. The princess asserted that "the heritage of Cyrus was the heritage of human understanding, tolerance, courage, compassion and, above all, human liberty". The Secretary General accepted the gift, linking the cylinder with the efforts of the United Nations General Assembly to address "the question of Respect for Human Rights in Armed Conflict". Since then the replica cylinder has been kept at the United Nations Headquarters in New York City on the second floor hallway, and the text has been translated into all six official U.N. languages.

Scholarly Views

The interpretation of the cylinder as a "charter of human rights" has been criticized by many scholars and characterized as political propaganda on the part of the Pahlavi regime. The German historian Josef Wiesehöfer comments that the image of "Cyrus as a champion of the UN human rights policy... is just as much a phantom as the humane and enlightened Shah of Persia." Neil MacGregor, the Director of the British Museum, wrote that the cylinder was used by the Shah as "a mantra of his newly constructed national identity" that "must have startled many who had tried to assert their human rights under his regime." Writing in the immediate aftermath of the Shah's commemorations, the British Museum's C.B.F. Walker comments that the "essential character of the Cyrus Cylinder [is not] a general declaration of human rights or religious toleration but simply a building inscription, in the Babylonian and Assyrian tradition, commemorating Cyrus's restoration of the city of Babylon and the worship of Marduk previously neglected by Nabonidus." Two linguists of the ancient Near East, Bill T.

Arnold and Piotr Michalowski, comment: "Generically, it belongs with other foundation deposit inscriptions; it is not an edict of any kind, nor does it provide any unusual human rights proclamation as is sometimes claimed." Cyrus's policies towards subjugated nations have been contrasted to those of the Assyrians and Babylonians, who had treated subject peoples harshly; he permitted the resettling of those who had been previously deported and sponsored the reconstruction of religious buildings. While the Shah cited this as evidence of respect for human rights, the Iranologist Elton L. Daniel has described such an interpretation as "rather anachronistic" and tendentious.

T.C. Mitchell, a former Keeper of Western Asiatic Antiquities at the British Museum, takes the view that interpreting the cylinder as the first charter of human rights "reflects a misunderstanding." Curtis, Tallis, and Salvini note that despite the cylinder's reference to a just and peaceful rule, and repatriation of deported peoples, the modern concept of human rights would have been quite alien to Cyrus's contemporaries and is not mentioned by the cylinder. Neil MacGregor, the British Museum's Director, comments: Comparison by scholars in the British Museum with other similar texts, however, showed that rulers in ancient Iraq had been making comparable declarations upon succeeding to the [Babylonian] throne for two millennia before Cyrus it is one of the museum's tasks to resist the narrowing of the object's meaning and its appropriation to one political agenda. He cautions that while the cylinder is "clearly linked with the history of Iran", it is "in no real sense an Iranian document: it is part of a much larger history of the ancient Near East, of Mesopotamian kingship, and of the Jewish diaspora." Cyrus has often been depicted as a particularly humane ruler, based on his characterization by ancient sources such as Persian texts, the Old Testament of the Bible and Herodotus,. M.A. Dandamaev, the leading Russian scholar of the neo-Babylonian and Persian periods, has written that "almost all the texts... which praise Cyrus have the character of propagandistic writings and demand a very critical approach... by accepting everything said in the texts which were composed by Babylonian priests, we ourselves become the victims of Cyrus's propaganda." Nonetheless, some scholars have supported the Shah's interpretation of the cylinder as a human rights charter. Neil MacGregor has written "the Cylinder may indeed be a document of human rights".

The Iranian lawyer Hirad Abtahi argues that viewing the cylinder as merely "an instrument of legitimizing royal rule" is unjustified, as Cyrus issued the document and granted those rights when he was at the height of his power, with neither popular opposition nor visible external threat to force his hand. The former Iranian prime minister Hassan Pirnia describes the cylinder as "discuss human rights in a way unique for the era, dealing with ways to protect the honour, prestige, and religious beliefs of all the nations dependent to Iran in those days."

DECLARATION OF THE RIGHTS OF MAN AND CITIZEN OF 1793

The Declaration of the Rights of Man and Citizen of 1793 is a French political document. It was written by the commission that included Louis Antoine Léon de Saint-Just and Marie-Jean Hérault de Séchelles during the period of the French Revolution. The main distinction between the Declaration of 1793 and the Declaration of the Rights of Man and of the Citizen of 1789 is its egalitarian tendency: equality is the prevailing right in this declaration. The text is often said to have been mainly written by Hérault de Séchelle, whose style and writing can be found on most of the documents of the commission that also wrote the French Constitution of 1793 that was never applied, but whose application was steadfastly demanded by the French left until the beginning of the 20th century. The first project of the Constitution of the French Fourth Republic also referred to this version of the Declaration of the Rights of Man and Citizen.

EQUALITY AS THE FIRST NATURAL RIGHT OF MAN

Equality is the most important aspect of the Declaration of 1793. In its second article, equality is the first right mentioned. In Article 3 states "All men are equal by nature and before the law". As such, for the authors of this declaration equality is not only before the law but it is also a natural right, that is to say, a fact of nature. There was already at that time a school of thought that stated that liberty and equality can quickly become contradictory: indeed liberty doesn't solve social inequalities since there exist some natural inequalities.

That school of thought considered that the government had only to protect liberty and to only proclaim natural equality, and eventually liberty would prevail over social equality since all people have different talents and abilities and are free to exercise them. The question raised by this declaration is how to solve social inequalities. Article 21 states that every citizen has a right to public help, that society is indebted to each citizen and therefore has the duty to help them. Citizens have there a right to work and society has a duty to provide relief to those who cannot work. Article 22 declares a right to education. These rights are considered "2nd generation rights of Man", economical and social rights. These rights entail a greater government intervention in order to reach society's goal, stated in article 1: common welfare.

THE PROTECTIONS OF LIBERTY

Individual liberty is still a primary right and some aspects are more precisely defined than in Declaration of 1789. The declaration explicitly states the freedom of religion, of assembly and of the press, of commerce, of petition. It also prohibits slavery "Every man can contract his services and his time, but he cannot sell himself nor be sold: his person is not an alienable property."

THE PROTECTIONS OF THE CITIZENS AGAINST THEIR OWN GOVERNMENT

If in a way, this declaration has a more liberal bend in the modern American sense since it states that there ought to be public policies for the general welfare, it also contains some very strong libertarian aspects. Article 7 states "The necessity of enunciating these rights supposes either the presence or the fresh recollection of despotism." Article 9: "The law ought to protect public and personal liberty against the oppression of those who govern." Article 33 states that resisting tyranny is a logical consequence of the rights of man: "Resistance to oppression is the consequence of the other rights of man. Article 34 states that if one is oppressed, everyone is. Article 27 states "Let any person who may usurp the sovereignty be instantly put to death by free men."

Though the usurpation of sovereignty is not detailed, sovereignty is explained in article 25 as residing "in the people". There is no doubt that this way of thinking deeply influenced the revolutionary government during the Terror. Finally, article 35 states "When the government violates the rights of the people, insurrection is for the people and for each portion of the people the most sacred of rights and the most indispensable of duties." Though this declaration was never enforced, History has shown that the French people has followed this advice with many successful and unsuccessful revolutions throughout the 19th century.

DRAFTING OF THE UNIVERSAL DECLARATION OF HUMAN RIGHTS

The Universal Declaration of Human Rights was drafted from early 1947 to late 1948 by Canadian John Peters Humphrey of the United Nations Secretariat and representatives of countries which were members of the first

United Nations Commission on Human Rights, which was until 2006, when it was replaced by the United Nations Human Rights Council, a standing body of the United Nations. Well known members of the Commission who contributed significantly to the creation of the Declaration included Eleanor Roosevelt of the United States, who was Chairman, Jacques Maritain and René Cassin of France, Charles Malik of Lebanon, and P. C. Chang of China, among others.

MEMBERSHIP OF THE COMMISSION

The membership of the Commission was designed to be broadly representative of the global community with representatives of the following countries serving: Australia, Belgium, Byelorussian Soviet Socialist Republic, Chile, China, Egypt, France, India, Iran, Lebanon, Panama, Philippines, United Kingdom, United States, Union of Soviet Socialist Republics, Uruguay and Yugoslavia.

THE HUMPHREY DRAFT

Humphrey was newly appointed as Director of the Division of Human Rights within the United Nations Secretariat. In this role he produced the first draft of a list of rights that were to form the basis of the Declaration.

THE CASSIN DRAFT

The underlying structure of the Universal Declaration was introduced in its second draft which was prepared by Rene Cassin. Cassin worked from a first draft prepared by John Peters Humphrey. The structure was influenced by the Code Napoleon, including a preamble and introductory general principles. Cassin compared the Declaration to the portico of a Greek temple, with a foundation, steps, four columns and a pediment. Articles 1 and 2 are the foundation blocks, with their principles of dignity, liberty, equality and brotherhood. The seven paragraphs of the preamble, setting out the reasons for the Declaration, are represented by the steps. The main body of the Declaration forms the four columns. The first column constitutes rights of the individual, such as the right to life and the prohibition of slavery. The second column constitutes the rights of the individual in civil and political society. The third column is concerned with spiritual, public and political freedoms such as freedom of religion and freedom of association.

The fourth column sets out social, economic and cultural rights. In Cassin's model, the last three articles of the Declaration provide the pediment which binds the structure together. These articles are concerned with the duty of the individual to society and the prohibition of use of rights in contravention of the purposes of the United Nations.

SUBSEQUENT DRAFTING

The Cassin draft was submitted to the Commission on Human Rights and was to undergo editing in the Commission, then in further drafts considered by the Third Committee of the United Nations, and finally in a draft before the General Assembly of the United Nations, which ultimately adopted the Declaration on 10 December 1948.

UDHR CHRONOLOGY

1945:

- United Nations Conference on International Organization, San Francisco

1946:

- 15 February, Establishment of "Nuclear Committee" of Commission on Human Rights.
- 29 April - 20 May 1946 - First Meeting of the Nuclear Committee.
- 21 June 1946 - ECOSOC adopts terms of reference of permanent Commission on Human Rights

1947:

- 27 January - 10 February - First Meeting of the Commission on Human Rights, Lake Success, New York. Drafting Committee established.
- 9 June - 25 June - First Meeting of the Drafting Committee, Lake Success, New York. Draft outline of an International Bill of Human Rights prepared

by the UN Secretariat. Drafting Committee splits work into two documents: preparation of a declaration of human rights and a working document on a draft international convention on human rights.

- 2 December - 17 December - Second Session of the Commission on Human Rights, Geneva. Commission begins to consider work on three projects: a declaration on human rights, and international convention on human rights and measures for implementation and enforcement

1948:

- 3 May - 21 May, Second Session of the Drafting Committee, Lake Success, New York.
- 24 May - 18 June, Third Session of the Commission on Human Rights, Lake Success, New York. Commission adopts a draft Declaration and transmits it to the Economic and Social Council.
- 26 August, Economic and Social Council transmits draft to the General Assembly.
- 30 September - 7 December, Third Committee of General Assembly spends 81 meetings considering the Declaration. 168 resolutions for amendments to the draft, submitted and considered.
- 1-4 December, Sub-committee of Third Committee charged with cross checking 5 official language versions.
- 10 December, Universal Declaration of Human Rights adopted by the United Nations General Assembly

EX OFFICIO OATH

The ex-officio oath was an English ecclesiastical and judicial weapon developed in the first half of the 17th century, and used as a form of coercion, persecution, and forcible self-incrimination in the religious trials of that era. The format was a religious oath imposed upon the accused prior to questioning, to answer truthfully all questions that might be asked. It gave rise to what became known as the "cruel trilemma" where the accused would find themselves trapped between a breach of religious oath, contempt of court for silence, or self-incrimination. The name derives from the questioner putting the accused on oath ex officio, meaning by virtue of his office or position. Outcry against this practice led to the establishment of the right to not incriminate oneself in common-law.

This was the direct precursor of similar rights in modern law, including the right to silence and non-self-incrimination in the Fifth Amendment to the United States Constitution. The right itself appears as item 16 in the Levellers Agreement of the Free People of England and first appeared in US law in the Massachusetts Body of Liberties and the Connecticut Code of the same era. The Star Chamber itself, as a judicial body, was abolished by Parliament as part of the Habeas Corpus Act 1640. Early examples of a codified right appears in the Levellers manifesto Agreement of the Free People of England: "t shall not be in the power of any Representative, to punish, or cause to be punished, any person or persons for refusing to answer questions against themselves in Criminal cases", The right first appeared in US law in the Massachusetts Body of Liberties and the Connecticut Code of the same era. The United States Supreme Court summarized the events of the time as part of the historical background in the landmark case Miranda v. Arizona:

- Perhaps the critical historical event shedding light on its [ie, the privilege against self-incrimination] origins and evolution was the trial of one John Lilburn, a vocal anti-Stuart Leveller, who was made to take the Star Chamber Oath in 1637. The oath would have bound him to answer to all questions posed to him on any subject. He resisted the oath and declaimed the proceedings, stating: "Another fundamental right I then contended for, was, that no man's conscience ought to be racked by oaths imposed, to answer to questions concerning himself in matters criminal, or pretended to be so."
- On account of the Lilburn Trial, Parliament abolished

the inquisitorial Court of Star Chamber and went further in giving him generous reparation. The lofty principles to which Lilburn had appealed during his trial gained popular acceptance in England. These sentiments worked their way over to the Colonies and were implanted after great struggle into the Bill of Rights.

FOUR FREEDOMS

The Four Freedoms were goals articulated by US President Franklin D. Roosevelt on January 6, 1941. In an address known as the Four Freedoms speech, he proposed four fundamental freedoms that people "everywhere in the world" ought to enjoy:

1. Freedom of speech and expression
2. Freedom of religion
3. Freedom from want
4. Freedom from fear

His inclusion of the latter two freedoms went beyond the traditional US Constitutional values protected by its First Amendment, and endorsed a right to economic security and an internationalist view of foreign policy that have come to be central tenets of modern American liberalism. They also anticipated what would become known decades later as the "human security" paradigm in social science and economic development.

THE DECLARATIONS

The speech delivered by President Roosevelt incorporated the following:

- "In the future days, which we seek to make secure, we look forward to a world founded upon four essential human freedoms.
- The first is freedom of speech and expression—everywhere in the world.
- The second is freedom of every person to worship God in his own way—everywhere in the world.
- The third is freedom from want—which, translated into world terms, means economic understandings

which will secure to every nation a healthy peacetime life for its inhabitants—everywhere in the world.

- The fourth is freedom from fear—which, translated into world terms, means a world-wide reduction of armaments to such a point and in such a thorough fashion that no nation will be in a position to commit an act of physical aggression against any neighbour—anywhere in the world.

That is no vision of a distant millennium. It is a definite basis for a kind of world attainable in our own time and generation.

That kind of world is the very antithesis of the so-called new order of tyranny which the dictators seek to create with the crash of a bomb".

FOUR FREEDOMS MONUMENT

The Four Freedoms Monument was commissioned by President Franklin D. Roosevelt following his articulation of the "Four Freedoms" in his 1941 State of the Union Address. Roosevelt felt that, through the medium of the arts, a far greater number of people could be inspired to appreciate the concept of the Four Freedoms. The statue was created by sculptor Walter Russell later that year, and was dedicated in 1943 before a crowd of 60,000 people at Madison Square Garden in New York City.

It was dedicated to Colin P. Kelly, the first recognized American hero of World War II. On June 14, 1944 the monument was re-dedicated in Kelly's hometown of Madison, Florida, with a speech by Governor Spessard Holland. Another American artist, Norman Rockwell, was inspired by Roosevelt's vision to create his own visual depiction of the Four Freedoms — in his case, through a series of four paintings completed in early 1943.

In Evansville, Indiana there is another Four Freedoms monument designed by Rupert Condict built in 1976, four Indiana Limestone columns. It has become the defacto photo image of the city. Another monument to the Four Freedoms stands in the Tremont neighbourhood of Cleveland, Ohio. It is a single column, with one of the Freedoms printed on each side. On top of the column is a sculpture of two hands holding a globe of the Earth.

MAGNA CARTA

Magna Carta is an English charter, originally issued in the year 1215, and reissued later in the 13th century in modified versions which omit certain temporary provisions, including the most direct challenges to the monarch's authority. The charter first passed into law in 1225. The 1297 version, described as The Great Charter of the Liberties of England, and of the Liberties of the Forest, still remains on the statute books of England and Wales.

The 1215 Charter required King John of England to proclaim certain liberties, and accept that his will was not arbitrary, for example by explicitly accepting that no "freeman" could be punished except through the law of the land, a right which is still in existence today. Magna Carta was the first document forced onto an English King by a group of his subjects in an attempt to limit his powers by law and protect their privileges. It was preceded and directly influenced by the 1100 Charter of Liberties, when King Henry I had specified particular areas where his powers would be limited. Despite its recognised importance, by the second half of the 19th century nearly all of its clauses had been repealed in their original form.

Three clauses remain part of the law of England and Wales, however, and it is generally considered part of the uncodified constitution. In a recent ruling Lord Laws used Magna Carta as an example of a constitutional statute, one which could only be repealed by a later statute with that clear intention.

The charter was an important part of the extensive historical process that led to the rule of constitutional law in the English speaking world, although it was "far from unique, either in content or form". In practice, Magna Carta in the medieval period did not in general limit the power of kings, but by the time of the English Civil War it had become an important symbol for those who wished to show that the King was bound by the law. It influenced the early settlers in New England and inspired later constitutional documents, including the United States Constitution.

HUMAN RIGHTS

Magna Carta was originally written in Latin. A large part of Magna Carta was copied, nearly word for word, from the Charter of Liberties of Henry I, issued when Henry became king in 1100, in which he said he would respect certain rights of the Church and the barons, for example not forcing heirs to pay a fee when they inherited.

Rights Still in Force Today

Magna Carta supports the right which became known as habeas corpus through clauses 36, 38, 39, and 40 of the 1215 Charter. Similar rights had existed before Magna Carta, and writs with the same effect had been issued as early as the 12th century, but Magna Carta was the first recording in writing of royal recognition of these rights. As the most recent version, it is the 1297 Charter which remains in legal force in England and Wales. In the 1297 charter: Clause 1 guarantees the freedom of the English Church. Although this originally meant freedom from the King, later in history it was interpreted differently. Clause 9 guarantees the "ancient liberties" of the City of London. Clause 29 guarantees a right to due process.

Feudal Rights Still in Place in 1225

Several clauses were present in the 1225 charter but are no longer in force and would have no real place in the post-feudal world. Clauses 2 to 7 refer to feudal death duties, defining their amounts and the provisions that applied if an heir to a fiefdom was under age or was a widow. Clause 23 provides that no town or person should be forced to build a bridge across a river. Clause 33 requires the removal of all fish weirs. Clause 43 gives special provision for tax on reverted estates and Clause 44 states that forest law should only apply to those in the king's forest.

Feudal Rights not in the 1225 Charter

Some provisions have no bearing in the world today, since they are feudal rights and were not even included in the 1225 charter. Clauses 9 to 12, 14 to 16, and 25 to 26 deal with debt and taxes and Clause 27 with intestacy. The other clauses state that no one may seize land in debt except as a last resort; that under age heirs and widows should not pay interest on inherited loans; that county rents will stay at their ancient amounts; and that the crown may only seize the value owed in payment of a debt, that aid must be reasonable, and that scutage may only be sought with the consent of the kingdom. Clause 14 states that the common consent of the kingdom was to be sought from a council of the archbishops, bishops, earls and greater Barons. This later became the great council, which led to the first parliament.

Judicial Rights

Clauses 17 to 22 allows for a fixed law court, which became the chancellery, and defines the scope and frequency of county assizes. They also state that fines should be proportionate to the offence, that they should not be influenced by ecclesiastical property in clergy trials, and that people should be tried by their peers.

Many think that this gave rise to jury and magistrate trial, but its only manifestation in the modern world was the right of a lord to a criminal trial in the House of Lords at first instance. Clause 24 states that crown officials may not try a crime in place of a judge. Clause 34 forbids repossession without a writ precipe. Clauses 36 to 38 state that writs for loss of life or limb are to be free, that one may use reasonable force to secure one's own land, and that no one can be tried on their own testimony alone.

Clauses 36, 38, 39 and 40 collectively define the right of Habeas Corpus. Clause 36 requires courts to make inquiries as to the whereabouts of a prisoner, and to do so without charging any fee. Clause 38 provides that a person could not be put on trial by the mere word of an official. Clause 39 gives the courts exclusive rights to punish anyone. Clause 40 disallows the selling of or delay to justice. Clauses 36 and 38 were removed from the 1225 version, but were reinstated in later versions. The right of Habeas Corpus as such was first invoked in court in the year 1305. Clause 54 says that no man may be imprisoned on the testimony of a woman except on the death of her husband.

Anti-corruption and Fair Trade

Clauses 28 to 32 state that no royal officer may take any commodity such as grain, wood or transport without payment or consent or force a knight to pay for something the knight could do himself, and that the king must return any lands confiscated from a felon within a year and a day. Clause 35 sets out a list of standard measures, and Clauses 41 and 42 guarantee the safety and right of entry and exit of foreign merchants. Clause 45 says that the King should only appoint royal officers suitable for the post. In the United States, the Supreme Court of California interpreted clause 45 in 1974 as establishing a requirement at common law that a defendant faced with the potential of incarceration is entitled to a trial overseen by a legally trained judge. Clause 46 provides for the guardianship of monasteries.

Temporary Provisions

Some provisions were for immediate effect and were not in any later charter. Clauses 47 and 48 abolish most of Forest Law. Clauses 49, 52 to 53 and 55 to 59 provide for the return of hostages, land and fines taken in John's reign. Article 50 states that no member of the d'Athée family may be a royal officer. Article 51 calls for all foreign knights and mercenaries to leave the realm. Articles 60, 62 and 63 provide for the application and observation of the Charter and say that the Charter is binding on the King and his heirs forever, but this was soon deemed dependent on each succeeding king reaffirming the Charter under his own seal.

Jews in England

Magna Carta contained two articles related to money

lending and Jews in England. Jewish involvement with money lending caused Christian resentment, because the Church forbade usury; it was seen as vice and was punishable by excommunication, although Jews, as non-Christians, could not be excommunicated and were thus in a legal grey area. Secular leaders, unlike the Church, tolerated the practice of Jewish usury because it gave the leaders an opportunity for personal enrichment.

This resulted in a complicated legal situation: debtors were frequently trying to bring their Jewish creditors before Church courts, where debts would be absolved as illegal, while the Jews were trying to get their debtors tried in secular courts, where they would be able to collect both principal and interest. The relations between the debtors and creditors would often become very nasty.

There were many attempts over centuries to resolve this problem, and Magna Carta contains one example of the legal code of the time on this issue:

- If one who has borrowed from the Jews any sum, great or small, die before that loan be repaid, the debt shall not bear interest while the heir is under age, of whomsoever he may hold; and if the debt fall into our hands, as suggested, not take anything except the principal sum contained in the bond. And if anyone die indebted to the Jews, his wife shall have her dower and pay nothing of that debt; and if any children of the deceased are left under age, necessaries shall be provided for them in keeping with the holding of the deceased; and out of the residue the debt shall be paid, reserving, however, service due to feudal lords; in like manner let it be done touching debts due to others than Jews.

After the Pope annulled the 1215 Magna Carta, future versions contained no mention of Jews.

Great Council

The first long-term constitutional effect arose from Clauses 14 and 61, which permitted a council composed of the most powerful men in the country to exist for the benefit of the state rather than in allegiance to the monarch. Members of the council were also allowed to renounce their oath of allegiance to the King in pressing circumstances and to pledge allegiance to the council and not to the King in certain instances. The common council was responsible for taxation, and although it was not representative, its members were bound by decisions made in their absence. The common council, later called the Great Council, was England's proto-parliament. The Great Council only existed to give input on the opinion of the kingdom as a whole, and it only had power to control scutage until 1258 when Henry III got into debt fighting in Sicily for the Pope.

The barons agreed to a tax in exchange for reform, leading to the Provisions of Oxford. But Henry obtained a papal bull allowing him to set aside these provisions and in 1262 commanded royal officers to ignore the provisions and only to obey Magna Carta. The barons revolted and seized the Tower of London, the Cinque ports and Gloucester.

Initially the King surrendered, but when Louis IX of France arbitrated in favour of Henry, Henry crushed the rebellion. Later he made some concessions, passing the Statute of Marlborough in 1267, which allowed writs for breaches of Magna Carta to be free of charge, enabling anyone to have standing to apply the Charter.

This secured the position of the Great Council forever, but its powers were still very limited. The council originally only met three times per year and so was subservient to the King's council, Curiae Regis, which, unlike the Great Council, followed the king wherever he went. Still, in some ways the council was an early form of parliament. It had the power to meet outside the authority of the King and was not appointed by him. While executive government descends from the Curiae Regis, parliament descends from the Great Council, which was later called the parliamentum. However, the Great Council was very different from modern parliament. There were no knights, let alone commons, and it was composed of the most powerful men, rather than elected citizens.

Magna Carta had little effect on subsequent development of parliament until the Tudor period. Knights and county representatives attended the Great Council, and the council became far more representative under the model parliament of Edward I which included two knights from each county, two burgesses from each borough and two citizens from each city. The Commons separated from the Lords in 1341. The exclusive right of the Commons to sanction taxes was re-asserted in 1407, although it was not in force in this period. The power vested in the Great Council by, albeit withdrawn, Clause 14 of Magna Carta became vested in the House of Commons but Magna Carta was all but forgotten for about a century, until the Tudors.

UN DECLARATION ON SEXUAL ORIENTATION AND GENDER IDENTITY

The proposed United Nations declaration on sexual orientation and gender identity is a Dutch/French-initiated, European Union-backed statement presented to the United Nations General Assembly on 18 December 2008. The statement, originally intended to be adopted as resolution, prompted an Arab League-backed statement opposing it. Both statements remain open for signatures and none of them has been officially adopted by the United Nations General Assembly.

The proposed declaration includes a condemnation of violence, harassment, discrimination, exclusion, stigmatization, and prejudice based on sexual orientation and gender identity. It also includes condemnation of killings and executions, torture, arbitrary arrest, and deprivation of economic, social, and cultural rights on those grounds. The proposed declaration was praised as a breakthrough for human rights, breaking the taboo against speaking about LGBT rights in the United Nations. Opponents criticized it as an attempt to legitimize same-sex civil partnerships or marriage, adoption by same sex couples, pedophilia and other "deplorable acts" and curtail freedom of religious expression against homosexual behaviour. As of December 2008, homosexuality is illegal in

77 countries and punishable by death in seven. In its 1994 decision in Toonen v. Australia, The UN Human Rights Committee, which is responsible for the International Covenant on Civil and Political Rights, declared that such laws are in violation of human rights law. In 2003 a number of predominantly European countries put forward the Brazilian Resolution at the UN Human Rights Commission stating the intention that lesbian and gay rights be considered as fundamental as the rights of all human beings.

In 2006, with the effort of its founder, Louis George Tin, International Day Against Homophobia launched a worldwide campaign to end the criminalisation of same-sex relationships. The campaign was supported by dozens of international public figures including Nobel laureates, academics, clergy and celebrities. In 2008, the 34 member countries of the Organization of American States unanimously approved a declaration affirming that human rights protections extend to sexual orientation and gender identity. Following meetings between Tin and French Minister of Human Rights and Foreign Affairs Rama Yade in early 2008, Yade announced that she would appeal at the UN for the universal decriminalization of homosexuality; the appeal was quickly taken up as an international concern.

Co-sponsored by France, which then held the rotating presidency of the European Union, and The Netherlands on behalf of the European Union, the declaration had been intended as a resolution; it was decided to use the format of a declaration of a limited group of States because there was not enough support for the adoption of an official resolution by the General Assembly as a whole. The declaration was read out by Ambassador Jorge Argüello of Argentina on 18 December 2008, and was the first declaration concerning gay rights read in the General Assembly.

SUPPORT

Several speakers addressing a conference on the declaration noted that in many countries laws against homosexuality stemmed as much from the British colonial past as from religion or tradition. Voicing France's support for the draft declaration, Rama Yade asked: "How can we tolerate the fact that people are stoned, hanged, decapitated and tortured only because of their sexual orientation?" UK-based activist Peter Tatchell said of the declaration:

- "This was history in the making... Securing this statement at the UN is the result of an inspiring collective global effort by many LGBT and human rights organisations. Our collaboration, unity and solidarity have won us this success. As well as IDAHO, I pay tribute to the contribution and lobbying of Amnesty International; ARC International; Centre for Women's Global Leadership; COC Netherlands; Global Rights; Human Rights Watch; International Committee for IDAHO; International Gay and Lesbian Human Rights Commission; International Lesbian and Gay Association; International Service for Human Rights; Pan Africa ILGA; and Public Services International."

Signatories

67 of the United Nations' 192 member countries have sponsored the declaration, including every member of the European Union and most Western nations:

Africa:

- Cape Verde
- Central African Republic
- Gabon
- Guinea-Bissau
- Mauritius
- São Tomé and Príncipe

Americas:

- Argentina
- Bolivia
- Brazil
- Canada
- Chile
- Colombia

- Cuba
- Ecuador
- Mexico
- Nicaragua
- Paraguay
- United States
- Uruguay
- Venezuela

Asia:

- Israel
- Japan
- Nepal
- Timor-Leste

Europe:

- Albania
- Andorra
- Armenia
- Austria
- Belgium
- Bosnia and Herzegovina
- Bulgaria
- Croatia
- Cyprus
- Czech Republic
- Denmark
- Estonia
- Finland
- France initiative
- Georgia
- Germany
- Greece
- Hungary
- Iceland
- Ireland
- Italy
- Latvia
- Liechtenstein
- Lithuania

- Luxembourg
- Macedonia
- Malta
- Montenegro
- Netherlands initiative
- Norway
- Poland
- Portugal
- Romania
- San Marino
- Serbia
- Slovakia
- Slovenia
- Spain
- Sweden
- Switzerland
- United Kingdom

Oceania:

- Australia
- New Zealand

OPPOSITION

Among the first to voice opposition for the declaration, in early December, 2008, was the Holy See's Permanent Observer at the United Nations, Archbishop Celestino Migliore, who claimed that the declaration could be used to force countries to recognise same-sex marriage:

- "If adopted, they would create new and implacable discriminations. For example, states which do not recognise same-sex unions as 'matrimony' will be pilloried and made an object of pressure."

A key part of the Vatican opposition to the draft Declaration relates to the concept of gender identity.

In a statement on 19 December, Archbishop Migliore noted:

- "In particular, the categories 'sexual orientation' and 'gender identity', used in the text, find no recognition or clear and agreed definition in international law. If they had to be taken into consideration in the

> proclaiming and implementing of fundamental rights, these would create serious uncertainty in the law as well as undermine the ability of States to enter into and enforce new and existing human rights conventions and standards."

However, Archbishop Migliore also made clear the Vatican's opposition to legal discrimination against homosexuals: "The Holy See continues to advocate that every sign of unjust discrimination towards homosexual persons should be avoided and urges States to do away with criminal penalties against them."

In an editorial response, Italy's La Stampa newspaper called the Vatican's reasoning "grotesque", claiming that the Vatican feared a "chain reaction in favour of legally recognised homosexual unions in countries, like Italy, where there is currently no legislation."

The United States, citing conflicts with US law, originally opposed the adoption of the nonbinding measure, as did Russia, China, the Holy See, and members of the Organization of the Islamic Conference. The Holy See's Permanent Observer Mission issued a statement saying that the draft declaration "challenges existing human rights norms." The Obama administration changed the US position to support the measure in February 2009.

An alternative statement, supported by 57 member nations, was read by the Syrian representative in the General Assembly. The statement, led by the Organization of the Islamic Conference, rejected the idea that sexual orientation is a matter of genetic coding and claimed that the declaration threatened to undermine the international framework of human rights, adding that the statement "delves into matters which fall essentially within the domestic jurisdiction of states" and could lead to "the social normalization, and possibly the legitimization, of many deplorable acts including pedophilia."

The Organization failed in a related attempt to delete the phrase "sexual orientation" from a Swedish-backed formal resolution condemning summary executions.

SIGNATORIES

57 UN member nations have co-sponsored the opposing statement:

Africa:

- Algeria
- Benin
- Cameroon
- Chad
- Comoros
- Côte d'Ivoire
- Djibouti
- Egypt
- Eritrea
- Ethiopia
- Gambia
- Guinea
- Kenya
- Libya
- Malawi
- Mali
- Mauritania
- Morocco
- Niger
- Nigeria
- Rwanda
- Senegal
- Sierra Leone
- Somalia
- Sudan
- Swaziland
- Tanzania
- Togo
- Tunisia
- Uganda
- Zimbabwe

Americas:

- Saint Lucia

Asia":
- Afghanistan
- Bahrain
- Bangladesh
- Brunei
- Indonesia
- Iran
- Iraq
- Jordan
- Kazakhstan
- Kuwait
- Lebanon
- Malaysia
- Maldives
- North Korea
- Oman
- Pakistan
- Qatar
- Saudi Arabia
- Syria initiative
- Tajikistan
- Turkmenistan
- United Arab Emirates
- Yemen

Oceania:
- Fiji
- Solomon Islands

VIRGINIA DECLARATION OF RIGHTS

The Virginia Declaration of Rights is a document drafted in 1776 to proclaim the inherent natural rights of men, including the right to rebel against "inadequate" government. It influenced a number of later documents, including the United States Declaration of Independence, the United States Bill of Rights, and the French Revolution's Declaration of the Rights of Man and of the Citizen. The Declaration was adopted unanimously by the Virginia Convention of Delegates on June 12, 1776 as a separate document from the Constitution of

Virginia adopted on June 29, 1776. It was later incorporated within the Virginia State Constitution as Article I, and a slightly updated version may still be seen in Virginia's Constitution, making it legally in effect to this day. It was initially drafted by George Mason ca. March 22, 1765; James Madison assisted him with the part on religious freedom. It was later amended by Thomas Ludwell Lee and the Convention to add Section 14 on the Right to uniform government.

Mason based his document on the rights of citizens described in earlier works such as the English Bill of Rights, and the Declaration can be considered the first modern Constitutional protection of individual rights for citizens of North America. It rejected the notion of privileged political classes or hereditary offices such as the members of Parliament and House of Lords described in the English Bill of Rights. The Declaration consists of sixteen articles on the subject of which rights "pertain to [the people of Virginia]...as the basis and foundation of Government." In addition to affirming the inherent nature of natural rights to life, liberty, and property, the Declaration both describes a view of Government as the servant of the people, and enumerates various restrictions on governmental power.

Thus, the document is unusual in that it not only prescribes legal rights, but it also describes moral principles upon which a government should be run. Articles 1-3 address the subject of rights and the relationship between government and the governed. Article 1 states that "all men are by nature equally free and independent, and have certain inherent rights of which...[they cannot divest;] namely, the enjoyment of life and liberty, with the means of acquiring and possessing property, and pursuing and obtaining happiness and safety," a statement later made internationally famous in the first paragraph of the U.S. Declaration of Independence, as "we hold these truths to be self-evident, that all men are created equal, and are endowed by their Creator with certain unalienable rights, that among these are life, liberty, and the pursuit of happiness." Articles 2 and 3 note the revolutionary concept that "all power is vested in, and consequently derived from, the people..." and that "whenever any government shall be found inadequate or contrary to these purposes, a majority of the community hath an indubitable, unalienable, and indefeasible right to reform, alter or abolish it, in such manner as shall be judged most conducive to the public weal." This latter concept effectively asserted the right of the people of Virginia to revolt against the British Empire.

Article 4 asserts the equality of all citizens, rejecting the notion of privileged political classes or hereditary offices - another criticism of British institutions such as the House of Lords and the privileges of the peerage: "no set of men, are entitled to exclusive or separate emoluments or privileges from the community, but in consideration of public services; which, not being descendible, neither ought the offices of magistrate, legislator, or judge be hereditary." Articles 5 and 6 recommend the principles of separation of powers and free elections, "frequent, certain, and regular" of executives and legislators: "That the legislative and executive powers of the state should be separate and distinct from the judicative; and, that the members of the two first...should, at fixed periods, be reduced to a private station, return into that body from which they were originally taken...by frequent, certain, and regular elections." Articles 7-16 propose restrictions on the powers of the government, declaring the government should not have the power of suspending or executing laws, "without consent of the representatives of the people,"; establishing the legal rights to be "confronted with the accusers and witnesses, to call for evidence in his favour, and to a speedy trial by an impartial jury of his vicinage," and to prevent a citizen from being "compelled to give evidence against himself."

Protections against "cruel and unusual punishments", baseless search and seizure, and the guarantees of a trial by jury, freedom of the press, freedom of religion "all men are equally entitled to the free exercise of religion,", and "the proper, natural, and safe defence of a free state" rested in a well regulated militia composed of the body of the people, trained to arms, that standing armies in time of peace, should be avoided as dangerous to liberty.

The following is the complete text of the Virginia Declaration of Rights:

- That all men are by nature equally free and independent, and have certain inherent rights, of which, when they enter into a state of society, they cannot, by any compact, deprive or divest their posterity; namely, the enjoyment of life and liberty, with the means of acquiring and possessing property, and pursuing and obtaining happiness and safety.
- That all power is vested in, and consequently derived from, the people; that magistrates are their trustees and servants, and at all times amenable to them.
- That government is, or ought to be, instituted for the common benefit, protection, and security of the people, nation or community; of all the various modes and forms of government that is best, which is capable of producing the greatest degree of happiness and safety and is most effectually secured against the danger of maladministration; and that, whenever any government shall be found inadequate or contrary to these purposes, a majority of the community hath an indubitable, unalienable, and indefeasible right to reform, alter or abolish it, in such manner as shall be judged most conducive to the public weal.
- That no man, or set of men, are entitled to exclusive or separate emoluments or privileges from the community, but in consideration of public services; which, not being descendible, neither ought the offices of magistrate, legislator, or judge be hereditary.
- That the legislative and executive powers of the state should be separate and distinct from the judicative; and, that the members of the two first may be restrained from oppression by feeling and participating the burthens of the people, they should, at fixed periods, be reduced to a private station, return into that body from which they were originally

taken, and the vacancies be supplied by frequent, certain, and regular elections in which all, or any part of the former members, to be again eligible, or ineligible, as the laws shall direct.

- That elections of members to serve as representatives of the people in assembly ought to be free; and that all men, having sufficient evidence of permanent common interest with, and attachment to, the community have the right of suffrage and cannot be taxed or deprived of their property for public uses without their own consent or that of their representatives so elected, nor bound by any law to which they have not, in like manner, assented, for the public good.
- That all power of suspending laws, or the execution of laws, by any authority without consent of the representatives of the people is injurious to their rights and ought not to be exercised.
- That in all capital or criminal prosecutions a man hath a right to demand the cause and nature of his accusation to be confronted with the accusers and witnesses, to call for evidence in his favour, and to a speedy trial by an impartial jury of his vicinage, without whose unanimous consent he cannot be found guilty, nor can he be compelled to give evidence against himself; that no man be deprived of his liberty except by the law of the land or the judgement of his peers.
- That excessive bail ought not to be required, nor excessive fines imposed; nor cruel and unusual punishments inflicted.
- That general warrants, whereby any officer or messenger may be commanded to search suspected places without evidence of a fact committed, or to seize any person or persons not named, or whose offense is not particularly described and supported by evidence, are grievous and oppressive and ought not to be granted.

- That in controversies respecting property and in suits between man and man, the ancient trial by jury is preferable to any other and ought to be held sacred.
- That the freedom of the press is one of the greatest bulwarks of liberty and can never be restrained but by despotic governments.
- That a well regulated militia, composed of the body of the people, trained to arms, is the proper, natural, and safe defence of a free state; that standing armies, in time of peace, should be avoided as dangerous to liberty; and that, in all cases, the military should be under strict subordination to, and be governed by, the civil power.
- That the people have a right to uniform government; and therefore, that no government separate from, or independent of, the government of Virginia, ought to be erected or established within the limits thereof.
- That no free government, or the blessings of liberty, can be preserved to any people but by a firm adherence to justice, moderation, temperance, frugality, and virtue and by frequent recurrence to fundamental principles.
- That religion, or the duty which we owe to our Creator and the manner of discharging it, can be directed by reason and conviction, not by force or violence; and therefore, all men are equally entitled to the free exercise of religion, just as to the dictates of conscience; and that it is the mutual duty of all to practice Christian forbearance, love, and charity towards each other.

INFLUENCE

The Virginia Declaration of Rights heavily influenced later documents. Thomas Jefferson is thought to have drawn on it when he drafted the United States Declaration of Independence one month later. James Madison was also influenced by the Declaration while drafting the Bill of Rights as was the Marquis de Lafayette in voting the French

Revolution's Declaration of the Rights of Man and of the Citizen. The importance of the Virginia Declaration of Rights is that it was the first constitutional protection of individual rights, rather than protecting just members of Parliament or consisting of simple laws that can be changed as easily as passed.

QUOTATIONS DERIVED FROM THE DECLARATION

- "We hold these truths to be self-evident, that all men are created equal, that they are endowed by their Creator with certain unalienable Rights, that among these are Life, Liberty and the pursuit of Happiness. —That to secure these rights, Governments are instituted among Men, deriving their just powers from the consent of the governed" — United States Declaration of Independence
- "Men are born and remain free and equal in rights. Social distinctions can be founded only on the common utility." — Declaration of the Rights of Man and of the Citizen

YOGYAKARTA PRINCIPLES

The Yogyakarta Principles on the Application of International Human Rights Law in relation to Sexual Orientation and Gender Identity is a set of international principles relating to sexual orientation and gender identity, intended to address documented evidence of abuse of rights of lesbian, gay, bisexual, and transgender people, and further of intersexuality requested by Louise Arbour just as to the International Human Rights Law. The outline of the Principles was drawn at a meeting of International Commission of Jurists and human rights experts from around the world at Gadjah Mada University on Java from 6 to 9 November in 2006.

"It contains 29 Principles adopted unanimously by the experts, along with recommendations to governments, regional intergovernmental institutions, civil society, and the UN itself". The principles are named after Yogyakarta, the smallest province of Indonesia located on the island of Java.

Among 29 signatories of the principles, there are Mary Robinson, Manfred Nowak and Martin Scheinin. The principles are intended to be and have become a universal guide to human rights. In alignment with the movement towards establishing basic human rights for all people, the Principles specifically address sexual orientation and gender identity.

The Principles were developed in response to patterns of abuse reported from around the world. These included examples of rape, torture, extrajudicial executions, medical abuse, denial of free speech and assembly as well as a range of discriminations in work, health, education, housing, access to justice and immigration. These are estimated to affect millions of people targeted on the basis of perceived or actual sexual orientation or gender identity.

It is noted on the website carrying the principles that concerns have been voiced about a trend of people's human rights being violated because of their sexual orientation or gender identity. Extrajudicial killing, torture and ill-treatment, sexual assault and rape, invasion of privacy, arbitrary arrest and imprisonment, denial of employment and education opportunities are cited.

It is explained that the United Nations human rights instruments detail the obligations States are under to ensure people are protected from discrimination, which includes people's expression of sexual orientation or gender identity. It is pointed out that implementation of these rights has been fragmented and inconsistent internationally. It is set out how the Principles provide a consistent understanding about application of international human rights law in relation to sexual orientation and gender identity. From 6 to 9 November 2006, an international seminar of legal experts on human rights took place at Yogyakarta, Indonesia. The seminar clarified the nature, scope and implementation of States' human rights obligations under existing human rights treaties and law, in relation to sexual orientation and gender identity. The Principles that developed out of this meeting were adopted by human rights experts from around the world, and included judges, academics, a former UN High Commissioner for Human Rights, NGOs and others. Michael O'Flaherty was rapporteur responsible for drafting and development of the Yogyakarta Principles produced from the meeting. At the meeting, Vitit Muntarbhorn and Sonia Onufer Corrêa were the co-chairpersons.

The compilers explain that the Principles detail how international human rights law can be applied to sexual orientation and gender identity issues, in a way that affirms international law and to which all States can be bound to. They suggest that the motivation is so that where ever people are recognised as being born free and equal in dignity and rights, this should include LGBT people as well. They argue that human rights standards also cover issues of sexual orientation and gender identity touch on issues of torture and violence, extrajudicial execution, access to justice, privacy, freedom from discrimination, freedom of expression and assembly, access to employment, health-care, education, and immigration and refugee issues. The intention outlined is for the Principles to explain that States are obliged to ensure human rights, and each principle recommends how to achieve this, highlighting international agencies' responsibilities to promote and maintain human rights.

The Principles are based on the recognition of the right against non-discrimination. The Committee on Economic, Social and Cultural Rights has dealt with the matter in its General Comments, the interpretative texts it issues to explicate the full meaning of the provisions of the Covenant on Economic, Social and Cultural Rights. In General Comments Nos 18 of Nos 18 of 2005, 15 of 2002 and 14 of 2000, it has indicated that the Covenant proscribes any discrimination on the basis of, inter-alia, sex and sexual orientation 'that has the intention or effect of nullifying or impairing the equal enjoyment or exercise of [the right at issue]'. The Committee on the Elimination of Discrimination against Women, notwithstanding that it has not addressed the matter in a General Comment or otherwise specified the applicable provisions of the Convention on the Elimination of

All Forms of Discrimination Against Women, on a number of occasions has criticised States for discrimination on the basis of sexual orientation. For example, it also addressed the situation in Kyrgyzstan and recommended that, 'lesbianism be reconceptualised as a sexual orientation and that penalties for its practice be abolished'.

The finalised Yogyakarta Principles was launched as a global charter for gay rights on 26 March 2007 in Geneva. Michael O'Flaherty, spoke at the International Lesbian and Gay Association Conference in Lithuania on 27 October 2007; he explained that "All human rights belong to all of us. We have human rights because we exist – not because we are gay or straight and irrespective of our gender identities", but that in many situations these human rights are not respected or realised, and that "the Yogyakarta Principles is to redress that situation". The Yogyakarta Principles was presented at a United Nations event in New York on November 7, 2007, co-sponsored by Argentina, Brazil and Uruguay.

Human Rights Watch explain that the first step towards this would be the de-criminalisation of homosexuality in 77 countries that still carry legal penalties for people in same-sex relationships, and repeal of the death penalty in the seven countries that still have the death penalty for such sexual practice. Human and LGBT Rights groups took up the Principles, and discussion has featured in the gay press. The Principles, while explaining the way existing Human Rights Statutes need to be applied in specific situations relevant to LGBT people's experience, influenced the proposed UN declaration on sexual orientation and gender identity in 2008. Piero A.

Tozzi, of the Catholic Family and Human Rights Institute, issued a briefing document 'Six Problems with the Yogyakarta Principles'. He argues that where Principle 24 seeks to recognize the diversity of family forms, this could devalue the concept of the family by including any grouping of two people. He also argues that Principles 20 and 21 could be used to restrict freedom of speech. The Council of Europe states in "Human Rights and Gender Identity" that Principle 3 of the

Yogyakarta Principles is of "of particular relevance": Because same sex marriage is possible only in five member states of the Council of Europe, transgender persons who are already married usually have to divorce prior to their new gender being officially recognised, although in many cases they would prefer to remain a legally recognised family unit, especially if they have children. Such enforced divorces may have a negative impact on the children of the marriage.

They recommend that member states "abolish sterilisation and other compulsory medical treatment as a necessary legal requirement to recognise a person's gender identity in laws regulating the process for name and sex change." As well as to "make gender reassignment procedures, such as hormone treatment, surgery and psycological support, accessible for transgender person, and ensure that they are reimbursed by public health insurance schemes."

3

Human Security in Theory and Practice

THE CONCEPT OF HUMAN SECURITY AND ITS ADDED VALUE

The Concept of Human Security as defined by the Commission on Human

SECURITY

Why Human Security Now

As argued by the Commission on Human Security, the need for a new paradigm of security is associated with two sets of dynamics:

1. First, human security is needed in response to the complexity and the interrelatedness of both old and new security threats – from chronic and persistent poverty to ethnic violence, human trafficking, climate change, health pandemics, international terrorism, and sudden economic and financial downturns. Such threats tend to acquire transnational dimensions and move beyond traditional notions of security that focus on external military aggressions alone.
2. Second, human security is required as a comprehensive approach that utilizes the wide range of new opportunities to tackle such threats in an integrated manner. Human security threats cannot be tackled through conventional mechanisms alone.

Instead, they require a new consensus that acknowledges the linkages and the interdependencies between development, human rights and national security.

What is Human Security

The CHS, in its final report Human Security Now, defines human security as:

- "...to protect the vital core of all human lives in ways that enhance human freedoms and human fulfillment. Human security means protecting fundamental freedoms – freedoms that are the essence of life. It means protecting people from critical and pervasive threats and situations. It means using processes that build on people's strengths and aspirations. It means creating political, social, environmental, economic, military and cultural systems that together give people the building blocks of survival, livelihood and dignity."

Overall, the definition proposed by the CHS re-conceptualizes security in a fundamental way by:

- Moving away from traditional, state-centric conceptions of security that focused primarily on the safety of states from military aggression, to one that concentrates on the security of the individuals, their protection and empowerment;
- Drawing attention to a multitude of threats that cut across different aspects of human life and thus highlighting the interface between security, development and human rights; and
- Promoting a new integrated, coordinated and people-centered approach to advancing peace, security and development within and across nations.

What are the Main Features of Human Security

Human security brings together the 'human elements' of security, rights and development.

As such, it is an inter-disciplinary concept that displays the following characteristics:

- Comprehensive
- Context-specific
- Multi-sectoral
- People-centered
- Prevention-oriented

As a people-centered concept, human security places the individual at the 'centre of analysis.' Consequently, it considers a broad range of conditions which threaten survival, livelihood and dignity, and identifies the threshold below which human life is intolerably threatened. Human security is also based on a multi-sectoral understanding of insecurities. Therefore, human security entails a broadened understanding of threats and includes causes of insecurity relating for instance to economic, food, health, environmental, personal, community and political security.

Table. Possible Types of Human Security Threats

Type of Security	Examples of Main Threats
Economic security	Persistent poverty, unemployment
Food security	Hunger, famine
Health security	Deadly infectious diseases, unsafe food, malnutrition, lack of access to basic health care
Environmental security	Environmental degradation, resource depletion, natural disasters, pollution
Personal security	Physical violence, crime, terrorism, domestic violence, child labour
Community security	Interethnic, religious and other identity based tensions
Political security	Political repression, human rights abuses

Moreover, human security emphasizes the interconnectedness of both threats and responses when addressing these insecurities. That is, threats to human security are mutually reinforcing and interconnected in two ways. First, they are interlinked in a domino effect in the sense that each threat feeds on the other. For example, violent conflicts can lead to deprivation and poverty which in turn could lead to resource depletion, infectious diseases, education deficits, etc. Second, threats within a given country or area can spread into a wider region and have negative externalities for regional and international security.

This interdependence has important implications for policy-making as it implies that human insecurities cannot be tackled in isolation through fragmented stand-alone responses. Instead, human security involves comprehensive approaches that stress the need for cooperative and multisectoral responses that bring together the agendas of those dealing with security, development and human rights. "With human security [as] the objective, there must be a stronger and more integrated response from communities and states around the globe".

In addition, as a context-specific concept, human security acknowledges that insecurities vary considerably across different settings and as such advances contextualized solutions that are responsive to the particular situations they seek to address. Finally, in addressing risks and root causes of insecurities, human security is prevention-oriented and introduces a dual focus on protection and empowerment.

What do Protection and Empowerment Mean for Achieving Human Security

Protection and empowerment of people are the two building blocks for achieving the goal of human security. They are proposed by the CHS as the bi-parts of any human security policy framework.

- Protection is defined by the CHS as "strategies, set up by states, international agencies, NGOs and the private sector, [to] shield people from menaces". It refers to the norms, processes and institutions required to protect people from critical and pervasive threats. Protection implies a "top-down" approach. It recognises that people face threats that are beyond their control. Human security therefore requires protecting people in a systematic, comprehensive and preventative way. States have the primary responsibility to implement such a protective structure. However, international and regional organizations; civil society and non-governmental actors; and the private sector also play a pivotal role in shielding people from menaces.

- Empowerment is defined by the CHS as "strategies [that] enable people to develop their resilience to difficult situations". Empowerment implies a "bottom up" approach. It aims at developing the capabilities of individuals and communities to make informed choices and to act on their own behalf. Empowering people not only enables them to develop their full potential but it also allows them to find ways and to participate in solutions to ensure human security for themselves and others.

As clearly stated by the CHS, protection and empowerment are mutually reinforcing and cannot be treated in isolation: "both are required in nearly all situations of human insecurity, though their form and balance will vary tremendously across circumstances".

HUMAN SECURITY DIFFER FROM TRADITIONAL SECURITY, HUMAN DEVELOPMENT AND HUMAN RIGHTS APPROACHES

"Human Security complements state security, strengthens human development and enhances human rights". Yet the question often arises as to what are the substantive differences between these concepts.

Significant among these are the following:

- Whereas state security concentrates on threats directed against the state, mainly in the form of military attacks, human security draws attention to a wide scope of threats faced by individuals and communities. It focuses on root causes of insecurities and advances people-centered solutions that are locally driven, comprehensive and sustainable. As such, it involves a broader range of actors: *e.g.* local communities, international organizations, civil society as well as the state itself. Human security, however, is not intended to displace state security. Instead, their relationship is complementary: "human security and state security are mutually reinforcing and dependent on each other. Without human security, state security cannot be attained and vice versa".

- To human development's objective of 'growth with equity', human security adds the important dimension of 'downturn with security'. Human security acknowledges that as a result of downturns such as conflicts, economic and financial crises, ill health, and natural disasters, people are faced with sudden insecurities and deprivations. These not only undo years of development but also generate conditions within which grievances can lead to growing tensions. Therefore, in addition to its emphasis on human well-being, human security is driven by values relating to security, stability and sustainability of development gains.
- Lastly, too often gross violations of human rights result in conflicts, displacement, and human suffering on a massive scale. In this regard, human security underscores the universality and primacy of a set of rights and freedoms that are fundamental for human life. Human security makes no distinction between different kinds of human rights – civil, political, economic, social and cultural rights thereby addressing violations and threats in a multidimensional and comprehensive way. It introduces a practical framework for identifying the specific rights that are at stake in a particular situation of insecurity and for considering the institutional and governance arrangements that are needed to exercise and sustain them.

THE ADDED VALUE OF HUMAN SECURITY AS AN OPERATIONAL TOOL

Human security is increasingly being adopted as a

doctrine to guide foreign policies and international development assistance, as well as a policy tool for programming in the fields of security, development and humanitarian work. The strength and appeal of human security as an operational tool for analysis, explanation and programming lies in the following components:

A Framework for Protection and Empowerment

Human security derives much of its strength from its dual policy framework resting upon the two Operationalization of this framework introduces a hybrid approach which:

- Combines top-down norms, processes and institutions, including the establishment of the rule of law, good governance, accountability and social protective instruments with a bottom-up focus in which democratic processes support the important role of individuals and communities as actors in defining and implementing their essential freedoms.
- Helps identify gaps in the existing security infrastructure and detects ways to mitigate the impact of existing security deficits.
- Ensures the sustainability of programmes and policies as protection and empowerment are introduced in a systematic and preventative manner with a look to long-term stability.
- Reinforces peoples' ability to act on their own behalf.
- Strengthens the resilience of individuals and communities to conditions of insecurity.
- Encourages participatory processes.

Comprehensive

Human security addresses the full scope of human insecurities. It recognises the multi-dimensional character of security threats – including but not limited to violent conflict and extreme impoverishment – as well as their interdependencies.

In particular, as an operational approach, human security:

- Attributes equal importance to civil, political, economic, social, and cultural rights.

- Sets rudimentary thresholds below which no person's livelihood, survival and dignity should be threatened.
- Provides a practical framework for the identification of a wide range threats in given crisis situations.
- Addresses threats both within and across borders.
- Encourages regional and multilateral cooperation.

Multi-sectoral

Coherence is needed between different interventions in order to avoid negative harms while choosing multiplying effects of positive interventions.

To this end, human security develops a true multi-sectoral agenda which:

- Captures the ultimate impact of development or relief interventions on human welfare and dignity.
- Provides a practical framework for assessing positive and negative externalities of interventions supported through policies, programmes and projects.
- Enables comprehensive and integrated solutions from the fields of human rights, development and security in a joint manner.
- Helps to ensure policy coherence and coordination across traditionally separate fields and doctrines.
- Allows for knowledge-sharing and results-oriented learning.

Contextualization

Insecurities vary significantly across countries and communities. Both their causes and expressions depend on a complex interaction of international, regional, national and local factors.

Addressing peoples' insecurities therefore always requires specification to capture variations over time and contexts. As a universally applicable, broad and flexible approach, human security provides a dynamic framework that:

- Addresses different kinds of insecurity as these manifest themselves in specific contexts.
- Builds on processes that are based on peoples' own perceptions of fear and vulnerability.

- Identifies the concrete needs of populations under stress.
- Enables the development of more appropriate solutions that are embedded in local realities.
- Unveils mismatches between domestic and/or international policies and helps identify priority security needs at the local level.
- Looks at the impact of global developments on different communities.
- Captures the rapidly changing international, regional and domestic security environments.

Emphasis on Prevention

A distinctive element of human security is its focus on early prevention to minimize the impacts of insecurity, to engender long-term solutions, and to build human capacities for undertaking prevention.

In this regard, human security:

- Addresses root causes of human insecurities.
- Emphasises early prevention rather than late intervention – thereby, more cost-effective.
- Encourages strategies concerned with the development of mechanisms for prevention, the mitigation of harmful effects when downturns occur and, ultimately, with helping victims to cope.

Partnerships and Collaboration

With its emphasis on the interconnectedness of threats, human security requires the development of an interconnected network of diverse stakeholders, drawing from the expertise and resources of a wide range of actors from across the UN as well as the private and public sectors at the local, national, regional and international levels.

Human security can therefore lead to the establishment of synergies and partnerships that capitalise on the comparative advantages of each implementing organization and help empower individuals and communities to act on their own behalf.

Benchmarking, Evaluation and Impact Assessment

Analyses based on human security can be of widespread importance. By providing a holistic and contextual account of peoples' concrete needs and the factors endangering their security, the information obtained through such analyses can be used in assessing existing institutional arrangements and policies as well as a benchmark for impact evaluation.

HOW TO OPERATIONALISE THE HUMAN SECURITY CONCEPT

HUMAN SECURITY PRINCIPLES AND APPROACH

From an operational perspective, human security aims to address complex situations of insecurity through collaborative, responsive and sustainable measures that are:

- People-centered,
- Multisectoral,
- Comprehensive,
- Context-specific, and
- Prevention-oriented.

In addition, human security employs a hybrid approach that brings together these elements through a protection and empowerment framework. Subsequently each human security principle informs the human security approach and must be integrated into the design of a human security programme.

HS Principle	HS Approach
People-centered	• Inclusive and participatory. • Considers individuals and communities in defining their needs/vulnerabilities and in acting as active agents of change. • Collectively determines which insecurities to address and identifies the available resources including local assets and indigenous coping mechanisms.
Multi-sectoral	• Addresses multi-sectorality by promoting

	dialogue among key actors from different sectors/fields. • Helps to ensure coherence and coordination across traditionally separate sectors/fields. • Assesses positive and negative externalities of each response on the overall human security situation of the affected community(ies).
Comprehensive	• Holistic analysis: the seven security components of human security. • Addresses the wide spectrum of threats, vulnerabilities and capacities. • Analysis of actors and sectors not previously considered relevant to the success of a policy/ programmme/project. • Develops multi-sectoral/multi-actor responses.
Context-specific	• Requires in-depth analysis of the targeted situation. • Focuses on a core set of freedoms and rights under threat in a given situation. • Identifies the concrete needs of the affected community(ies) and enables the development of more appropriate solutions that are embedded in local realities, capacities and coping mechanisms. • Takes into account local, national, regional and global dimensions and their impact on the targeted situation.
Prevention-oriented	• Identifies risks, threats and hazards, and addresses their root causes. • Focuses on preventative responses through a protection and empowerment framework.

HUMAN SECURITY PROGRAMME PHASES

To design a human security programme, the following phases must be considered. Each phase requires a set of goals and tasks which provide the actions needed to ensure the integrity of the human security programme.

Phase	Goals and Tasks
Phase 1: Analysis, Mapping and Planning	• Establish participatory processes and collectively identify the needs/ vulnerabilities and the capacities of the affected community(ies). • Map insecurities based on actual vulnerabilities and capacities with less focus on what is feasible and more emphasis on what is actually needed. • Establish priorities through needs/ vulnerabilities and capacity analysis in consultation with the affected community(ies). • Identify the root causes of insecurities and their inter-linkages. • Cluster insecurities based on comprehensive and multi-sectoral mapping and be vigilant of externalities. • Establish strategies/responses that incorporate empowerment and protection measures. • Outline short, medium, and long-term strategies/outcomes even if they will not be implemented in the particular programme. (Outlining strategies at different stages with the community is an important foundation for sustainability.) • Establish multi-actor planning to ensure coherence on goals and the allocation of responsibilities and tasks.
Phase 2: Implementation	• Implementation in collaboration with local partners, ensuring that actions do no unintentionally undermine any other human security component/ principles and respect the local norms

	and practices of the affected community(ies). • Implementation that considers the changing dynamics of risks and threats and is flexible to adjust to such changes as necessary for the protection and empowerment of the affected community(ies). • Capacity building of the affected community(ies) and local institutions. • Monitoring as part of the programme and the basis for learning and adaptation.
Phase 3: Impact Assessment	• Are we doing the right thing as opposed to whether or not we are doing things right? • Does the programme alleviate identified human insecurities while at the same time avoiding negative externalities? • Deriving lessons learned from failures and successes and improving the programme.

Phase I: Analysis, Mapping and Planning

During the initial analysis, mapping and planning phase of a human security programme, it is critically important to ensure that the programme addresses the actual needs/vulnerabilities and capacities of the affected community(ies) and presents strategies that are based on the protection and empowerment framework with the active participation and implementation of the affected community.

Specifically, the goals of the analysis, mapping and planning phase are to:

- Collectively identify the needs/vulnerabilities and the capacities of the affected community and develop programme priorities in consultation with the affected community;

- Identify the root causes of insecurities and their inter-linkages across sectors, and establish comprehensive responses that generate positive externalities for the affected community.
- Ensure coherence on the goals and the allocation of responsibilities among the various actors; and
- Include short, medium, and long-term strategies.

The Human Security Analytical Framework to Needs/ Vulnerabilities and Capacity Analysis

A human security analytical framework to needs/ vulnerabilities and capacity analysis is necessary to guide the development and the implementation of the data collection process as well as to inform the analysis of the data from a human security perspective.

Specifically, the human security approach to needs/ vulnerabilities and capacity analysis will be determined by the following actions under each of the human security principles:

- People-centered
  - Involve the affected community(ies) when gathering data on the needs/ vulnerabilities and the capacities of the affected community(ies).
  - Identify root causes through analysis of the 'degree of cause'.
  - Develop empowerment strategies based on the capacities needed.
  - Strengthen the resilience of individuals and communities.
- Multi-sectoral/Comprehensive
  - Consider the broad range of threats and vulnerabilities both within and across communities.
  - Develop a comprehensive and integrated analysis that incorporates the fields of security, development and human rights.
  - Identify the lack of policy coherence and coordination across sectors/fields that can have

a negative impact on achieving the human security needs of the affected community(ies).

- Context-specific
  - Ensure that analysis incorporates context specific local information.
  - Include community perception of the threats and vulnerabilities in addition to other quantitative indicators.
  - Highlight potential mismatch between domestic and/or international policies and the priority security needs of the affected community(ies).
  - Identify gaps in the existing security infrastructure.
- Prevention-oriented
  - Identify the root causes and the primary protection and empowerment gaps so as to develop sustainable solutions.
  - Emphasize prevention as well as response when developing priorities.
  - Focus on empowerment measures that build on local capacities and resilience.

Once the data has been gathered, the Human Security Needs, Vulnerabilities and Capacity Matrix provides the spatial presentation for mapping, identifying and analysing the identified threats, needs and capacities of the affected community(ies). Mapping is well-suited to the analytical needs of the human security approach.

Not only does it manage complexity well, mapping also provides the opportunity to visually:

- Identify and link the most severe and widespread threats and vulnerabilities;
- Offer the strategies for addressing the identified insecurities; and
- Consider the capacities and the resources of the affected community(ies) vis-à-vis each type of threat and vulnerability.

The spatial representation of mapping is also crucial for identifying differences within and among communities in resource distribution. Finally, by providing a more comprehensive view of insecurities in a particular situation or community, mapping allows for stronger identification of the gaps in the existing protection and empowerment infrastructures as well as the priorities for action among the identified insecurities. Based on the mapping exercise, the inter-linkages and dynamics among the various threats, vulnerabilities and capacities are identified. It is in these intersections that the most effective and comprehensive strategies can be developed.

Therefore, it is important to identify these intersections in order to:

- Establish priorities for action;
- Assess the sectors and strategies for externalities; and
- Develop multi-actor integrated plans.

Human Security Strategies

The human security approach not only requires a thorough assessment of the vulnerabilities and the capacities of the affected community, it also demands an assessment of the strategies needed to help prevent and mitigate the recurrence of insecurities.

It is through this dual assessment that the inter-connectedness between threats, vulnerabilities, capacities and strategies can be most effectively examined.

The Human Security Multi-Sectorality and Externalities Framework

To develop effective human security strategies, the Human Security Multi-Sectorality and Externalities Framework provides the necessary tool for developing policy and programme coherence among the relevant sectors involved in a programme intervention. By assessing the potential externalities of the proposed intervention, the framework entails multiple key functions in the design and improvement of human security programmes.

Why undertake an analysis of multi-sectorality?

- Intervention in one area can have negative impacts

in other areas of equal importance to human security.

- Coherence is needed between different interventions in order to avoid negative externalities.
- To multiply positive externalities.
- To take advantage of available expertise, lessons learnt, etc.
- To share knowledge and improve the efficiency and effectiveness of responses.
- To be more efficient in terms of pooling of resources.
- To provide information for monitoring, evaluation and impact assessment.

What are the challenges of employing multi-sectorality?

- Turf war between organizations.
- Grand strategies that are top down, political and on document.
- Forced mainstreaming without explaining rationale.
- Multiplication of overlays of management, accountability, committees, etc.
- Different financing modalities as well as monitoring, evaluation and impact assessment.

How can Policy and Programme Coherence be Addressed

For the most part, most organizations and institutions are attempting to address multi-sectorality through coordination and a focus on effectiveness. This however is quite difficult in the face of differing mandates. Therefore, rather than organizational coordination, a human security approach requires working in an integrated manner by directly assessing externalities and focusing on legitimacy, efficiency and effectiveness.

A successful multi-sectoral approach requires:

- An analytical, comprehensive, and integrated framework.
- A strategic approach to change.
- Permanent networking among programmes that have thematic or target population overlaps.
- Overcoming tensions between short, medium, and long-term strategies and planning.
- Joint interdisciplinary research.

The Human Security "Protection and Empowerment" Framework

The analysis, mapping and planning phase of a human security programme also requires employing the "protection and empowerment" framework by designing strategies that address both top-down and bottom-up measures.

- Protection involves strategies that enhance the capacities of the institutional/governance structures needed to protect the affected community(ies) against the identified threats.
- Empowerment includes strategies that build upon the capacities of the affected community(ies) to cope with the identified threats and to strengthen their resilience and choices so as to act on their own behalf and those of the others.

How to Develop 'Protection and Empowerment' Strategies?

Having identified several strategies and assessed the potential positive and negative externalities among each, it is crucial to subsequently assess the identified strategies for their employment of the 'protection and empowerment' framework.

The key questions at this stage are:

- What are the relationships between the specific protection and empowerment strategies?
- Which empowerment strategies build upon the capacities of the local population to best resist and respond to the identified threats and vulnerabilities while also enlarging their choices?
  - What community capacity(ies) and assets provide solid foundations for empowerment strategies?
  - What community strengths have been neglected? How can they best be employed?
- Which protection strategies target the existing gaps in the human security infrastructure and reinforce the capacities of the institutional structure to ensure the protection of the affected community(ies) against the most severe and widespread threats?
  - Based on the assessment of resources and gaps

in the human security infrastructure, which strategies are most likely to have positive externalities on other sectors?

- Which protection strategies have the greatest positive externalities on empowerment? Which empowerment strategies have the greatest positive externalities on protection strategies?

Phase II. Implementation

One of the goals of the implementation phase is to ensure ownership by the beneficiaries and local counterparts through capacity building and partnership. A strong human security programme should be evaluated against the level of local ownership in the implementation phase and the sustainability of the programme, which is increased through collaborative implementation.

Participatory Approaches and Local Capacity Building

Participation by the affected beneficiaries and local counterparts is vital to the successful implementation and sustainability of any human security programme. Human security programmes must be informed by inputs from the local population in order to be both legitimate and effective in achieving the objectives of the affected community(ies). Participatory processes also provide forums for partnerships that are necessary for addressing complex situations of human insecurity.

Today, there is a large toolkit of participatory approaches available and the decision on which to employ should be determined by the specificities of the circumstances.

Nevertheless, some of the factors that will impact strategic choices regarding participation include:

- Access to the local population.
- Cultural/community barriers to participation.
- Existing inequalities amongst the local population.
- External hazards or hostile conditions.
- Funding constraints.
- Timeframe.

For UN actors, participation is an important element for advancing multi-agency programme and/or project development.

As a result, participatory processes are undertaken with multiple partner agencies in order to ensure:

- Clear delineation of responsibilities and tasks.
- Harmonized monitoring and reporting mechanisms.
- Shared goals, objectives, strategies, outcomes, and impact in programme/project development.

Meanwhile for multi-actor groups, participation broadens the scope of the potential participants and emphasizes local and national participatory processes as much as possible.

In these groups, participation:

- Provides a foundation for capacity-building and empowerment strategies.
- Provides a medium for mainstreaming best practices and lessons learned.
- Provides opportunities for building and/or strengthening networks of action.
- Supports implementation by local actors in collaboration with other agencies.

The Stages of Participatory Implementation

The building of local capacities and the emphasis on empowerment measures are fundamental to the advancement of human security.

This can occur during all phases of a human security programme. However, the implementation phase provides significant opportunities for building upon and developing new local capacities through participation in project activities and implementation by community members and local counterparts.

Participation subsequently needs to be actively mainstreamed through:

- Allowing for leadership to emerge from the affected community(ies) and building upon and supporting legitimate local and community-based structures.
- Careful planning that integrates strategies and activities which highlight and build upon the

capacities and the resources of the affected community(ies).

- Implementing, reporting and monitoring mechanisms in a manner that makes technical assistance readily accessible and shares ownership for successful implementation with the affected community(ies).

4

International Human Rights Law

INTRODUCTION

In June 1993 a United Nations World Conference was held in Vienna to address the differences in national perceptions of international human rights. The goal was to reach a mutual understanding and universal approach to human rights norms, fundamental freedoms and enforcement mechanisms

As a preliminary to this global gathering of nations, an Asian regional meeting was held in Bangkok, gathering together the respective governments. One premise was to challenge the idea of 'universal human rights standards', which the Vienna Conference sought to establish. To Asia, their language of human rights differed fundamentally to that defined by the international community of the United Nations, given their unique culture, history and economy. Their discussions culminated in the Bangkok Declaration, proposing a culturally relative approach in favour of globally applicable standards.

In the aftermath of the Vienna Conference there appeared to be no resolution that appeased all parties. Ambassador Kausikan summed this view up when he declared that the World Conference on Human Rights in Vienna, on June 1993 did not promote "a genuine and fruitful dialogue" between the West and East.

- The West went to Vienna accusing Asia of trying to undermine the ideal of universality and determined to blame Asia if the conference failed. Inevitably Asia resisted. The result after weeks of wrangling was a

> predictable diplomatic compromise ambiguous enough so that all could live with it, but settled very few things. There was no real dialogue between Asia and the West, no genuine attempt to address the issues or forge a meeting of minds. If anything, the Vienna Conference may have only hardened attitudes on both sides and increased the deep scepticism which many Asian countries regard Western posturing on human rights

Over a decade later the debate continues, aligning itself upon an East/West axis, with the Western world cultivating a vision of human rights with a core of civil and political rights shaped by a liberal western tradition, and the East challenging this view with cultural, political and economic dimensions. Ultimately "What appears from the Western perspective, to be a noble campaign for universal rights is interpreted from the Asian perspective, as cultural imperialism".

China lies amid this opposing Eastern faction and although it has experienced enormous economic and social progress, political reform has lagged behind, and the repression of citizens seeking to exercise their internationally recognised fundamental freedoms continues to be problematic.

This document seeks to understand China's aversion to the application of international human rights principles by analysing the main opposing arguments. Given the apparent reluctance of accedence to universal standards the focus will then turn to the International Community and their proposed mechanisms of improving the human rights dilemma. Within this the action taking by America, the European Union and the United Nations will be specifically noted. In addition the mechanisms that are currently in place to deal with the human rights problem by China itself will be looked to, to assess their capability of truly rectifying the problem.

CHINA'S OPPOSITION TO A UNIVERSAL STANDARD OF HUMAN RIGHTS

As a full member of the United Nations and a signatory to the Charter of the United Nations, China have pledged themselves to co-operate with the international community to achieve universal respect for, and observance of human rights and fundamental freedoms, and to accept the jurisdiction of the UN in cases of human rights abuse. Considering China's apparent commitment to the international community, its opposition to a universal agreement on human rights calls for clarification.

DIFFERENCE IN CULTURE AND THE CONCEPTION OF HUMAN RIGHTS

It is the perception of western society and the majority of the international community that being human is reason enough to be attributed certain inalienable rights. China asserts a contrasting dogma whereby man is born only with social and political duties, which should be carried out in service to the community. Rights are not derived from ones' status as a human being but rather they "flow from the state in the form of a gratuitous grant that can be subjected to conditions or abrogation by the unilateral decision of the state". These views stem from the Confucian tradition in China that humanity is not an innate quality but rather something which is achieved through socialization and contribution to the harmony of society. The granting of inalienable rights at birth would be a considered a subversion of established Chinese ideals.

Democracy is a further facet of Western traditions that fits uneasily with Chinese heritage. The Western world favours a system with the population as a ruling class, and an ultimate goal of individual rights and political liberty. From a western perspective the Confucian ideal could only be deemed corrupt as it mandates great discretionary power for one ruler, with a society accepting their decisions as being in the best interest of the community. There exists no need for political human rights as it is unnecessary to keep check on the authority of the leader. In principle, the teachings of Confucius are manifest in China's past only, but history produces tradition and tradition shapes people's thinking and behaviour. The rationality, morality, and values of human beings are embedded in the particular cultural tradition in which they find themselves and from this the picture of human rights is shaped. China has sculpted its view of human rights from a culture at variance with that of the west, and so it contends that it cannot be governed by the same standards. The situation of China sharpens a long standing dilemma amongst various regions such as Indonesia and Africa, who articulate their inability to subsume a universalistic approach to human rights on account of there culture and traditions.

The fundamental question is whether there can be a truly universal doctrine of human rights applicable to all nations, and to what extent culture can justify a different application of human rights thinking and discourse? This is not a problem to which the consensus can agree upon and it may be necessary for the West to accept that states can legitimately agree to disagree without being guilty of gross misdeeds. An attempt to impose the Western definitions of 'liberty' and 'freedom' may only prove to be destructive in the face of Chinese opposition, best foregone in the interest of promoting genuine human rights. What can be said is that culture should not be used as a device to commit human rights violations and to reject entirely political and civil rights; "abuse is not part of any nation's cultural heritage".

It is a point worth noting that a persuasive case exists by which China can create a strong human rights foundation in line with global standards by drawing on its own political culture and beliefs. There are many aspects of Chinese culture which are indicative of values akin to those of the west such as value for life, and strong familial bonds. What is more is that the traditional culture advanced to justify cultural relativism far too often no longer exists. It is important to be astute to cynical, manipulation of a dying cultural past, "communitarian rhetoric too often cloaks the depredations of corrupt and often Westernized or deracinated elites."

IMPORTANCE OF ECONOMICOVER SOCIAL RIGHTS

The 1948 Universal Declaration of Human Rights proclaimed both political and economic rights, but the subsequent drafting of two separate protocols divided rights into civil and political on one hand, and economic, social and cultural on the other. Although the preambles of both the International Covenant on Civil and Political Rights, and the International Covenant on Economic, Social and Cultural Rights refer to the enjoyment of both classes of rights many countries have advocated only one division. In 1998 China became a signatory to the ICCPR yet it makes the ongoing representation that given its poor economy it is unable to support the political freedoms mandated therein and instead chooses to advocate the economic and social rights embodied in the IESCR

In 2004, Liu Zhenghua spoke on behalf of Chinese Delegation on Economic, Social and Cultural Rights at the 60 Session of the Commission on Human Rights.

In his speech he called upon the International Community to:

- Respond positively to the legitimate demand of the developing countries for greater prominence to be given to economic, social and cultural rights so as to promote fuller enjoyment of all human rights and fundamental freedoms by all peoples.

During the same session Du Zhonxing, adviser of the Chinese delegation on Civil and Political Rights made the following statement:

- As a developing country with a large population, great regional disparities, and a comparatively low level of economic development and education, China is facing various difficulties and challenges in its effort to realise civil and political rights. No matter what method or model a country adopts in realising human rights, the enjoyment of civil and political rights by individuals in that country cannot possibly exceed the level of its overall social development.

Such proclamations affirm that China grants primacy to economic development to the detriment of political freedoms. In the past the government has stated that "it is a simple truth that, for any country or nation, the right of subsistence is the most important of all human rights, without which the other rights are out of the question." Such statements suppose a false dilemma of having to choose between starvation and oppression, as economic development flourishes when it is without the hindrance of political freedoms. There is a lack of empirical support for a contention that suppression of freedoms yields significant benefits in terms of economic performance.

In fact the opposite is more likely to be true, as countries with authoritarian governments are the only nations to have suffered famine. Promoting political rights if anything only proves to improve the economy, it allows the people to have a voice to define their economic needs, enabling a better government response. Academics continue to dispute the dichotomy of economic and political rights stating that economic development and freedoms are inseparable and that no country can legitimately prioritize economic conditions over political freedoms.

SOVEREIGNTY

China mandates that respect for each country's sovereignty and non-interference with their internal affairs is a universal principle, and that this principle extends to all fields of international relations, including human rights. Section 7 of Article 2 of the Charter of the United Nations provides foundation for this assertion, stipulating that "Nothing contained in the present charter shall authorize the United Nations to intervene in matters which are essentially within the domestic jurisdiction of the state".

China is weary of other countries using human rights as a guise so that they may impose upon them their own political standards and modes of development. Consequently any criticism of its human rights by the international community is deemed to impinge their sovereignty.

The weakness of China's objection is twofold. Firstly the issue is not whether the international protection of human rights infringes domestic sovereignty, but whether it does so unlawfully. Secondly, the question arises as to whether the benefits to the world community outweigh the measure of national sovereignty that is relinquished. In addressing human rights the international community is not unlawfully interfering with China's internal jurisdiction. Human Rights issues cross national boundaries and so are valid international concerns; they deal with interactions between states and individuals, not relations between nations. One need only look at the many Christians, Tibetans and Falun Gong practitioners that fled China under the regime of Jiang Zemin to escape religious persecution. They now reside as refugees in countries external to China, an example of the domestic affairs spilling into the international arena.

As already noted, China is a voluntary member of the UN and signatory to the UN Charter, and consequently subject to international human rights enforcement decisions. In pursuing a policy of fiercely protecting its domestic integrity, China ultimately ignores the element of sovereignty abdicated in becoming a full member of the International Community. It is suggested therefore that in resolving who should have ultimate control on these matters, a balancing test of potential benefits to harms tips the argument in favour of international protection and enforcement. To avidly protect the integrity of China's domestic sovereignty over human rights will lead to individual harm, thus negating the very fabric of the treaties to which China is a signatory.

RECTIFYING THE PROBLEM

China's human rights position is one requiring a delicate approach. Its preference may be one of isolation and entirely independent governing, but its poor human rights record and repressive regimes nullify such a prospect. In pressing for progress, the international community must be careful not to upset the fragile balance between enduring human rights and respecting cultural difference.

USA

The United States Department, as part of its Human Rights and Democracy Fund Project assigned more than $12,000,000 to China in 2004 and approximately $19,000,000 in 2005. Such expenditure is intended to encourage innovative programmes to uphold democratic principles, support democratic institutions and improve human rights. A substantial proportion of this fund is assigned to develop law and governance so as to create greater transparency in government and increase public participation.

This form of contribution carries weighted benefit. China continually mandates that economic instability is a major reason why political rights cannot be fully realised by their citizens. In providing a fund that has a sole focus of promoting a foundation for political rights, the United States is helping to remove one of China's greatest obstacles to fully ratifying the ICCPR.

In addition to funding, the United States recently published a report aimed at supporting democracy and human rights. Therein the US affirmed its commitment to continue to urge China to bring its human rights standards in line with that of the international community. As a means of securing this endeavour, US officials at all levels regularly engage with Chinese officials and researchers to discuss legal reform. The US mission in China has also brought internationally recognized speakers to China to address audiences on various topics, including democracy, human rights, religious freedom, corporate social responsibility and rule of law.

Such mechanisms facilitate the mutual exchange of ideas and create greater trust between China and the Western world. For China to commit to evolving its human rights it is important to encourage internal understanding as to what this will entail, otherwise it will be categorised as hostile imposition of foreign ideologies.

THE EUROPEAN UNION

The European Union has continually stood against China on account of its poor human rights regime. In 1997 the EU clarified its position by refusing to sponsor a human rights resolution on China at the United Nations Human Rights Commission. 2005 brought with it greater stress on the importance of dialogue and compromise between the EU and China with the holding of the 8th EU-China Summit in Beijing.

During this meeting both sides endorsed the importance of exchanges in the field of human rights on the basis of equality and mutual respect. The EU welcomed China's commitment to ratifying the ICCPR and both sides confirmed their commitment to co-operate with UN human rights and international human rights standards provided for in relevant international human rights instruments.

Debatably one of the greatest achievements of the rhetoric between these two parties has been the emergence of the EU-China Legal and Judicial Co-operation Programme. This has become one of the most important assistance programmes of its kind in China, aiming to support and strengthen the rule of law thorough citizen participation. This type of grass roots up approach grants greater insurance that the endeavours of the international community are in keeping with the best interests of the Chinese people. Smaller grass roots projects have also been established, such as the EU-China Village Governance Programme, so as to empower citizens with civil rights.

This programme aims to devolve power to small regions, so that they can establish their own 'mini government' in which they participate in voting and the election of representatives. Such a system allows a natural understanding of what political rights entail, and allows citizens to experience their values. If the ICCPR is ratified, the approaches endorsed by the European Union will greater allow for the practical application of the rights contained therein.

THE UN

The Office of the Hugh Commissioner for Human Rights has developed a Regional Programme with a main objective of providing support for the ratification and implementation of international human rights treaties through comparative analysis of law and practices in the regions. OHCHR's approach involves working closely with regional actors, including government, national institutions, international organisations and civil society. This type of programme acknowledges China's reluctance to fully engage with the international community on the grounds of cultural difference. By becoming more aware of the diversity of the East, and the practices of law already in place the UN is better equipping itself to encourage a culturally sensitive approach to treaty ratification. The effects of this regime are already resonating in the more formal steps that China took towards ratification of the ICCPR at the close of 2005. At this time, during a visit by the High Commissioner for Human Rights, Louise Arbour, China assented to an agreement that they would ratify the ICCPR in the near future.

CHINA

The People's Republic of China has made some positive moves towards the realisation of human rights. The United Nation's, China ranks seventh in the world in terms of the size of its economy· If we take the progress that China has made in terms of taking its people out of poverty, and compare it with the rest of the globe, statistics will show that in the last 20 years, China has been decreasing the number of poverty stricken people by 10 million per year.

In 1999 the World Bank and the UN development programme issued a report stating that "the number of poverty stricken people in the world is increasing in many places in the world, but China is an exception and China has achieved world renowned progress in solving the poverty problem" This makes China the leader in the world at reducing the number of poverty stricken people

The development of a comprehensive social security system and health service system is further affirmation of China's progression in terms of Socioeconomic Rights' as is the improved education system where the enrolment rate for primary school-age children now stands at 87.3 per cent. These figures exceed the average figures for developing countries in the corresponding period.

China's efforts in the realm of social and economic rights are admirable, but the dubious aspect of its rights portfolio lies in the area of civil and political rights. In the 2004 White Paper entitled "Building of Political Democracy in China",

China declared the adoption of a constitutional amendment by the Second Session of the 10th National People's Congress. The new addition proclaims that 'the state respects and protects human rights'. This insertion has been deemed by many as a positive move forward and is backed by Amnesty International, but it does negate the remaining inadequacy of the Constitution as a whole nor does it remedy the inadequate legal and institutional system which provides no practical mechanism for the Constitution's application.

China has become a signatory to the ICCPR, and although it has yet to be ratified, the intention to do so in the near future has been declared. There have already been some signs of a changing attitude towards political rights under the auspices of the Chinese authorities. At local levels democratic policy making is developing through the establishing of village committees.

Direct elections of members of villagers' committees take place and they themselves are encouraged to decide upon major affairs of their community through democratic dialogue. Since the promulgation of the new Organic Law on Villagers' Committees in 1999, nearly half of the provinces, municipalities directly under the Central Government and autonomous regions have published their own laws and regulations on the election of villagers' committees.

Many of these improvements have been outlined in the Chinese White Papers, publications which boast of the human rights endeavours that China has undertaken. One should be weary of taking these proclamations at face value. Sidney Jones, the Asian Director of Human Rights Watch has made prior statements of concern as to the motives of these documents and the substantiality of their claims. He has termed them a 'white wash' and suggested that they are a tactic used to placate the international community even though the reality of the situation in China is very different.

The Standing Committee of the 10th National People's Congress, China's top legislature has also stipulated an amendment to the criminal procedure in its five year legislature plan. It has been predicted that the amendment will include presumption of innocence, the right of the defendant to keep silent and seek legal council during questioning. Such amendments are a clear move towards improving the judicial system so as to support the upholding of human rights. As yet though there has been no clear move towards defining these amendments, nor any definite announcement on the part of any Chinese Official, so it remains to be seen whether they will be put in place in actuality.

5

Regional Systems of Protection and Promotion

In addition to the universal instruments of human rights protection several regional systems of human rights have developed, which usually provide a higher standard of rights and their implementation.

The advantage of regional systems is their capacity to address complaints more efficiently. In the case of courts, binding decisions with compensation can be given and also the recommendations of the Commissions on Human Rights are generally taken seriously by states.

They may result not only in "lead cases" to interpret and clarify provisions of human rights instruments, but also in changes of national law in order to bring it into conformity with international human rights obligations. In addition, regional systems tend to be more sensitive to cultural and religious concerns, if there are valid reasons for them.

EUROPE

The European human rights system has three layers, namely the system of the Council of Europe (presently 46 members), of the Organization for Security and Cooperation in Europe (55 members) and of the European Union (presently 25 members). The European system of human rights is the most elaborate regional system. It has developed as a reaction to the massive human rights violations during World War II. Human rights, the rule of law and pluralistic democracy are the cornerstones of the European legal order.

European Human Rights Instruments:

- Charter of Fundamental Rights of the European Union (2000)
- Convention for the Protection of Human Rights and Fundamental Freedoms (1950) and 14 additional protocols
- European Charter for Regional or Minority Languages (1992)
- European Convention for the Prevention of Torture and other Inhuman and Degrading Treatment (1987)
- European Social Charter (1961), as revised in 1991 and 1996 and Additional Protocols 1988 and 1995.
- Final Act of Helsinki (1975) and follow- up process of CSCE/OSCE with Charter of Paris for new Europe (1990)
- Framework Convention for the Protection of National Minorities (1994)

THE HUMAN RIGHTS SYSTEM OF THE COUNCIL OF EUROPE

An Overview

The main instrument is the European Convention on Human Rights (ECHR) of 1950 and its 13 additional protocols. Of particular importance are protocols No. 6 and 13 (not yet in force) on the abolition of the death penalty, which distinguish the European human rights approach from that of the United States, and protocol No. 11, which replaced the European Commission on Human Rights and the European Court of Human Rights by one permanent European Court of Human Rights. The ECHR mainly contains civil and political rights.

The European Social Charter of 1961 set out to add economic and social rights, but never gained the same importance as the ECHR. From the beginning it suffered from a weak and inefficient system of implementation. However, parallel to the growing attention to economic and social rights on the universal level since the late 1980s, new attention has been given also to the European Social Charter which was amended twice in 1988 and 1995 and now also offers the possibility of collective complaints based on an additional protocol. A major innovation has been introduced by the European Convention for the Prevention of Torture and Inhuman or Degrading Treatment or Punishment of 1987, which established a European Committee for the Prevention of Torture and Inhuman or Degrading Treatment or Punishment.

The Committee sends delegations to all member states of the Convention to undertake regular or special visits to all places of detention. The logic of the system is its preventive effect as opposed to ex post facto protection, which is still taken care of by the ECHR and its court. In December 2002, the UN General Assembly adopted an additional protocol to the UN Convention against Torture which foresees a similar mechanism to operate worldwide.

The European Framework Convention for the Protection of National Minorities (1995) was elaborated after the summit meeting of the Council of Europe in Vienna 1993 as a reaction to the increasing problems with minority rights in Europe.

These problems are the result of the dissolution of the Soviet Union and the Socialist Republic of Yugoslavia and more generally of the process of self-determination in Europe in the 1990s. States have to protect the individual rights of members of national minorities, but also to provide conditions which allow minorities to maintain and develop their culture and identity.

The enforcement mechanism however is limited to a reporting system and an Advisory Committee of Experts in charge of reviewing the reports. The Council of Europe in 1999 also established a "Commissioner on Human Rights", who gives information about his or her activities in an annual report.

Furthermore, there is a confidential monitoring system of the performance of members in different areas of human rights, which is the responsibility of the Council of Ministers on the basis of reports prepared by the Secretariat.

European Human Rights Institutions and Bodies Council of Europe:

- European Court of Human Rights (single court 1998)
- European Committee on Social Rights (as revised 1999)
- European Committee for the Prevention of Torture or Other Inhuman or Degrading Treatment (CPT, 1989)
- Advisory Committee of the Framework Convention on National Minorities (1998)
- European Commission on Racism and Intolerance (ECRI, 1993)
- European Commissioner for Human Rights (1999)
- Committee of Ministers of the Council of Europe

OSCE:

- Office for Democratic Institutions and Human Rights (ODIHR, 1990)
- High Commissioner on National Minorities (OSCE, 1992)
- Representative for the Freedom of the Media (OSCE, 1997)

European Union:

- European Court of Justice
- European Monitoring Centre on Racism and Xenophobia (EUMC, 1998)
- European Agency for Fundamental Rights (2007)

The European Court of Human Rights

The main instrument of protection of human rights in Europe is the European Court of Human Rights in Strasbourg, the obligatory jurisdiction of which today is recognised by all member states of the Council of Europe. The number of judges is equal to the number of member states of the Council of Europe.

In each case a so-called "national judge" is involved in order to facilitate the understanding of the national legislation. However, judges once appointed serve only in their personal capacity.

In order for a complaint to be admissible, four major pre-conditions have to be fulfilled:

- Violation of a right protected by the ECHR and its additional protocols
- Complainant(s) being a victim of the violation
- Exhaustion of all effective domestic remedies
- Complaint to be made less than 6 months after exhaustion of domestic remedies

If considered admissible, a chamber of 7 judges decides about the merits of the case. Their judgment is final if the case is not considered as being of particular importance or representing a new line of jurisdiction, in which case a grand chamber of 17 judges serves in an appeal function.

The judgments are binding and may also provide compensation for damages. The supervision of the execution of the judgments is the task of the Committee of Ministers. The main problem of this system at present is the large number of complaints received which has increased from about 1.000 in 1989 to more than 44.000 in 2004, resulting in an overloading of the system. The Protocol No. 14 to the ECHR of 2004 has been adopted to address this problem.

HUMAN RIGHTS SYSTEM OF THE ORGANIZATION OF SECURITY AND COOPERATION IN EUROPE (OSCE)

The OSCE, which replaced the Conference on Security and Cooperation in Europe in 1994, is a very particular organisation. It neither has a legal charter nor international legal personality and its declarations and recommendations are only of a political nature and not legally binding on states. Nonetheless, the often very detailed catalogues of obligations adopted in various follow-up conferences or expert meetings and monitored by the Council of representatives of member states and regularly organized follow-up conferences is a rather successful monitoring mechanism.

The "Helsinki Process" played a major role in building cooperation between East and West during the Cold War and providing a basis for cooperation in the wider Europe of 55 countries. Under the title of "human dimension", the OSCE undertakes a number of activities in the field of human rights and minority rights in particular. These also play a major role in the various field missions as in the case of Bosnia and Herzegovina or Serbia and Montenegro as well as Kosovo. For this purpose OSCE missions have a human rights department and human rights officers are deployed throughout the country to monitor and report on the human rights situation, but also to promote human rights and to assist in certain cases of protection.

The OSCE also supports national institutions of human rights in the countries where it maintains a mission like the ombudspersons in Bosnia and Herzegovina or in Kosovo. Special mechanisms have been developed in the form of the High Commissioner for Minorities and the Representative for the Freedom of the Media (Freedom of Expression and Freedom of the Media), which have their offices in The Hague and Vienna, respectively. The High Commissioner on National Minorities is an instrument of conflict prevention with the mandate to deal with ethnic tensions at the earliest possible stage.

The OSCE also had a major role in monitoring democratic elections in a number of countries in Europe transforming into pluralist democracies. The democratisation process and the promotion of human rights is supported by the Office of Democratic Institutions and Human Rights (ODIHR) located in Warsaw. The OSCE also plays a major role in conflict resolution and post-conflict reconstruction in Europe.

HUMAN RIGHTS POLICY OF THE EUROPEAN UNION

Whereas the European Economic Community created in 1957 originally did not concern itself with political issues like human rights, the political integration of Europe towards a European Union since the 1980s has enabled human rights and democracy to become key-concepts of the common European legal order. A major role was played by the European Court of Justice which developed a human rights jurisdiction derived from "common constitutional traditions of member states" and international treaties to which those member states were parties, notably the European Convention on Human Rights. Several human rights were constructed as general principles of community law, like the right to property, freedom of association and religion or the principle of equality, which is of particular importance in European community law. Since the 1980s the European Community also developed a human rights policy in its relations with third countries, which is also reflected in the so-called Copenhagen criteria for the recognition of new states in South- Eastern Europe.

Art. 6 and 7 of the 1995 Treaty on European Union explicitly refer to the European Convention of 1950 and it is foreseen that the European Union will accede to that convention as a member. In 2000 a Convention was convened to draft the Charter of Fundamental Rights of the EU, adopted by the Nice summit in 2000. Presently this Charter is the most modern human rights document in Europe and includes civil and political as well as economic, social and cultural rights similar to the UDHR.

So far, it has no legally binding status. However, as it enshrines a number of human rights obligations which also form part of various international treaties of which the European Union member states are parties, the Charter can be understood as an interpretation and clarification of those binding obligations. Since 1995 the EU includes human rights clauses in its bilateral agreements, such as the "Stability and Association Agreements", the Cotonou Agreement or the Euromed Agreement.

Although a new European constitution, which should have given the European Charter on Fundamental Human Rights a binding status has not (yet) come into force, a stronger focus on human rights might be achieved in other ways. The European Union has developed a human rights policy both for its internal relations as well as its international relations, where it forms part of its Common Foreign and Security Policy. The Annual Report on Human Rights published by the Council of the European Union reflects the importance of this human rights policy for the European Union in general. The Council makes public statements, but is also active behind the scenes in a case-oriented "human rights diplomacy" and together with the European Commission pursues "human rights dialogues" with several countries like China and Iran. The European Parliament has taken a lead in keeping human rights high on the EU agenda and also issues annual reports on human rights.

On its initiative financial support for projects of NGOs in the field of human rights and democracy is available from the European Initiative for Democracy and Human Rights, operated by Europe Aid on behalf of the European Commission, which defines the political strategy. Special emphasis is given to the struggle against torture and the death penalty, or the campaign for the International Criminal Court. The European Union Monitoring Centre on Racism and Xenophobia (EUMC), created by the European Union to address the growing problem of racism and xenophobia in Europe and established in Vienna in 1998, monitors the situation in Europe and promotes activities against racism and xenophobia.

A European Agency for Fundamental Rights will be established in Vienna in 2007 to monitor the human rights treated in the European Charter. Based on the work of EUMC, it will collect data and provide reports on Human Rights situations on request and thus support European Union Human Rights policies. In 1998, Art. 13 was introduced into the on the European Community Treaty empowering the Community to combat discrimination on the grounds of racial or ethnic origin, religion or belief, age, disability or sexual orientation.

In 2000, the Council adopted directive 2000/43/ EC on the implementation of the principle of equal treatment irrespective of racial or ethnic origin, in particular, in the fields of employment, access to education and training, and social advantages, which applies both to public and private sectors within the EU. Similarly, the European Union has a particular focus on equality. The European Community Treaty member states have to apply the principle of "equal payment for men and women" and to adopt measures providing equality of opportunity. Additionally, this principle has been further developed in regulations and directives like the updated equal treatment directive 2002/73/EC.

THE AMERICAS

The Inter-American system of Human Rights started with the American Declaration of the Rights and Duties of Man, which was adopted in 1948, together with the Charter of the Organization of American States (OAS). The Inter-American Commission on Human Rights, created by OAS in 1959 and consisting of 7 members, is the main body of the system. In 1978, the American Convention on Human Rights, adopted in 1969, came into force, and since has been complemented by two additional protocols, one on economic, social and cultural rights and one on the abolition of the death penalty. The United States is not a member of the Convention, although the seat of the Commission is in Washington. The Convention also provided for the Inter-American Court on Human Rights, which was established in 1979 with its seat in Costa Rica, where the "Inter-American Institute of Human Rights" is also located. There are several legal instruments granting rights to women, but the Inter-American Convention on the Prevention, Punishment and Eradication of Violence against Women (Convention of Belém do Pará), which came into force in 1995, deserves special mentioning. It has already been ratified by 31 of the 34 member-states of OAS. This Convention regular national reports are to be submitted to the Inter-American Commission of Women, established already in 1928. There is also a Special Rapporteur on the Rights of Women (since 1994).

Inter-American System of Human Rights:

- American Declaration on the Rights and Duties of Man (1948)
- Inter-American Commission on Human Rights (1959)
- American Convention on Human Rights (1969/1978)
- Additional Protocol on Economic, Social and Cultural Rights (1988)
- Additional Protocol on the Abolition of the Death Penalty (1990)

- Inter-American Court on Human Rights (1979/1984)
- Inter-American Commission on Women (1928)
- American Convention on the Prevention, Punishment and Eradication of Violence against Women (1994)

Individuals, groups or NGOs can make complaints, called "petitions" to the Inter-American Commission on Human Rights, which may also request information on human rights measures taken. The Inter-American Court cannot be addressed directly, but only through the Commission, which can decide which cases are to transfer to the Court. In this way, in the past, the Court did not get many cases, which now seems to have changed. The Court can also give advisory opinions, *i.e.* on the interpretation of the Convention.

Like the Commission it has seven members and works on a non-permanent basis. The Commission can also undertake on-site investigations and issues special reports on particular issues of concern. There are several NGOs, which assist victims of human rights violations to take cases to the Inter- American Commission on Human Rights and the Court.

AFRICA

The African system of human rights was created in 1981 with the adoption by the then OAU of the African Charter on Human and Peoples' Rights, which came into force in 1986. It provides for the African Commission on Human and Peoples' Rights, consisting of 11 members, which has its seat in Banjul, the Gambia.

Today, all 53 member states of the African Union (AU), which succeeded the OAU in 2001, have ratified the African Charter, which follows the approach of the Universal Declaration of Human Rights uniting all categories of human rights in one document.

Its preamble refers to the "values of African civilization", which is intended to inspire the African concept of human and peoples' rights. Besides individual rights it also enunciates peoples' rights. Furthermore, it spells out duties of individuals, for example towards the family and society, which, however, have little relevance in practice.

African System of Human Rights:

- African Charter on Human and Peoples' Rights (1981, in force 1986)
- African Commission on Human and Peoples' Rights (1987)
- Protocol on the Establishment of an African Court on Human and People's Rights (1997, in force 2003)
- Protocol on the Rights of Women (2003, in force 2005)
- African Charter on the Rights and Welfare of the Child (1990, in force 1999)

The Commission has a large mandate in the field of promotion of human rights, but can also receive complaints from states (which has never happened so far) and individuals or groups. Admissibility criteria are wide and also allow for communications from NGOs or individuals on behalf of victims of violations. However, the Commission cannot issue legally binding decisions, which is one reason why a protocol to the Charter on the establishment of the African Court on Human and Peoples' Rights has been adopted, which came into force in 2003. It can receive complaints only through the Commission as in the Inter- American System.

The Court can be directly addressed by individuals only if states make a special declaration in that respect, which is the exception so far. However, in 2004, the Assembly of Heads of State and Government decided to merge the Court with the Court of the African Union on the basis of a new legal instrument, while all necessary measures for the functioning of the Human•Rights Court can already be taken. A regular monitoring of the national situation of human rights is to take place on the basis of the examination of state reports by the Commission, which, however, are often irregular and unsatisfactory.

Following the UN practice, the Commission has appointed special rapporteurs on extra-judicial, summary and arbitrary executions, on prisons and conditions of detention, on the rights of women, on human rights defenders and on freedom of expression. The Commission also sends fact-finding missions and promotional missions organises extraordinary sessions in particular cases, such as after the execution of nine members of the Movement for the Survival of the Ogoni People in 1995 and their unfair trial. An important part of the momentum of the Commission comes from Non-Governmental Organizations from Africa and beyond, which are allowed to participate in all public meetings of the Commission.

They often bring cases of violations and support the work of the Commission and its special rapporteurs. It is also important that governments make the Charter directly applicable in their national legal systems. This has happened, for example, in the case of Nigeria with the result that Nigerian NGOs as, for example, "Constitutional Rights Project" successfully brought cases of violations of the Charter before Nigerian Courts.

Following the adoption of the UN-Convention on the Rights of the Child in 1989 an African Charter on the Rights and Welfare of the Child was adopted in 1990. However, it only came into force in 1999 and in 2005 had been ratified by only 35 AU-states. The Charter foresees the establishment of an African Committee of Experts on the Rights and Welfare of the Child which has to meet at least once a year. In view of the slow ratification process it remains to be seen whether this convention and its committee will produce good results.

OTHER REGIONS

For the Islamic countries, the "Cairo Declaration on Human Rights in Islam" of 1990 needs to be mentioned, which was drawn up by the Foreign Ministers of the Organization of the Islamic Conference, but never adopted officially? All rights stipulated in this Declaration are subject to the Islamic Sharia. Furthermore, an Arab Charter on Human Rights has been elaborated by Arab human rights experts and adopted by the Council of the League of Arab States in 1994 but has never entered into force for lack of ratifications. In Asia, in spite of several attempts, it has not yet been possible to adopt a regional Human Rights instrument or to establish an Asian Human Rights Commission, mainly because of the diversity within the region. However, there are efforts within regional integration areas like ASEAN, which may finally also lead to an Asian Commission on Human Rights in the future. On the level of civil society, more than 200 Asian NGOs under the leadership of Asian Legal Resources Centre in Hong Kong, on the occasion of the 50th Anniversary of the UDHR in 1998, elaborated an "Asian Human Rights Charter" as a "Peoples' charter".

There is also a Euro-Asian Dialogue between the European Union and 10 ASEM states on human rights, which has already had four sessions. A similar dialogue exists between the European Union and China. As an inter-regional agreement, the Cotonou Partnership Agreement between 78 African, Caribbean and Pacific (ACP) States and the 15 members of the European Union of 2000, in Art. 9 (2) recalls that "respect for human rights, democratic principles and the rule of law constitute the essential elements of this agreement."

6

Freedom from Poverty

INTRODUCTION

Although poverty has been seen as a historical phenomenon, the forms in which it manifests itself today are becoming increasingly complex. This complexity is a result of many factors, including the changing nature of relationships between humans, the relationship between society and factors and processes of production, and the outlook of governments and international institutions like the World Bank, the International Monetary Fund, or the United Nations on various dimensions of poverty.

The concept of poverty has evolved over time. Poverty, which used to be seen as income-related only, is now viewed as a multi-dimensional concept that derives from and is closely linked to politics, geography, history, culture and societal specificities.

In developing countries, poverty is pervasive and is characterised by hunger, lack of land and livelihood resources, inefficient redistribution policies, unemployment, illiteracy, epidemics, lack of health services and safe water. In developed countries, poverty manifests itself in the form of social exclusion, in rising unemployment and low wages. In both cases, poverty exists because of lack of equity, equality, human security and peace.

Poverty means a drought of access in a world of plentiful opportunity. The poor are not able to change their situation as they are denied the means of that capability due to lack of political freedom, inability to participate in decision-making processes, lack of personal security, inability to participate in the life of a community and threats to sustainable and intergenerational equity. Poverty is the denial of economic, social and political power and resources that keeps the poor immersed in poverty.

DEFINITION AND DESCRIPTION OF THE ISSUE DEFINING POVERTY

There are various definitions of poverty and its manifestations:

- From the income perspective, poverty defines a person as poor if, and only if, their income level is below the defined poverty line. Many countries have adopted income poverty lines to monitor the progress in reducing the incidence of poverty. The cut-off poverty line is defined in terms of having enough income for a specified amount of food. The UNDP Human Development Report (HDR) 1997, "poverty means that opportunities and choices most basic to human development are denied - to lead a long, healthy, creative life and to enjoy a decent standard of living, freedom, dignity, self-respect and the respect of others."
- The Human Poverty Index (UNDP, HDR 1997) uses indicators of the most basic dimensions of deprivation - a short life, a lack of basic education and a lack of access to public and private resources, thereby acknowledging that human poverty is more than income poverty.
- From a human rights perspective, the Office of the High Commissioner for Human Rights views poverty as "a human condition characterized by the sustained or chronic deprivation of the resources, capabilities, choices, security and power necessary for the enjoyment of an adequate standard of living and other fundamental civil, cultural, economic, political and social rights."
- In the Draft Guidelines: A Human Rights Approach

to Poverty Reduction Strategies by the Office of the High Commissioner for Human Rights, September 2002, poverty is viewed as an "extreme form of deprivation". The Report suggests that only those capability failures should count as poverty that are deemed to be basic in some order of priority. While these may differ from one society to another, the common set of needs considered basic in most societies include the need of being adequately nourished, avoiding preventable morbidity and premature mortality, being adequately sheltered, having basic education, being able to ensure the security of the person, having equitable access to justice, being able to appear in public without shame, being able to earn a livelihood and taking part in the life of a community.

Debates on how to index and measure poverty persist, but the complexity of human life means that poverty will always remain in search of a definition.

Vulnerability and deprivation, being essentially subjective, cannot be narrowed to a rigid framework that is universally applicable.

DIMENSIONS OF POVERTY

The phenomenon of poverty is understood and articulated differently depending on the specific economic, social, cultural and political context. Going a step forward, we shall now try to relate the words included in definitions of poverty (*e.g.* justice, vulnerability, dignity, security, opportunities etc.) to real-life issues, which would help explain the different dimensions of poverty.

Livelihoods

Denial of access to land, forests, water, *e.g.* in rural areas, state forest laws do not allow indigenous people to collect food and fodder that rightfully belong to them. In the urban context, the city wants rural migrants for their labour, but does not take responsibility for their shelter, health and educational needs, pushing them further into vulnerability and insecurity. Discrimination based on caste, ethnicity and race have also been critical factors for denying communities and groups access to natural resources vital for their livelihoods and therefore their human right to live in dignity.

Basic Needs

Denial of food, education, healthy living and housing, *e.g.* the commercialisation of water, electricity, school and hospital services pushes the prices of essential services beyond the reach of the poor, forcing them to sell their meagre assets and live a sub-human existence, which ultimately robs them of the right to living in dignity.

Justice

Denial of justice *per se* or timely justice, *e.g.* the poor in many countries cannot access the judicial system due to the high costs associated with it. Youngsters from slums, ethnic, racial or religious minorities are the first to be rounded up as easy suspects for crimes not even committed by them, or women who seek intervention by the police in matters of domestic violence are disregarded on the pretext of the issue being a private matter.

Often, due to pressure from the state and other powerful lobbies, courts are seen to delay judicial matters relating to workers' compensation or the rehabilitation of displaced people, which costs the poor their livelihoods.

Organisation

Denial of the right to organise, assume power and to resist injustice, *e.g.* poverty interferes with the freedom of workers to organise themselves for better working conditions.

Participation

Denial of the right to participate in and influence decisions that affect life, *e.g.* growing collusion of political and corporate interests usurps the space of citizens to effectively participate in public matters such as the provision of basic services.

Illiteracy and lack of information due to displacement deny refugees the right to determine their future. Most Roma, due to their migratory nature, are often not even listed on electoral registers and therefore cannot vote.

Human Dignity

Denial of the right to live a life in respect and dignity, *e.g.* in rural areas, caste, ethnic, racial and other minority groups who form a large part of the landless or marginal landowners are forced to compromise their dignity for earning meagre wages.

Children, instead of being at school, are forced into exploitative labour such as waste recycling, leather tanning or agriculture.

Groups Susceptible to Poverty

Though poverty is a widely spread phenomenon and affects people all over the world, it is particularly acute for women and children. Feminisation of poverty has become a significant problem in countries with economies in transition due to the increase in male migration, unemployment and due to the proliferation of household export-oriented economies that are underpaid for their labour.

Most female labour is undocumented and unpaid. Women are preferred to men as workers in many sectors of economy as they are seen as a 'docile workforce.' In many communities, women do not possess and do not have control over land, water, property and other resources and face social and cultural barriers in realising their human rights.

Poverty denies children the opportunity to fulfil their potential as human beings and makes them vulnerable to violence, trafficking, exploitation and abuse. Higher infant and child mortality is often caused by malnutrition; high child/adult ratios are an additional cause for income poverty. With the rapid rise of urbanisation, the number of children living on the streets is increasing.

Around 113 million children all over the world (97% of which are in developing countries) have never been to school and fall easy prey to different forms of exploitation or child labour. Furthermore, increasing commercialisation of education and health services deprives children of their basic constitutional rights in many countries.

Why Poverty Persists

Northern governments which control the governance of the world economy are content to tolerate and maintain trade and financial structures which concentrate wealth in the industrialised world and exclude the poorest countries and people from a share in global prosperity, resulting in inequality among nations of the North and South.

Interestingly enough, both within developed and developing countries there is a widening gap between the rich and the poor. The structural adjustment programmes (SAPs) of the World Bank and the stabilisation packages of the International Monetary Fund came with the promise of generating expanded opportunities of employment, income, wealth and economic development by integrating national economies into a global economic system.

SAPs that seek to eradicate poverty through fiscal discipline without addressing the inequities in the distributive systems may intensify poverty, as countries spend money paying off debts, thereby however neglecting expenditure on basic services like health, education and shelter.

The neo-liberal globalisation puts emphasis on production for exports and ignores the basic rights of people to fulfil their own needs and earn a livelihood with dignity. The rollback of the state from its welfare responsibilities of health, education, food and shelter and the absence of safety nets impact the poor. Inflation, contraction of employment and erosion of real wages brought out by liberalisation and privatisation of assets also affect the poor.

The UNDP Human Development Report 2002 points out that rapid economic growth in already rich countries of Western Europe, North America and Oceania combined with slow growth on the Indian Subcontinent and consistent slow growth in Africa contributed to the increase in global inequality in the second half of the 20th century. Even in the OECD (Organization for Economic Cooperation and Development) countries, the gains have been captured by the richest people, with the incomes of the top 1% of families growing 140%, three times the average, resulting in a dramatic increase in income inequality and the emergence of the "new poor".

- The richest 5% of the world's people have incomes 114 times larger than those of the poorest 5%.
- The income of the richest 25 million Americans is equal to that of almost 2 billion of the world's poorest people.

Today, a quarter of the world's people live in severe poverty confined to the margins of society.

The Human Development Report 2002 of UNDP, an estimated 1.2 billion people survive on less than the equivalent of $1,— a day. Interestingly, the Human Development Report 2005 states that this measurement method does not enjoy full recognition anymore, instead more specified data is needed in order to monitor the progress on the way to achieving the Millennium Development Goals.

Consequently, the examination of developments in this process also leads to highly alarming data, such as the prediction that in case the present policies are kept, the goal to reduce child mortality will be missed and the goal to ensure primary education will not be met, leaving 47 million children out of school by 2015.

While there has been progress as far as access to safe drinking water and the provision of basic vaccinations are concerned, some goals, like the achievement of literacy, still lack proper implementation.

The Human Development Report 2005, 800 million people remain illiterate worldwide. Another issue to be considered remains the pledge to combat child mortality, a challenge highlighted by the 2005 Human Development Report just as to which in 2002 every three seconds a child under 5 years of age died. More needs to be done, for example, in the fight against HIV/AIDS, and the policy of some of the worst-affected countries to deny and neglect the topic or even emphasise stereotypes will certainly not add to the achievement of the relevant MDG.

INTERCULTURAL PERSPECTIVES AND CONTROVERSIAL ISSUES

RELATIVE POVERTY AND ABSOLUTE POVERTY

Relative Poverty denotes that a person or group of people is poor in relation to others or in relation to what is considered to be a fair standard of living/level of consumption in a particular society. Absolute Poverty denotes that people are poor in relation to what is held to be the standard of minimum requirement.

An individual who is categorised as absolutely poor by American standards may be considered relatively poor, say, in the African context. Although Jim's basic economic needs are taken care of, he experiences exclusion and stagnation and is unhappy with his atomised existence and powerlessness. The latter indeed shows how Jim is relatively poor in comparison to others from his society who are socially and politically active.

Social Exclusion

Social Exclusion is often used synonymously with 'relative poverty', but the concepts are not identical. Social exclusion may lead to poverty and at the same time, social exclusion may be the outcome of poverty.

In the case of Jim, social exclusion has resulted in paralysing his political existence, whereas in the case of the Sahariya community of Rajasthan, their economic poverty and destitution have been instrumental for their social exclusion.

IMPLEMENTATION AND MONITORING

During the UN Millennium Assembly session in 2000, heads of states and governments acknowledged their collective responsibility to uphold the principles of human dignity, equality and equity at the global level. They set eight goals for development and poverty eradication to be achieved by 2015. These include: to eradicate extreme poverty and hunger, achieve universal primary education, promote gender equity and empower women, reduce child mortality, improve maternal health, ensure environmental sustainability and develop a global partnership for development. The decade of 1997–2006 has been declared the First United Nations Decade for the Eradication of Poverty.

Each year, 17 October is celebrated as the UN International Day for the Eradication of Poverty. Globalisation and its controversial implications are generating new forms of poverty.

Moreover, these new forms are manifested in societies that are at different levels of socio-political and economic development, comprising people of different faiths, beliefs and cultures. For example, the impact of globalisation on Africa is quite unlike that on India mainly due to the different socio-political and economic conditions in Africa as compared to India.

These distinct differences between cultures and geographic regions have also had an impact on how people have perceived threats emerging from impoverishment and social marginalisation. The critical issue, therefore, is to further develop the framework that monitors these different forms of poverty at the global and local levels and also to empower people to strengthen their resistance and struggle against exploitative forces.

The UN Charter and the Universal Declaration of Human Rights sought to provide the moral framework for constructing a new system of rights and obligations, placing highest emphasis on guaranteeing human dignity, peace and human security for all people in the period after the second World War.

It is the holistic approach to human rights that enables a response to the multi-dimensional nature of poverty. This approach goes beyond charity, recognising that freedom from poverty is only possible when the poor are empowered through human rights education. It affirms that the poor have legal entitlements and that state and non-state actors have legal obligations to fulfil. While individual states have the main responsibility for realising the human rights of its citizens, other states and non-state actors also have an obligation to contribute to and support this process.

This is of utmost importance for establishing equitable, just and non-protectionist systems of multilateral trade, an adequate flow of financial assistance, and for ensuring that the poor have a stake in the development process in this globalising world.

These values find expression in political statements such as the Rio Declaration, Agenda 21, the Copenhagen Declaration, the Beijing Platform for Action and the Habitat Agenda, designed by states as an international developmental architecture to eradicate poverty and make an indispensable requirement for sustainable development.

Treaty Bodies Monitoring Poverty

The monitoring bodies examine the state reports at regular intervals, may accept complaints, and make observations and recommendations to states, economic institutions, UN agencies and others to take steps to improve their human rights record, including poverty alleviation.

The Concluding Observations on various State Party Reports by the Committee on Economic, Social and Cultural Rights show that lack of clarity of the status of the Covenant in domestic law, lack of enforcement of laws based on international human rights commitments and lack of information on the treaty instrument are impeding factors.

Reports observe that debt burden, the absence of disaggre-gated data, widespread corruption in state authorities, military regimes undermining judiciary, and entrenched conservative religious influences imposing discrimination get in the way of implementing poverty reduction strategies.

Though the number of countries ratifying the conventions has increased dramatically since 1990, there is a huge gap between commitments, policy intentions and actual implementation. The lack of political will of governments, conflicting commitments made on international platforms like the WTO (*e.g.* TRIPS which could result in increasing the costs of medicines to satisfy corporate greed, and thus denying individuals their basic human right to a healthy life and living in dignity) and inadequate resource allocation for realising various commitments are major threats.

SPECIAL RAPPORTEURS AND INDEPENDENT EXPERTS

The Commission on Human Rights has appointed two Independent Experts – one has the mandate to report to a special working group on the implementation of the right to development (Resolution 1998/72) while the other has the responsibility for investigating and making recommendations regarding the effect extreme poverty has on human rights (Resolution 1998/25).

The Independent Expert on Human Rights and Extreme Poverty evaluates the measures taken at the national and international levels to promote the full enjoyment of human rights by people living in extreme poverty, examines the obstacles encountered and the progress made by women and men living in extreme poverty, and also makes recommendations and proposals in the sphere of technical assistance and other areas for the reduction and eventual elimination of poverty.

In her Report to the Commission on Human Rights, the Independent Expert presented essential findings on how the situation of the poor can be changed. To fulfil those requirements, human rights education is necessary to empower the poor and help them change their destiny. The human rights education process promotes and enhances critical analysis of all the circumstances and realities that confront the poor.

It provides appropriate knowledge, skills and capacities to deal with the forces that keep them poor. It enables the building of organisations and the creation of self-help networks so that they can claim and pursue the progressive realisation of all human rights and fully eradicate poverty. In her 2004 report, the Independent Expert on human rights and extreme poverty, Ms. A.-Z. Lizin of Belgium, pointed out that "The total world military budget for 2003 alone would cover the cost of building all the schools that Africa needs for young people aged from 0 to 18 years and pay their teachers for 15 years".

7

Human Rights by Issue

ADULTISM

Adultism is a predisposition towards adults, defined as "behaviours and attitudes based on the assumptions that adults are better than young people, and entitled to act upon young people without agreement".

It is also seen as, "an addiction to the attitudes, ideas, beliefs, and actions of adults." Adultism is popularly used to describe any discrimination against young people and is distinguished from ageism, which is simply prejudice on the grounds of age; not specifically against youth. Adultism is ostensibly caused by fear of children and youth.

ETYMOLOGY AND USAGE

Coinage

The word adultism first appears in psychology literature in 1933, when it was defined as a condition wherein a child possessed adult-like "physique and spirit".

It was exemplified by:

- A boy of 12 and a girl of 13 who had the spirit and personality of adults.... They were placed in institutions because of stealing and prostitution. These forms of precocity lead the individual into difficulties and should be recognized early in the development of the individual.

This definition has been superseded by another from a late 1970s journal article proposing that adultism is the abuse of the power that adults have over children. The author identified examples of adultism not only in parents but in teachers, psychotherapists, the clergy, police, judges, and juries. Co-Counseling adopted the term in the late 1980s to describe "the oppression of and discrimination against people who are young." Since then the term has come to describe any mistreatment or silencing of children and/or youth. In 1996, Jenny Sazama, an adultism expert with an organization called Youth On Board, explained that,

- Young people are systemically mistreated and disrespected by society, with adults as the agents of the oppression. The basis of young people's oppression is disrespect. Manifestations of the oppression include: systematic invalidation, denial of voice or respectful attention, physical abuse, lack of information, misinformation, denial of any power, economic dependency, lack of rights, and any combination of the above.

This definition is now used widely by youth-serving organizations and education institutions seeking to counter the effects of adultism. The Child Welfare League of America writes,

- "[Adultism is] an adult practice of forming certain beliefs about young people and practicing certain behaviours towards them because of societal views, usually negative, that are based on their age. Adultism happens when this prejudice is combined with the ability of adults to exert control over the lives of young people. When adults practice adultism, young people are viewed as objects instead of resources. The end result is that young people become disempowered and disenfranchised.

While not meeting universal acceptance, one national media organization promotes the notion that "adultism is the foundation for all forms of oppression," due to the commonality of every person's having experienced said discrimination. Illustrating the commonality of this problem, local youth-serving organizations increasingly address adultism. A programme in Oakland, California, describes the impact of adultism, which "hinders the development of youth, in particular, their self-esteem and self-worth, ability to form positive relationships with caring adults, or even see adults as allies." The Texas Network of Youth Services offers a list of traits associated with adultism.

Similar Terms

Adultism is a generalization of paternalism, allowing for the broad force of adulthood beyond males, and may be witnessed in the infantalization of children and youth. It has been proposed pedophobia (the fear of children) and ephebiphobia (the fear of youth) are antecedents to adultism. Tokophobia, the fear of childbirth, may also be a precursor; gerontophobia, or its antonym, gerontocracy, may be extensions of adultism. Similar terms such as adult privilege, adultarchy, and adultcentrism/adultocentrism have been proposed as alternatives which are more morphologically parallel. Some activists alternatively call adultism "youthism," equating it to sexism and heterosexism.

The dilemma inherent in this term is present in other activist circles, where "youthism" is employed to indicate "one form of ageism which describes people who hold beliefs or take actions advocating unfavourable balance of power or resources towards the 'younger' generations." At least one prominent organization describes discrimination against youth as ageism, which is any form of discrimination against anyone due to their age. The National Youth Rights Association argues that ageism is a more natural and understandable term than adultism and thus is more commonly used among the young people affected by this discrimination.

Advocates of using 'ageism' also believe it makes common cause with older people fighting against their own form of age discrimination. However, a national organization called Youth On Board counters this, arguing that "addressing adultist behaviour by calling it ageism is discrimination against youth in itself." The opposite of adultism is jeunism, which is defined as the preference of young people and adolescents over adults.

CAUSES

In his seminal 1978 article, Flasher explained that adultism is born of the belief that children are inferior, professing that adultism can be manifested as excessive nurturing, possessiveness, or over-restrictiveness, all of which are consciously or unconsciously geared towards excessive control of a child. Recently, theologians Heather Eaton and Matthew Fox proposed, "Adultism derives from adults repressing the inner child." John Holt stated, "An understanding of adultism might begin to explain what I mean when I say that much of what is known as children's art is an adult invention."

That perspective is seemingly supported by Maya Angelou, who remarked:

- We are all creative, but by the time we are three or four years old, someone has knocked the creativity out of us. Some people shut up the kids who start to tell stories. Kids dance in their cribs, but someone will insist they sit still. By the time the creative people are ten or twelve, they want to be like everyone else.

EVIDENCE OF ADULTISM

A 2006/2007 survey conducted by the Children's Rights Alliance for England and the National Children's Bureau asked 4,060 children and young people whether they have ever been treated unfairly based on various criteria (race, age, sex, sexual orientation, etc). A total of 43% of British youth surveyed reported experiencing discrimination based on their age, far eclipsing other categories of discrimination like sex (27%), race (11%), or sexual orientation (6%).

CLASSIFICATION OF ADULTISM

Experts have identified multiple forms of adultism, offering a typology that includes internalized adultism, institutionalized adultism, cultural adultism, and other forms.

Internalized Adultism

University of Michigan professor Barry Checkoway asserts that internalized adultism causes youth to "question their own legitimacy, doubt their ability to make a difference" and perpetuate a "culture of silence" among young people. "Adultism convinces us as children that children don't really count," reports an investigative study, and it "becomes extremely important to us [children] to have the approval of adults and be 'in good' with them, even if it means betraying our fellow children.

This aspect of internalized adultism leads to such phenomena as tattling on our siblings or being the 'teacher's pet,' to name just two examples." Other examples of internalized adultism include many forms of violence imposed upon children and youth by adults who are reliving the violence they faced as young people, such as corporal punishment, sexual abuse, verbal abuse, and community incidents that include store policies prohibiting youth from visiting shops without adults, and police, teachers, or parents chasing young people from areas without just cause.

Institutional Adultism

Institutional adultism may be apparent in any instance of systemic bias, where formalized limitations or demands are placed on people simply because of their young age. Policies, laws, rules, organizational structures, and systematic procedures each serve as mechanisms to leverage, perpetuate, and instill adultism throughout society. These limitations are often reinforced through physical force, coercion or police actions and are often seen as double-standards. This treatment is increasingly seen as a form of gerontocracy.

Institutions perpetuating adultism may include the fiduciary, legal, educational, communal, religious, and governmental sectors of a community.

For examples see:

- Access to contraceptives
- Access to healthcare
- adoption of new parents
- Age of candidacy
- Age of consent
- Child soldiers

- Cohabitation with relatives/close friends
- Compulsory education
- Criminalization
- Curfews
- Drinking age
- Emancipation laws in each state/country
- Freedom of religion
- Mosquito sound devices
- Over-medicating children
- Policing
- Public school choice
- The Draft (Men's rights)
- Voluntary employment when legal or approved by parent/the state
- Voting age

Cultural Adultism

Cultural adultism is a much more ambiguous, yet much more prevalent, form of discrimination or intolerance towards youth. Any restriction or exploitation of people because of their young age, as opposed to their ability, comprehension, or capacity, may be said to be adultist.

These restrictions are often attributed to euphemisms afforded to adults on the basis of age alone, such as "better judgment" or "the wisdom of age." A parenting magazine editor comments, "Most of the time people talk differently to kids than to adults, and often they act differently, too." This summarizes cultural adultism.

For examples:

- Academic misconceptions of youth
- Child abuse
- Child labour
- Child prostitution
- Commercialization
- Controversy over sagging
- Corporal punishment
- Drinking age
- Generation gap

- Literature
- Mass marketing to youth
- Mental illness
- Moralism
- Online filters
- Peer pressure
- poverty
- Runaways
- Scapegoating
- Stereotypes about Youth subculture
- Teen sex
- Unemployment gaps in ages 18 to 25

RESULTS

Social Stratification

Discrimination against age is increasingly recognized as a form of bigotry in social and cultural settings around the world. An increasing number of social institutions are acknowledging the positions of children and youth as an oppressed minority group. Many youth are rallying against the adultist myths spread through mass media from the 1970s through the 1990s. Research compiled from two sources (a Cornell University nation-wide study, and a Harvard University study on youth) has shown that social stratification between age groups causes stereotyping and generalization; for instance, the media-perpetuated myth that all adolescents are immature, violent and rebellious.

Opponents of adultism contend that this has led to growing number of youth, academics, researchers, and other adults rallying against adultism and ageism, such as organizing education programmes, protesting statements, and creating organizations devoted to publicizing the concept and addressing it. Simultaneously, research shows that young people who struggle against adultism within community organizations have a high rate of impact upon said agencies, as well as their peers, the adults who work with them, and the larger community to which the organization belongs.

Cultural Responses

There may be many negative effects of adultism, including ephebiphobia and a growing generation gap. A reactive social response to adultism takes the form of the children's rights movement, led by young people who strike against being exploited for their labour. Numerous popular outlets are employed to strike out against adultism, particularly music and movies. Additionally, many youth-led social change efforts have inherently responded to adultism, particularly those associated with youth activism and student activism, each of which in their own respects have struggled with the effects of institutionalized and cultural adultism.

Academic Developments

A growing number of governmental, academic, and educational institutions around the globe have created policy, conducted studies, and created publications that respond to many of the insinuations and implications of adultism. Much of popular researcher Margaret Mead's work can be said to be a response to adultism. Current researchers whose work analyses the effects of adultism include sociologist Mike Males and critical theorist Henry Giroux.

ADDRESSING ADULTISM

Any inanimate or animate exhibition of adultism is said to be "adultist". This may include behaviours, policies, practices, institutions, or individuals. Educator John Holt proposed that teaching adults about adultism is a vital step to addressing the effects of adultism, and at least one organization and one curriculum do just that. Several educators have created curricula that seek to teach youth about adultism, as well. Currently, organizations responding to the negative effects of adultism include the United Nations, which has conducted a great deal of research in addition to recognizing the need to counter adultism through policy and programmes. The CRC has particular Articles (5 and 12) which are specifically committed to combating adultism. The international organization Human Rights Watch has done the same. Common practice accepts the engagement of youth voice and the formation of youth-adult partnerships as essential steps to resisting adultism. In the USA, adultism hasn't yet became a major political issue or seen to interfere with the American concept of equality, but if it were, it would be equally as divisive and controversial like the historic issues of racism and classism, and current-day issues like combating homophobia and ageism against the elderly.

CULTURAL RIGHTS

The cultural rights movement has provoked attention to protect the rights of groups of people, or their culture, in similar fashion to the manner in which the human rights movement has brought attention to the needs of individuals throughout the world. Cultural rights are different from human rights specifically because they are vested in groups of people, whereas human rights deal with individuals.

PROTECTING A CULTURE

Cultural rights focus on groups such as religious and ethnic minorities and indigenous societies that are in danger of disappearing. Cultural rights include a group's ability to preserve its way of life, such as child rearing, continuation of language, and security of its economic base in the nation, which it is located.

The related notion of indigenous intellectual property rights has arisen in attempt to conserve each society's culture base and essentially prevent ethnocide. The cultural rights movement has been popularized because much traditional cultural knowledge has commercial value, like ethno-medicine, cosmetics, cultivated plants, foods, folklore, arts, crafts, songs, dances, costumes, and rituals.

Studying ancient cultures may reveal evidence about the history of the human race and shed more light on our origin and successive cultural development. However, the study, sharing and commercialization of such cultural aspects can be hard to achieve without infringing upon the cultural rights of those who are a part of that culture.

CULTURAL BIGOTRY

The notion of cultural rights is not too cultural. Cultural rights has many ways that it can be looked upon. "Cultural rights are vested not in individuals but in groups, such as religious and ethnic minorities and indigenous societies." All cultures are brought up differently, therefore cultural rights include a group's ability to preserve its culture, to raise its children in the ways its forebears, to continue its language, and to not be deprived of its economic base by the nation in which it is located." Anthropologist sometimes choose not to study some cultures beliefs and rights, because they believe that it may cause misbehaviour, and they choose not to turn against different diversities of cultures. Although anthropologist sometimes do turn away from studying different cultures they still depend a lot on what they study at different archaeological sites.

AGEISM

Ageism is a form of discrimination which is based on someone's chronological age. Many people use this term specifically to refer to discrimination against older people, but ageism can strike people of all ages. Like other forms of discrimination, ageism can be extremely harmful, especially when it is viewed as culturally normal and acceptable. In some regions of the world, campaigns to fight ageism have been initiated in an attempt to educate people and stamp out ageism. The term was coined in 1969 by Robert Butler, who likened discrimination against the elderly to discrimination on the basis of gender, creed, or ethnic identity.

He hoped that by creating a specific term to discuss age discrimination, he could bring such a discussion out into the open, making people more aware of it. By defining ageism, he also made it possible to create legislation which is designed to make it illegal. Like other "-isms" such as racism and sexism, ageism often involves heavy stereotyping. For example, someone may think that older people make poor employees because of their perceived fragility, or that a young person would not make a good employee because he or she would be irresponsible. Often, such stereotypes are heavily reinforced in the community at large, with people internalizing values, beliefs, and norms which support age discrimination. Ageism in the workplace is a serious issue for many elderly and youth activists. Seniors often face hiring discrimination because employers think that they are not worth training, or not fit to perform a job, while young people often find themselves marginalized when they seek employment. Some people refer to ageism in employment as "adultism," referencing the preference for "adults" in the workplace. However, "jeunism," discrimination in favour of the young, can also strike; some workplaces, for example, want to have younger staffs because they think young people are easier to control, more attractive, or because they think that a young staff will appeal to their target demographic.

Both seniors and children are marginalized in many societies. Seniors, for example, are presumed to be incapable of making decisions because of their advanced age, while children are not allowed to make choices because they are perceived as too young. Some regions of the world have laws which are considered ageist by activists, such as laws limiting the drinking age, or laws mandating retirement at a specific age. Ageism can be difficult to fight. Recognizing and combating ageism in yourself is an important first step, as is discussing the issue with the people around you. By making people more aware of ageism as an issue, you can help to reduce the amount of ageism in your community and society at large.

FUNCTION

Ageism functions to strip individuals of their rights or worth solely based on their age. This is unfair to senior citizens because it trivializes their wisdom and experience that they have gained over the course of a lifetime. This is also unfair to teenagers and children because it assumes that their opinions and ideas do not hold any value simply because they have not been alive long enough to gain the experiences that would properly educate their beliefs.

IDENTIFICATION

Ageism is identified in a lot of ways. It can be seen in simply the formation of generalizations that postulate that members of a certain age group act a particular way. These generalizations can then be extended to prompt prejudice and discriminatory behaviours against individuals simply because of the age of an individual. It is often seen in the workplace, as senior citizens are often denied jobs due to their age. Such cases have been brought to lawsuits over discrimination.

MISCONCEPTIONS

There is a common misconception that only young people can exhibit ageist outlooks. This is not the case, simply because the idea of "aging" is so subjective depending on who is defining the concept. The word "old" can be defined as any number, depending on who is using the word. There is also the misconception that the elderly never exhibit ageist tendencies towards the young. This is also not the case, as often the inexperience of youth will lead people to trivialize the interest and behaviours of the youth.

PREVENTION/SOLUTION

Prevention is the best option to battling ageism. Those who are made aware of the dangers of ageist outlooks are less likely to exhibit ageist views that can cause discrimination in the workplace and the rest of society. By encouraging others to practice acceptance and tolerance of other people and cultures, things like discrimination and hate become easier to fight.

CONSIDERATIONS

The world is become an increasingly more litigious place. Following an ageist outlook and applying that outlook to discrimination within the workplace and greater society is a dangerous way to behave as it may lead to legal issues being filed by those who feel they have been treated unjustly. On a moral level, ageism trivializes the abilities of individuals based on their age. On a personal and financial level, ageism can lead to upheaval and devastation.

DEMOCRACY

Human rights and democracy have historically been viewed as separate, albeit parallel, concepts. However, understandings of both human rights and democracy are dynamic and varied, and recent re-conceptualizations of both ideas have led to the emergence of a discourse that recognizes their interdependence. Specifically, definitions of democracy have expanded from the traditional procedural democracy to encompass the ideals of a substantive, liberal democracy. Likewise, the human rights framework has begun to further develop conceptions of social, economic, and cultural rights, in addition to civil and political rights, thus expanding the notion of human rights to include human security, and extending human rights to the collective as well as the individual level.

These renewed definitions present opportunities for recognizing the convergence of the theories and fields related to human rights and democracy. The necessity of acknowledging the interdependence of democracy and human rights is becoming especially important in emerging democracies such as Palestine. In these cases, in which the development and reform of democratic institutions is starting to take place, it is imperative to ensure that such institutions are built on foundations of both human rights and democracy if they are to be sustainable.

To be sure, previous attempts at democracy by the Palestinian Authority in the 1990s proved to be ephemeral, largely due to the absence of protection for human rights. Likewise, human rights advocates have found it difficult to affect systemic change in the absence of a legitimate democracy. Thus, as Palestine looks ahead to new opportunities for democracy in the future, it is necessary to integrate the broadened human rights framework, including human security, with the ideals and institutions of a liberal, participatory democracy. This document begins with a theoretical discussion of the principles of democracy, distinguishing between substantive and procedural democracy and identifying key elements and institutions inherent in a liberal democracy. The next part examines the emerging re-conceptualization of the human rights framework, including the human security perspective, which has enhanced the complementarity between human rights and democracy. The following part discusses the convergence of the democracy and human rights fields and theories, and concludes that the two concepts are not only complementary, but are indeed interdependent. The second half of the document focuses on the application of this theory in the case of Palestine by analysing past and present experiences with democracy and human rights in the Occupied Territories, including obstacles and points of progress, and discussing recommendations for future implementation.

THEORETICAL ANALYSIS

Defining Democracy: Principles and Institutions

The idea of democracy has been understood and applied in different ways, both temporally and culturally, with democracy taking various forms in different societies. From a historical perspective, the direct democracy of ancient Athens has been transformed into the representative democracy that is common today. Likewise, former restrictions on the political participation of women and other marginalized groups have been challenged in modern times to allow for more inclusive democracies.

Most recently, both theorists and practitioners of democracy are starting to further articulate differences between procedural democracies and substantive, liberal democracies. However, all of these forms of democracy are based to some extent on the original Greek notion of demokratia, that is, "government by the people," from the words demos and kratos.

This core concept still forms the crux of modern definitions of democracy, including the 1993 Vienna Declaration's statement that "democracy is based on the freely expressed will of the people to determine their own political, economic, social and cultural systems and their full participation in all aspects of their lives." From this starting point, it is possible to identify several key principles and institutions that are inherent to a sustainable democracy. While historically there has been more emphasis on the political institutions and procedures that comprise democracy, namely elections, political parties, and governmental bodies, increased attention has recently been given to the ideals and principles that underscore those mechanisms. As stated by David Beetham, Director of the Centre for Democratization Studies at the University of Leeds, "to define democracy simply in institutional terms is to elevate means into ends, and to concentrate on the forms without the substance." Jack Donnelly, Professor of International Studies at the University of Denver, agrees, noting that "pure procedural democracy can easily denigrate into non-democratic or even anti-democratic formalism," thus, "substantive conceptions rightly insist that we not lose sight of the core values of popular authority and control over government."

However, Donnelly also notes that purely substantive approaches fail to recognize the "idea of the people ruling rather than just benefiting... The term 'democratic' easily slides into an essentially superfluous synonym for 'egalitarian.'" That is, government for the people is not synonymous with government by the people, and therefore may or may not be democratic. To be sure, substantive conceptions risk being susceptible to normative associations that identify any positive sociopolitical elements as indicators of democracy. This document takes the position that neither "substantive" nor "procedural" conceptions of democracy should be considered more important than the other; indeed, it is questionable if the two notions can even be separated.

Instead, substantive and procedural elements should be viewed as complementary and in fact essential to each other. The principles that underscore substantive democracy will only remain theoretical ideals unless mechanisms are present for translating those ideals into reality, while procedural institutions, however democratic in form, are meaningless if they do not yield ends that reflect democratic values. For the remainder of this document, the term "substantive democracy" will refer to democracies that embody both the principles and the institutions that form the foundation of democracy, in contrast to "electoral democracies," which may be democratic in name and form but not in practice. The basic elements of a substantive democracy, just as to Beetham, "are that the people have a right to a controlling influence over public decisions and decision makers, and that they should be treated with equal respect and as of equal worth in the context of such decisions."

Beetham refers to these concepts as popular control and popular equality, both of which contribute to the foundation of the principles and institutions that inform democracy. These primary elements, in conjunction with the rule of law, open government, and public participation, form the core of substantive democracies, as reflected in their mechanisms and institutions, and the presence of civil society and citizen rights.

Mechanisms

The primary indicator of democracy is the presence of popular elections. Beetham, "popular authorization is achieved through regular competitive elections just as to universal secret ballot, which ensures voters a choice of candidates and policies and gives them the opportunity to dismiss politicians who no longer command their confidence." As Shadrack Gutto, Director of the Centre for Applied Legal Studies at the University of Witwatersrand in Johannesburg, states however, "for elections to be substantially 'free and fair,' it is imperative that enabling principles and rights be observed," including "the rights to or freedom of association, opinion, expression, and assembly."

Gutto also notes the importance of available and adequate material and human resources to educate voters, register voters, monitor the voting process, count election results, and reconcile disputes. Indeed, the democratic nature of an electoral process should be assessed by "the reach, inclusiveness, independence, integrity, and impartiality of elections, as well as how equally the electoral process treats citizens, how much effective choice it offers them, how far the government actually fulfills the electoral choices made, and how many people in practice exercise the right to vote." In addition, political parties function as a mechanism within electoral systems by organizing different policies into cohesive programmes, nominating appropriate candidates, and advocating for the implementation of decisions supported by the electorate.

Institutions

As Beetham articulates, "although elections form a key mechanism for the popular control of government, they are of limited effectiveness on their own without institutions that secure a government's continuous accountability to the public." Gutto agrees, noting how "elected representatives can play a democratic role only to the extent that enabling institutions of governance with clear systems and procedures that are secured by a normative framework and laws exist." Open and accountable political institutions depend primarily on the decentralization of governance and the separation of powers between the executive, legislative, and judiciary spheres.

These branches should be monitored through a system of checks and balances by each other, through horizontal accountability, and also be answerable to the people as a whole through vertical accountability. These institutions' specific roles and functions can be best understood and implemented when articulated in a constitution or equivalent "rule of law." The constitution should also articulate the financial responsibilities of the legislature, as well as allow for a system of regional and local government.

Civil Society

As Gutto notes, "however effective public institutions and accountability processes may be in any society aspiring to democracy, their effectiveness and impact would nevertheless be diminished in the absence of a vibrant and activist civil society." Civil society, sometimes referred to as "democratic society," creates opportunities for active citizenship and direct involvement in the functioning of a democracy. The key elements of civil society include an independent media, sources of policy expertise independent of the state, and associations that may include organizations dedicated to social services, development, health, education, human rights, women's empowerment, or other issues. An active civil society has the additional benefit of fostering respect for the rights of other citizens by creating environments of diversity and dialogue.

Citizen Rights

Democracy also includes the presence of political and civil rights for citizens, especially freedom of expression, association, and assembly, which require the guarantee of due legal process and liberty and security of person to be effective. There has been recent debate on the necessity of economic, social, and cultural rights as conditions of democracy, however, it is becoming more widely accepted that "for civil and political rights and freedoms to have any value, citizens must possess the capacity to exercise them." The majority of political, civil, economic, social, and cultural rights at the national level relate directly or indirectly to the international human rights framework, as will be discussed further.

The Dynamism of Democracy

It should be noted that, despite these common elements, democracy can take a variety of forms; there is no "one size fits all" democracy. As Beetham explains, "different societies and diverse circumstances require different arrangements if democratic principles are to be effectively realised."

Abdul Aziz Said, Professor of International Peace and Conflict Resolution at American University, agrees, noting that "the form of democracy is always cast in the mold of the culture of a people;" he thus urges a "more democratic theory of democracy" that recognizes its potential for variation and dynamism. Relatedly, Said specifically emphasizes that "democracy is not a western product." As noted above, the principles and institutions that inform substantive democracy are based on tenets that transcend national and political ideologies; thus, democracy is not exclusive to the West. This point has several implications. First, it implies that there is no fundamental incompatibility between democracy and the Arab world, nor between democracy and Islam. As Said notes, "the lack of democracy in the Middle East is due more to a lack of preparation for it than to a lack of religious and cultural foundations."

Secondly, the idea that democracy is not exclusive to the West can serve to caution superpowers to avoid imposing their models of democracy on other societies, and encourage them to instead assume a supportive role in developing democracy in local contexts. Likewise, superpowers should be cautious of pursuing national interests under the guise of democracy to prevent the association of democracy with western imperialism. At the same time, local democracy advocates are called upon to consider how their social mechanisms, values, and contexts can inform culturally sustainable democracies.

Defining Human Rights: The Human Security Perspective

As Donnelly summarizes, "human rights are, literally, the rights that one has simply as a human being. As such they are equal rights, because we are all equally human beings. They are also inalienable rights, because no matter how inhumanely we act or are treated we cannot become other than human beings." Human rights are defined in several key documents, namely, the Universal Declaration of Human Rights, adopted by the United Nations General Assembly in 1948; the International Covenant on Civil and Political Rights, adopted in 1966; and the International Covenant on Economic, Social, and Cultural Rights, also adopted in 1966.

The Vienna Declaration, adopted at the World Conference on Human Rights in 1993, further expanded the meaning of human rights. Originally, human rights were developed to outline a set of individual rights that states were required to respect or provide for their citizens. The framework not only included the prohibition of certain acts, but also the "imposition of the duty to perform certain obligations in order to promote and protect the enjoyment of certain rights." In other words, abuse of human rights can take the form of both violations and denials. While the full realisation of human rights is still an ideal, much has been achieved in the name of human rights.

Anthony Langlois, Professor of International Relations at Flinders University in Adelaide, Australia, achievements include "international recognition of human rights as the basic set of norms of human behaviour, the internationalization of human rights institutions of various types, and the development of International Human Rights Law." The notion of human rights has begun to be broadened in recent years. First, the responsibility of ensuring human rights has been expanded beyond only state governments to include individuals, groups of people, and other non-state actors. Secondly, the common association of human rights law with peacetime has given way to the widespread recognition that human rights law applies in conflict situations, just as it does in periods of stability.

Finally, and perhaps most importantly for the context of this document, the past ten years have seen increased acknowledgment of the interdependence and indivisibility of human rights. While this has always been true in theory, in the past the two separate Covenants suggested divisions between political and civil rights and economic, social, and cultural rights. While some divisions still exist, the gaps between the two fields of rights were largely bridged in 1993 at Vienna, where it was declared that "human rights are universal, indivisible and interdependent and interrelated" and that the international community "must treat human rights globally in a fair and equal manner."

In other words, the notion of human rights is expanding to include the concept of human security in a more conscious and deliberate manner. The United Nations Development Report of 1994, "human security can be said to have two main aspects. It means, first, safety from such chronic threats as hunger, disease and repression. And second, it means protection from sudden and hurtful disruptions in the patterns of daily life—whether in homes, in jobs or in communities." This renewed interest in human security and development has accordingly placed increased emphasis on economic and social rights, thus contributing to the re-conceptualization of the human rights framework.

As Beetham summarizes: The idea of economic and social rights as human rights expresses the moral intuition that, in a world rich in resources and the accumulation of human knowledge, everyone ought to be guaranteed the basic means for sustaining life, and that those denied these are victims of a fundamental injustice. Expressing this intuition in the form of human rights both gives the deprived the strongest possible claim to that of which they are deprived and emphasizes the duty of responsible parties to uphold or help them meet their entitlement.

Democracy and Human Rights

Democracy and human rights are clearly different notions; "they are distinct enough for them to be viewed as discreet and differentiated political concepts." Whereas democracy aims to empower "the people" collectively, human rights aims to empower individuals. Similarly, human rights is directly associated with the how of ruling, and not just the who, which may be the case in an electoral democracy, though not in a substantive democracy.

Thus, "democracies" exist that do not necessarily protect human rights, while some non-democratic states are able to ensure some, though not all, human rights. On another level, the international acceptance, institutionalization, and legal aspects of human rights mentioned above do not apply to democracy.

These distinctions have influenced the traditional separation of the theories and fields of human rights and democracy. From the human rights perspective, many have adhered to the separationist theory, which argues that "democracy is not immediately needed for the observation of human rights and that the maintenance of an essential link between human rights and democracy may well have the effect of delaying the implementation of human rights norms in various states." A recent corollary of the separationist theory is the "democracy as neo-imperialism" notion that charges that "democracy is a 'Western-centric' approach to government that is not found indigenously in all societies and is not desirable for all peoples." These arguments are subject to several key counter arguments that show the interdependence of human rights and democracy.

First, in terms of the neo-imperialist argument, it is certainly true that Western superpowers should not impose their particular forms of democracy on other societies and expect them to be accepted and sustainable, as noted above. However, it is equally culturally insensitive to claim that democracy is only an option in the West, or that it is incompatible with other cultures. Secondly, in reference to the separationist theory, while it would be unwise to "wait" for democracy to start promoting human rights, it must also be recognized that some human rights are intrinsically linked with institutions and principles of democracy.

Furthermore, separating human rights from democracy undermines opportunities for implementation, in that it reduces human rights to standards or norms; as Langlois states, "human rights amount to little more than charity if they are not functioning in a democratic framework." Essentially, the inclination to separate human rights from democracy is rooted in the acceptance of their traditional definitions. An electoral democracy that lacks the other institutions and principles of a substantive democracy can function without necessarily guaranteeing human rights, just as some narrowly defined human rights can still be realised in the absence of democracy.

However, the re-conceptualization of democracy as substantive, and of human rights as being more far-reaching and inclusive, underscores the necessity of linking the two. This interdependence occurs on the levels of principle, enforcement, and specific rights. On the conceptual level, as Langlois notes, "both contemporary liberal democracy and human rights are derived from and express the assumptions of liberalism," which include individualism, egalitarianism, and universalism. Furthermore, both democracy and human rights pursue a common agenda, and it is "only within a democracy [that] human rights standards or norms transcended such that the values articulated by these norms or standards are genuine rights."

In addition, it is only in a well-functioning democracy that individual citizens have access to mechanisms to ensure the implementation of their rights. The relationship between human rights and democracy is perhaps most clear through an examination of civil and political rights, especially those articulated in Article 21 of the UDHR and Article 25 of the ICCPR, both of which ensure citizen participation in government through free and fair elections and through direct service and participation.

These rights are related to the rights of expression, association, assembly, and movement, which are also interdependent with democracy, as well as the rights to liberty, security of person, and the guarantee of due process of the law. Economic, social, and cultural rights are also being increasingly recognized as being mutually dependent, if not integral, with democracy. As Gutto writes, "the pursuit of the right to development and socio-economic rights is strongly associated with the social democracy vision of poverty eradication and the equitable distribution of ownership, control, and the benefits of wealth."

Indeed, political and civil rights can best be realised by citizens who meet a basic level of physical security in terms of access to shelter, water, sanitation, and food, as well as education, healthcare, and employment or income. Socially, democracy is interrelated with rights to equality and non-discrimination, especially for marginalized groups including women and minorities. Culturally, the respect for diversity and pluralism inherent to democracy is linked to the protection of rights related to language, religion, or ethnicity. It is thus clear that human rights and democracy are interdependent, especially when defined in the broader conceptualizations of democracy as substantive democracy, and human rights as civil, political, economic, social, and cultural rights. These different kinds of rights cannot be realised in a non-democratic system, and likewise, no democracy is sustainable without the presence of these rights. While this relationship is evident in theory, it is perhaps more useful to consider the inter-dependence of human rights and democracy through the case study of an emerging democracy.

HUMAN RIGHTS AND DEMOCRACY IN PALESTINE

The status of democracy in Palestine is somewhat open to interpretation. Many democracy advocates agree that Palestine is moving in the direction of becoming a substantive democracy, but that it still has ways to go. Specifically, the will of the people reflects a keen desire for democracy, but that has yet to translate into viable democratic institutions and principles. As Nathan J. Brown of the Carnegie Endowment for International Peace states, "Palestine is... a model liberal democracy.

Its most significant flaw is that it does not exist." That is, democracy in Palestine is evident in theory, but it has not been able to fully manifest itself in practice. Obstacles to realising both human rights and democracy are rooted in both external and internal factors. In terms of external factors, the Israeli occupation and the protracted Israeli-Palestinian conflict have posed obvious challenges to the development of democracy and human rights in Palestine.

To start with democracy, political reform is difficult in the midst of any ongoing violent conflict. In the case of Israel-Palestine, the challenge of political reform is further exacerbated by the nature of the occupation, which creates a complicated system of dual authority between Israel and the PA. Indeed, just as to democracy advocates interviewed for this report, the occupation remains the most prominent obstacle to Palestinian democracy. Challenges resulting from the external influence of the occupation are interrelated with internal factors as well, most notably corruption in the executive branch of the PA under Arafat and the failure of the security services to be effective. Indeed, the Oslo Accords "were predicated on the ability of the PA to enhance Israeli security and thus focused on enabling the executive and placing few fetters on the security services in internal matters." In addition to, and perhaps, because of the fact that the PA lacked sovereignty, it also lacked legitimacy. This problem emerged not only from the external fact of the occupation however, but also from internal shortcomings such as centralization of power, lack of accountability and transparency, corruption, and human rights violations. To be sure, human rights, like democracy, have suffered from both internal and external factors.

On the one hand, numerous human rights violations by Israel against Palestinians have been cited, including targeted assassinations, restrictions on movement, collective punishment, and home demolitions. On the other hand, Palestinian security forces under the PA have also been guilty of numerous human rights violations, including detention without trial and/or specific charges, improper trials, torture, maltreatment, and use of the death penalty.

Both human rights and democracy have also been hindered by poverty and the lack of human security in many communities in Palestine. As George Giacaman of Muwatin stated, "the democratic system is not sustainable with rampant poverty. Democracy requires a more equitable economic system based on a fair distribution of wealth." Khalid Nassif of the Civic Forum Institute agreed, noting that democracy regresses in the absence of economic and social rights that ensure human security. Nassif, "when the economy improves, people have a greater sense of freedom and safety, and they can give more time and attention to joining parties and organizations and taking an interest in democracy."

Clearly then, both human rights and democracy in Palestine have been hindered by both internal and external factors, primarily, the conflict with Israel and the limitations of the PA, and also by regional and international influences. Nevertheless, the will for both democracy and human rights in Palestine is strong on both individual and collective levels, and in fact, both exist to some extent in theory and on document. The current key issue before Palestinians at this time is to translate those conceptualizations into realised practices and institutions, which can only be possible through an integrative approach that recognizes the interdependence of human rights and democracy.

At the same time, Israel and the international community must acknowledge that a democratic state in Palestine requires the existence of a state, as well as democracy. The next part of this document examines the institutions and elements of a substantive democracy that are necessary for bringing the ideals of human rights and democracy in Palestine to fruition.

Elections

The presidential elections of January 2005 were a major step towards procedural democracy. The elections followed the death of president Yasser Arafat, who had been elected in January 1996, and provided an opportunity for new leaders and parties to emerge. Though the election of Mahmoud Abbas was predicted, the elections saw widespread participation, with 71 per cent of registered voters casting ballots, and were declared free and fair by local and international monitors.

To refer to Beetham's standards for democratic electoral processes, the January elections were deemed successful in terms of their reach, inclusiveness, independence, integrity, and impartiality. The Central Elections Commission was credited with making laudable efforts in registering voters, coordinating the monitoring of the voting process, and counting and implementing results. While the process was far from flawless, it was considered to be an overall success, and resulted in a smooth transfer of power and authority. The success of the election was largely made possible by pressure on both Israeli and Palestinian officials to protect rights to association, assembly, and expression, and the process itself underscored the procedural rights defined in Article 21 of the UDHR and Article 25 of the ICCPR. The municipal elections of May 2005 were likewise considered to be successful overall. In addition to being another step towards procedural democracy, these elections also affirmed support in the electoral system and thus contributed to the strengthening of substantive democracy. As journalist Bakr Abu Bakr wrote in the Palestinian daily Al-Hayat Al-Jadidah: It is important...to point out what these elections represent to a Palestinian people still struggling to be free, still fighting Israeli occupation, and exercising democracy... They represent: first, an assertion of a course and a way of life chosen by the Palestinian people exemplified by freedom, dignity, dialogue, responsibility, and respect for the will of the people; second, the will and aspiration of many popular leaderships to serve the people...; third, a demonstration of Palestinian solidarity...; fourth, the continuity of Palestinian political struggle towards common goals; fifth, a renewal of societal leaderships.

Clearly, the elections represented more than simply a procedure; they were a tangible expression of democratic ideals and principles. These ideals were intertwined with human rights, including the rights to dignity, freedom, and political participation. Furthermore, the electoral process, while reflecting human rights, also served to facilitate human rights by functioning as an expression of Palestinian unity. The next phase of elections, for the Palestinian Legislative Council, were originally scheduled for July 2005 but were postponed to allow more time to formalize amendments to the proposed new electoral law.

While most democracy advocates support the adoption of the new law and recognize the need for giving ample time for its passage, most view the indefinite postponement as a setback to democratic processes and momentum. Furthermore, the postponement was interpreted by many as an attempt by Fatah to consolidate its support to secure a victory over Hamas in particular. This widely accepted theory, regardless of its veracity, has unfortunately undermined the apparent commitment to democratic procedures established in the presidential and municipal elections.

Political Parties

Political parties are a mechanism that can facilitate free

and fair elections, and thus contribute significantly to a sustainable procedural democracy. Likewise they provide opportunities for citizen participation and expression, and thus contribute to the development of a substantive, liberal democracy as well. As Giacaman stated, "a multi-party system is essential for establishing a sustainable democracy."

In Palestine, there exists some foundation for a pluralist party structure. Although Fatah has remained the dominant party for some time, and has at times been difficult to distinguish from the PLO and the PA, other political parties have always remained in existence, and Islamist parties like Hamas in particular have gained considerable support in the past ten years. Thus, it is clear that "there is a plurality of parties; the parties are based on ideological differences but still operate within a national consensus; and they generally accept one another's legitimacy.

Missing, of course, are the democratic institutions that would induce existing parties to channel their energies towards electioneering and governance." That is, while various groups have long existed in Palestine, until recently they have lacked the electoral processes within which to operate. To be sure, the majority of parties in Palestine have traditionally considered themselves "movements" or "fronts," and thus focus their attention on activities not necessarily related to electoral processes.

In addition, the historical dominance of Fatah, and more recently, Hamas, have created challenges for the development of electoral parties in that "Fatah is too indistinguishable from the PA and Hamas too removed from it." Indeed, while Fatah has traditionally identified itself as the primary force for Palestinian liberation, its loose cohesion has suffered from various fractions, due both to its position as the central party of the PA and to its handling of the second intifada.

In contrast, Hamas has distanced itself from the PA, identifying itself as an "alternative to the status quo" and "the main opposition to Fatah and the PA." This contrast was not only established on the conceptual level but on the direct level as well, as Hamas provided numerous social services to communities that Fatah and the PA had been unable to supply. Also, Hamas has distinguished itself from Fatah by intentionally using religious rhetoric, in contrast to Fatah's secular nature. In the past six months however, the nature of Hamas's political involvement has been shifting from that of an independent movement to a perhaps viable party in that members participated for the first time in municipal elections and plan to participate in PLC elections. Many democracy advocates are now calling for a "third movement" that would provide an alternative to the so-called "old guard" of Fatah and the PA, and to fundamentalist groups like Hamas.

As Mustafa Barghouthi, Director of the Health, Development, Information, and Policy Institute on Palestine commented, "Palestinians do not have to choose between autocracy and fundamentalism. There is a democratic alternative. Palestine could be a state that is independent and sovereign." Dr. Lily Feidy of MIFTAH agreed, advocating for a third movement that is secular and democratic.

Nassif, who has observed numerous town meetings through the work of the Civic Forum Institute, it is evident that "people want change, and want more participation by political parties. They want real democracy, and they want political parties to function as a fundamental part of that democracy." It should be noted that electoral party systems can take many forms, and in fact, a strictly organized party system could actually be detrimental in Palestine since many active reformists in the PLC have functioned essentially as independents, in practice at least if not in name. However, it is clear that the development of institutions to support electoral parties is becoming a necessity.

Brown suggests three minimal steps to further democratic transition in the area of electoral parties. First, Fatah must be disentangled from the PA, for "when politicization of official positions runs deeply throughout the bureaucracy, and where there is a conflation of roles and ruling bodies... mechanisms of horizontal and vertical accountability begin to break down." Secondly, parties need to develop clear structures of internal governance and take "significant organizational steps, such as determining their membership, internal procedures, selection of candidates, and decision-making structures." Third, organizations need to re-orient themselves to function in electoral competition, that is, groups need to consciously decide if they are primarily violent movements or if they are electoral parties.

In order for these steps to take place, certain human rights must be ensured. The rights to assembly and movement are inherent to political party organization, and the rights to opinion and expression are necessary for allowing diverse parties to develop and mature. These rights must be protected by both the PA and by Israel. As Barghouthi stated, "[Israeli] suppression of secular democratic forces in Palestine will lead to a polarization... between Hamas fundamentalists and the PA." Indeed, the protection of human rights are essential for the emergence of a third movement.

Separation of Powers

As Hussein Sirriyeh, Professor of Arabic and Middle Eastern Studies at the University of Leeds, writes, "the definition of democracy should not merely be restricted to the narrower sense of free elections and a multi-party system. It should also encompass a broader spectrum of ingredients, including government by consent and accountability..." To be sure, in order for political parties to function in effective institutions, especially the legislature, there needs to be a clear separation of power between the executive, legislative, and judiciary branches, with a viable system of checks and balances between them, articulated in a Constitution.

This is necessary for ensuring transparency and accountability, and for enabling the different branches to fulfill their respective duties. In Palestine, power was largely concentrated in the executive branch under the leadership of Arafat, who developed a highly personalized system of authority. Under this system, Arafat managed to bypass the majority of institutions to extend his personal influence. While this strategy was arguably motivated by Arafat's attempt to unite various factions of Palestinians with different opinions and interests, and to bolster his status as the unifying symbol of Palestine, the centralization of power proved detrimental and only further crippled the already limited legitimacy of the PA. This centralization manifested itself in various ways. The most measurable indication was evident in the PA budget, in which over one quarter of the PA revenues were placed under the direct and unaccountable control of Arafat by 1997.

The executive's domination was also felt strongly by the legislative and judiciary branches. While the PLC had the authority to draft and pass laws, it had no mechanism to ensure that the president would approve them. Thus, numerous bills and laws that were passed by the PLC, including the Basic Law, were subject to interminable waiting for Arafat's approval. Similarly, the executive responded to many court orders from the judiciary by simply ignoring them. Sirriyeh proposes several theses to explain the authoritarian nature of the PA under Arafat.

Some of these reasons include the desire of the PA to make an impression on the Israelis by suppressing anti-Oslo opposition, the issue of internalized PNA insecurity, the "outsider" status of the original PA leadership, the lack of political experience of the PA, and the desire to promote national unity by subordinating divisions within Palestine. Whatever the reason, the failure to separate powers, compounded by widespread corruption within the PA, resulted in a system that lacked transparency, accountability, and ultimately, legitimacy. This crippled the development of democratic institutions in their early stages, and it is only recently that the new PA leadership under Abu Mazen has begun to confront the process of de-centralizing authority.

Judiciary

The branch of government that perhaps requires the most immediate attention is the judiciary. The judiciary was virtually nonexistent during the majority of the post-Oslo period, and it was only in 2002 with the passing of the judicial organizational law that the judiciary began to be managed by an independent judicial council. However, to date the council has consisted of judges who, while inexperienced in administrative matters, are intent on preserving their autonomy, thus causing them to lose the support of the bar association. The judiciary has also been embroiled in rivalries with the PLC and the executive branch's Ministry of Justice, with disputes occurring most recently over a draft judicial law for reform introduced by a special committee under Abu Mazen and currently referred to the legislature.

Despite these challenges, the fact that an independent judiciary council does exist provides a foundation for starting judicial reform. Although building a strong judiciary is a long, complex process, it is imperative for several reasons. On the conceptual level, judicial reform is symbolically significant because it can address the general lawlessness that directly affected many Palestinian communities during the second intifada and can thus restore confidence in the PA.

To be sure, an effective court system has the potential to restore order and thus serve as an indicator to Palestinians of the authenticity of reforms. Furthermore, "judicial reform is a logical priority because it can be a genuine tool—not simply a symbolic one—in addressing the corruption that is perhaps one of the most corrosive issues for Palestinian governance." Although laws exist regarding hiring for government positions, disclosing personal finances, and monitoring public funds, there have been no mechanisms for implementing them or prosecuting corrupt officials.

This problem can be addressed by focusing initial reform efforts on the office of public prosecution. A strong judiciary can serve other important functions as well, including being a leading force in constitutional reform and the development and application of the Basic Law. It also can function as a key body for placing checks and balances on the executive and legislative branches.

Indeed, just as to Hamdi Shaqqura of the Palestinian Centre for Human Rights, the empowerment of a strong and independent judiciary can alleviate current debates regarding concern over the popularity of Hamas as a political party. Shaqqura suggests that any hypothetical attempts by elected

Hamas officials to "Islamicize" the system or re-introduce violence as an acceptable policy would be countered by the judiciary. Finally, a strong, independent judiciary is necessary for preserving human rights. First, it would provide a legitimate institution for prosecuting cases of human rights abuses.

Lamis Alami of the Palestinian Independent Commission for Citizens' Rights, ombudsmen and monitoring groups like PICCR can document human rights violations, but they currently lack effective institutions for addressing them. Furthermore, an effective judiciary branch is necessary for protecting rights to fair and public hearings and trials, as articulated in Articles 10 and 11 of the UDHR.

Security

Closely related to the topic of judicial reform is the issue of security. Indeed, in order to ensure due process and avoid violations such as arbitrary arrests or torture, it is necessary that an effective security apparatus, including a police force, operates with legitimacy. Viable security services are necessary for preserving the rule of law, which is essential in a sustainable democracy.

The issue of security is particularly important in Palestine, as security continues to play a vital role in many aspects of the Israeli-Palestinian conflict. To be sure, "for some external actors—especially Israel—security forms the basic logic of the reform process," and many of Israel's actions and policies are justified by concern for security. In the post-Oslo period however, many Palestinians perceived that the thrust of the so-called security reforms in the Occupied Territories was to protect Israeli security at the expense of Palestinian security. Inside Palestine, security concerns were not only associated with Israel but with internal elements as well, as the security services came to be associated with authoritarianism, corruption, and human rights violations against fellow Palestinians, including illegal detentions, improper trials, torture, and executions. The failure of the Palestinian security services after Oslo is largely attributable to other flaws within the PA. Primarily, "the absence of an effective control by an identifiable institution led to the excessive manipulation of responsibilities by members and leaders of these organizations." To be sure, "the security services effectively answered to the president regardless of the content of the Basic Law. When Arafat was president, he encouraged multiple security services but declined to draw clear divisions of responsibilities among them."

This resulted in a lack of order and organization, lack of mandate, lack of professionalism, and consequently, lack of legitimacy. Indeed, over a dozen security organizations were operating under Arafat, and none of them proved effective in providing either internal or external security. As Brown suggests, "the myriad layers of overlapping forces and command structures need to be replaced with a consolidated and transparent organization with clear lines of command to a democratically accountable official or set of officials."

The president should still have some involvement, but other executive branch officials should include members of the Ministry of the Interior. Furthermore, the PLC should be involved by finishing the draft of the legal framework for the security services' operation, as well as by examining the security budget. In addition to these top-down measures, reforms need to occur directly within the security services, first through consolidation and re-organization, and also through improved trainings.

Specifically, security personnel trainings should be infused with human rights training, and ideally, should take place in conjunction with local human rights organizations. This model is helpful for facilitating a professional ethos within the security services; that is, "their training should focus not only on developing technical expertise but also on fostering a sense of what security services should not do."

Steps should also be taken to establish a multi-level system of monitoring and accountability, including:

- A system for security personnel and officers to report human rights abuses and violations;
- A procedure for families to appeal for investigations;

- A joint investigative body at the local level consisting of senior and junior security officers, human rights activists, and jurists to review cases of abuse allegations;
- A stronger Committee on Human Rights within the PLC;
- A stronger PICCR or similar ombudsman institution.

Some reforms have already taken place under Abu Mazen, but the process of security reform will inevitably be long and complex. Nevertheless, "Palestinian reform will clearly be moving forward if the Ministry of Interior exercises real oversight, if the PLC passes a set of laws governing security forces, and if the regular reporting of human rights groups and other NGOs suggests that the security forces are more respectful of the limits to their authority."

Civil Society

As discussed above, democracy depends largely on the presence of a vibrant civil society. In Palestine, the presence of a strong civil society can be considered one of the most promising assets for the development of a sustainable democracy. Numerous civil organizations have existed since the early years of the occupation, essentially "keeping the country going before the PA, and still very active" after Oslo and during the present period.

Dajani notes that, in Palestine, "in the absence of a state and central government, and without any formal, centrally organized political socialization via schools, the media, religion, friends or family, people began to organize themselves in civil groups—which subsequently became known as NGOs—and took over the role of a government."

These organizations have assumed a variety of roles and duties, including the provision of social services, political activism, human rights monitoring, education and advocacy, media and outreach, and others. Civil society groups have thus taken a number of forms, such as women's groups, media outlets, trade unions, human rights groups, religious groups, etc. While duplication, and at times, competition, are inevitable, many civil society organizations collaborate with each other and complement each others' work, and over 90 organizations belong to the Palestinian NGO Network, an umbrella group that seeks to support, strengthen, and consolidate Palestinian civil society.

Organizations that focus on women's rights and empowerment are especially important for ensuring the viability of a sustainable democracy. As Feidy explains, a strong Palestinian women's movement has existed since the 1920s, and women have been active in civil society throughout Palestinian history. However, women have been largely marginalized under the PA, with the old guard seeking to limit the participation of both women and youth.

Alami, the women's agenda has lagged at times because many active women believe that political activism against the occupation deserves more attention than the women's movement, although one cannot really separate one agenda from the other. Indeed, if women are to have an impact politically, they need to have the rights and access to participation. As Giacaman stated, "Equality is central to democracy."

In addition to political marginalization, women also face challenges related to employment, education, violence, early marriage, and inheritance rights. Many Palestinian Muslim women also confront unique issues related to certain interpretations of Islam. The range of challenges related to women has resulted in a variety of responses by different civil society groups. Some focus on advocating for legal reform, such as the establishment of a quota to ensure a certain percentage of local or PLC seats are reserved for women, while others focus more on assisting female candidates and encouraging women to run for office or to vote for candidates who are female or who support women's rights.

Other groups focus on making women aware of their civil and political rights through trainings, workshops, and conferences. As Musalim explains of his work with PCPD, "We are not speaking for people; rather, we empower people to speak on behalf of themselves. People have listened too long. They need to use their own voices now." This approach is especially important for women's empowerment. An obvious institution for channeling these voices is the media, and indeed, newspapers and media outlets are important institutions within Palestinian civil society. A strong foundation exists in Palestine for a free press; just as to Brown, "the basis for independent media that can facilitate reform [in Palestine] is solid." To be sure, the majority of media outlets in Palestine are privately owned, in contrast to the state-controlled media that dominates in some other parts of the Arab world and elsewhere.

Similarly, despite noted attempts by some PA officials to constrict discourse on certain topics such as Islamist parties, or certain stories, such as internal discord, the PA never fully stifled public expression. Nevertheless, there is still much room for improvement. Palestinian journalists should thus continue to build on their sound foundation of free media institutions to ensure that the media can function as a viable institution in a substantive democracy. Journalists and media outlets are not the only groups focusing on media concerns. Many organizations that advocate for democracy and reform are embracing media issues, as well as women's rights, as key areas of concentration for their work, under the larger goal of promoting democracy and working towards the development of sustainable institutions.

Some of the leading democracy organizations include MIFTAH, which focuses on democracy, human rights, gender equity, and participatory governance; Muwatin, which initiates intellectual debate on democratic issues and options; PCPD, which promotes human rights, tolerance, participation, accountability, empowerment, and rule of law; and Civic Forum Institute, which aims to increase citizens' awareness of democratic concepts and institutions and develop civil society institutions. This list is not intended to be exhaustive, but rather is meant to provide brief insight into the types of organizations that currently exist in the area of democracy advocacy. Civil society is just one vital aspect of a participatory democracy, in which citizens are active participants in their government and communities, rather than just passive recipients. It should be noted that democratic participation can take many forms, including voting, holding public office, volunteering a service, writing letters to officials and/or newspapers, participating in marches, protests, and other forms of direct activism, and countless others. It is not the objective of this document to evaluate the impact of various forms of participation; rather, it is to recognize the importance of citizen agency. Perhaps the best indication of the potential for participatory democracy in Palestine was the early years of the first intifada, which saw widespread popular participation of different forms.

Though the nonviolent "people power" strategies employed during that time have yet to be duplicated on the same scale, the spirit of that period is evident in the willingness of the people to express their opinions and voice their criticisms of both the PA and Israel. Participatory democracy, and thus civil society, are both inputs and outputs of human rights. First of all, as an output, the emergence of civil society depends on the rights to freedom of thought, opinion, and expression, the right to assembly and association, and the right to participation and service in government or country.

As an input, many civil society groups adopt missions that help to ensure economic, social, and cultural rights such as access to social services like food, clothing, housing, and medical care, education, and human security and others focus on securing civil and political rights. In addition, human rights organizations in particular, as a part of civil society, play an important role in monitoring and documenting human rights violations and advocating for the protection of rights.

Assessment of Democracy and Human Rights in Palestine

Foundations clearly exist in Palestine for the emergence of a substantive democracy, but the process still has far to go. A helpful way of conceptualizing Palestine's current level of democracy is the transition theory, advocated by Dankwart

Rustow. This theory, democratic development occurs in four main stages: "a stage when a national unity is being established; a preparatory phase of prolonged and inconclusive political struggle; a decision phase when a historical movement of choosing a democratic path is taken; and a habituation phase witnessing a consolidation of democracy."

In the case of Palestine, a national unity has long been established, and one might consider the post-Oslo period and second intifada to be periods of prolonged struggle. It is possible that, at present, Palestine is transitioning into the third stage, embarking upon a path of decision to work deliberately towards democracy. Most democracy advocates interviewed agreed, suggesting that Palestine is in a middle stage, on the way to democracy. It is thus important at this stage to identify obstacles that prevent Palestine from fully realising a substantive democracy.

First, it should be noted that any transition to democracy is a long, slow process. In the case of Palestine, there have also been additional setbacks in the form of clashes in reform visions, both internally and between internal and external actors. Another obstacle is the persistence of the old guard, who continue to occupy many key positions. The past six months have seen hope for progress in both of these areas however, with the election of Abu Mazen. The new president has committed himself to reform, and in doing so has reconciled differences between international and domestic agendas, and has opened up the PA and Fatah to be more transparent and accountable.

As Brown notes however, "the primary obstacle to further Palestinian reform lies in the international context: Political reform is difficult in the midst of an ongoing conflict." Specifically, it is not possible to establish a substantive democracy under occupation. Unfortunately, international actors like the United States have to date have "approached diplomacy and reform as sequential rather than interdependent... [though] it is precisely the mutual dependence of reform and peace that make both so difficult achieve." To be sure, the "peace now, democracy later" philosophy of Oslo proved to be ineffectual and perhaps even detrimental, and it is doubtful that the current logic of "democracy now, peace later" will be any different. As Brown notes, it is futile to build "public institutions that are expected to establish authority and accountability while placing them in a context of extremely limited autonomy."

Perhaps a better way to conceptualize the peace and democracy equation is to integrate the variable of human rights. As has been discussed in this document, democracy is necessary for human rights, and human rights are necessary for democracy.

Likewise, a real just peace cannot exist unless peace is integrated with the protection of human rights. Because human rights is thus a common variable to both peace and democracy, it makes sense to focus on the human rights framework when pursuing both diplomacy and institution-building. Only when human rights and democracy are pursued simultaneously will either be achieved, and it is only then that a just peace will be possible.

Human rights and liberal democracy are not merely complementary, rather, they are interdependent. A democracy that is substantive as well as procedural cannot function without human rights, just as human rights, meaning civil, political, economic, social, and cultural rights, cannot be ensured in the absence of democracy. In the case of Palestine, a foundation exists for both the realisation of human rights and the development of a substantive democracy, but both internal and external factors have hindered the building of viable institutions to actualize those ideals.

Greater attention thus needs to be given to the development of mechanisms such as elections, political parties, and separation of powers, and the restructuring of institutions including the judiciary branch and security sector. Despite the absence of these institutions to date, the will and perseverance of the Palestinian people, through both civil society and direct participation, has continued to push forward the democracy and human rights movements. Thus, attention must be given to these bottom-up efforts of popular participation, in addition to the top-down efforts of institution-building, if a liberal democracy is to be established. To be sure, no amount of institutional reform will be sustainable if it does not develop in tandem with popular will and public participation. For this reason, it is necessary for civil society organizations and actors to continue to facilitate political participation and raise public awareness, and it is imperative that individuals and communities seize opportunities to demonstrate their will. Media institutions in particular can play a key role in this process by serving as a means of popular communication, education, and mobilization.

The human rights framework can be helpful for developing direction and coordination for these efforts, and can integrate the distinct yet interdependent ideals of peace and justice, and human rights and democracy.

EDUCATION

The right to education is recognized as a human right by the United Nations and is understood to establish an entitlement to free, compulsory primary education for all children, an obligation to develop secondary education accessible to all children, as well as equitable access to higher education, and a responsibility to provide basic education for individuals who have not completed primary education. In addition to these access to education provisions the right to education encompasses also the obligation to eliminate discrimination at all levels of the educational system, to set minimum standards and to improve quality.

The right to education is enshrined in Article 26 of the Universal Declaration of Human Rights and Article 14 of the International Covenant on Economic, Social and Cultural Rights. The right to education has also been reaffirmed in the 1960 UNESCO Convention against Discrimination in Education, 1st Protocol of ECHR and the 1981 Convention on the Elimination of All Forms of Discrimination Against Women. The right to education may also include the right to freedom of education. Education narrowly refers to formal institutional instructions. Generally, international instruments use the term in this sense and the right to education, as protected by international human rights instruments, refers primarily to education in a narrow sense.

The 1960 UNESCO Convention against Discrimination in Education defines education in Article 1(2) as: "all types and levels of education, (including) access to education, the standard and quality of education, and the conditions under which it is given." In a wider sense education may describe "all activities by which a human group transmits to its descendants a body of knowledge and skills and a moral code which enable the group to subsist".

In this sense education refers to the transmission to a subsequent generation of those skills needed to perform tasks of daily living, and further passing on the social, cultural, spiritual and philosophical values of the particular community. The wider meaning of education has been recognised in Article 1(a) of UNESCO's 1974 Recommendation concerning Education for International Understanding, Co-operation and Peace and Education relating to Human Rights and Fundamental Freedoms.

The article states that education implies: "the entire process of social life by means of which individuals and social groups learn to develop consciously within, and for the benefit of, the national and international communities, the whole of their personal capabilities, attitudes, aptitudes and knowledge."

The European Court of Human Rights has defined education in a narrow sense as "teaching or instructions... in particular to the transmission of knowledge and to intellectual development" and in a wider sense as "the whole process whereby, in any society, adults endeavour to transmit their beliefs, culture and other values to the young."

FULFILLING THE RIGHT TO EDUCATION

The fulfilment of the right to education can be assessed using the 4 As framework, which asserts that for education to be a meaningful right it must be available, accessible, acceptable and adaptable. The 4 As framework was developed by the former UN Special Rapporteur on the Right to Education, Katarina Tomasevski, but is not necessarily the standard used in every international human rights instrument and hence not a generic guide to how the right to education is treated under national law.

The 4 As framework proposes that governments, as the prime duty-bearer, has to respect, protect and fulfil the right to education by making education available, accessible, acceptable and adaptable. The framework also places duties on other stakeholders in the education process: the child, which as the privileged subject of the right to education has the duty to comply with compulsory education requirements, the parents as the 'first educators', and professional educators, namely teachers.

The 4 As have been further elaborated as follows:

1. *Availability*: Education is free and government-funded and there is adequate infrastructure and trained teachers able to support education delivery.
2. *Accessibility*: The system is non-discriminatory and accessible to all, and positive steps are taken to include the most marginalised.
3. *Acceptability*: The content of education is relevant, non-discriminatory and culturally appropriate, and of quality. The school itself is safe and teachers are professional.
4. *Adaptability*: Education can evolve with the changing needs of society and contribute to challenging inequalities, such as gender discrimination, and can be adapted locally to suit specific contexts.

A number of international NGOs and charities work to realise the right to education using a rights-based approach to development.

DEVELOPMENT OF THE RIGHT TO EDUCATION

In Europe, before the Enlightenment of the eighteenth and nineteenth century, education was the responsibility of parents and the church. With the French and American Revolution education was established also as a public function. It was thought that the state, by assuming a more active role in the sphere of education, could help to make education available and accessible to all. Education had thus far been primarily available to the upper social classes and public education was perceived as a means of realising the egalitarian ideals underlining both revolutions. However, neither the American Declaration of Independence (1776) nor the French Declaration of the Rights of Man (1789) protected the right to education as the liberal concepts of human rights in the nineteenth century envisaged that parents retained the primary duty for providing education to their children. It was the states obligation to ensure that parents complied with this duty, and many states enacted legislation making school attendance compulsory.

Furthermore child labour laws were enacted to limit the number of hours per day children could be employed, to ensure children would attend school. States also became involved in the legal regulation of curricula and established minimum educational standards. In On Liberty John Stuart Mill wrote that an "education established and controlled by the State should only exist, if it exists at all, as one among many competing experiments, carried on for the purpose of example and stimulus to keep the others up to a certain standard of excellence."

Liberal thinkers of the nineteenth century pointed to the dangers to too much state involvement in the sphere of education, but relied on state intervention to reduce the dominance of the church, and to protect the right to education of children against their own parents. In the latter half of the nineteenth century, educational rights were included in domestic bills of rights. The 1849 Paulskirchenverfassung, the constitution of the German Empire, strongly influenced subsequent European constitutions and devoted Article 152 to 158 of its bill of rights to education. The constitution recognised education as a function of the state, independent of the church. Remarkable at the time, the constitution proclaimed the right to free education for the poor, but the constitution did not explicitly require the state to set up educational institutions. Instead the constitution protected the rights of citizens to found and operate schools and to provide home education. The constitution also provided for freedom of science and teaching, and it guaranteed the right of everybody to choose a vocation and train for it.

The nineteenth century also saw the development of socialist theory, which held that the primary task of the state was to ensure the economic and social well-being of the community through government intervention and regulation. Socialist theory recognised that individuals had claims to basic welfare services against the state and education was viewed as one of these welfare entitlements. This was in contrast to liberal theory at the time, which regarded non-state actors as the prime providers of education.

Socialist ideals were enshrined in the 1936 Soviet Constitution, which was the first constitution to recognise the right to education with a corresponding obligation of the state to provide such education. The constitution guaranteed free and compulsory education at all levels, a system of state scholarships and vocational training in state enterprises. Subsequently the right to education featured strongly in the constitutions of socialist states. As a political goal, right to education was declared in F. D. Roosevelt's 1944 speech on the Second Bill of Rights.

IMPLEMENTATION

International law does not protect the right to pre-primary education and international documents generally omit references to education at this level. The Universal Declaration of Human Rights states that "everybody" has the right to education, hence the right accures to all individuals, although children are understood as the main beneficiaries.

The rights to education are separated into three levels:

- Primary (Elemental or Fundamental) Education. This shall be compulsory and free for any child regardless of their nationality, gender, place of birth, or any other discrimination. Upon ratifying the International Covenant on Economic, Social and Cultural Rights

States must provide free primary education within two years.

- Secondary Education must be generally available and accessible.
- Higher Education (at the University Level) should be provided just as to capacity. That is, anyone who meets the necessary education standards should be able to go to university.

Both secondary and higher education shall be made accessible "by every appropriate means, and in particular by the progressive introduction of free education". The only country that has declared reservations about introducing free secondary or higher education is Japan.

Role of the State

Today education is considered an important public function and the state is seen as the chief provider of education through the allocation of substantial budgetary resources and regulating the provision of education. The pre-eminent role of the state in fulfilling the right to education is enshrined in the 1966 International Covenant on Economic, Social and Cultural Rights. Traditionally, education has been the duty of a child's parents, however with the rise of systems of education, the role of parents has diminished. With regards to realising the right to education the World Declaration on Education for All, adopted at the 1990 World Conference on Education for All states that "partnerships between government and non-governmental organisations, the private sector, local communities, religious groups, and families" are necessary.

Compulsory Education

The realisation of the right to education on a national level may be achieved through compulsory education, or more specifically free compulsory primary education, as stated in both the Universal Declaration of Human Rights and the International Covenant on Economic, Social and Cultural Rights.

ANTI-HOMELESSNESS LEGISLATION

Anti-homelessness legislation can take two forms; legislation that aims to help and re-house homeless people, and legislation that is intended to criminalize homelessness and/or send the homeless to homeless shelters compulsively.

INTERNATIONAL LAW

Since the publication of the Universal Declaration of Human Rights (Charter of the United Nations — UN) in 1948, the public perception has been increasingly changing to a focus on the human right to housing, travel and migration as a part of individual self-determination rather than the human condition.

The Declaration, an international law reinforcement of the Nuremberg Trial Judgements, upholds the rights of one nation to intervene in the affairs of another if said nation is abusing its citizens, and rose out of a 1939–1945 World War II Atlantic environment of extreme split between "haves" and "have nots." The modern study of homeless phenomena is most frequently seen in this historical context.

LAWS SUPPORTING THE HOMELESS

Laws supporting homeless people generally place obligations on the state to support or house homeless people.

Scotland

The Scottish parliament passed the Homelessness Etc (Scotland) Act 2003 which has an aim of ensuring that by 2012 everyone assessed as being unintentionally homeless will be entitled to permanent accommodation. In addition, the Homeless Persons (Unsuitable Accommodation) (Scotland) Order came into force in December 2004 and requires councils to ensure that pregnant women and households with children are not placed in unsuitable temporary accommodation, unless there are exceptional circumstances.

United States

The charter of the McKinney-Vento Homeless Assistance

Act of 1986 (Stewart B. McKinney Homeless Assistance Act) is to "coordinate the Federal response to homelessness and to create partnerships between the Federal agencies addressing homelessness and every level of government and every element of the private sector".

LAWS CRIMINALIZING THE HOMELESS

Use of the law that criminalizes the homeless generally takes on one of four forms:

- Restricting the public areas in which sitting or sleeping are allowed.
- Removing the homeless from particular areas.
- Prohibiting begging.
- Enforcing laws on the homeless and not on those who are not homeless. (The French novelist Anatole France noted this phenomenon as long ago as 1894, famously observing that "the law, in its majestic equality, forbids the rich as well as the poor to sleep under bridges".)

England and Wales

The Vagrancy Act 1824 makes it an offence to sleep on the streets or to beg. In essence, therefore, it is a crime in England and Wales to be homeless or to cadge subsistence money. When the Act was passed, criticism of it centred on the fact that it created a catch-all offence. To sleep on the streets or to beg subsistence became a crime, whatever reason an individual might have had for being in such a predicament. That provision still pertains today in England and Wales. So far as it extended to Scotland, it was repealed by the Civic Government (Scotland) Act 1982.

COMMUNICATION RIGHTS

Rights relating to communication have been central to the concept of universal human rights emerging in the mid-20th century, and its consolidation in the United Nations Charter and the Universal Declaration of Human Rights (UDHR). But Jean d'Arcy is generally credited with being the first to explicitly make the case for a "right to communicate" In 1969, then Director of Radio and Visual Services in the UN Office of Public Information, he wrote: "The time will come when the (UDHR) will have to encompass a more extensive right than man's right to information, first laid down 21 years ago in Article 19. This is the right of man to communicate. It is the angle from which the future development of communications will have to be considered if it is to be fully understood".

INTERGOVERNMENTAL PLATFORMS: NWICO, UNESCO, AND THE MACBRIDE COMMISSION

The issue was catapulted to the forefront of geopolitics soon after. Soon the idea of a "right to communicate"was at the centre of an international diplomatic row that lasted several years the debate over what became known as a New World Information and Communication Order - NWICO. Against a backdrop of the emergent role of media and communication, many countries became seriously concerned at the impact on national identity, ¬cultural ¬integrity, and political and economic sovereignty. NWICO, spearheaded by the Non-Aligned Movement (NAM) of UN countries focused on:

- The "free flow" doctrine of information flow, which was reinforcing the dominance of western media and news content;
- The growing concentration of the media and communication industry translating into more foreign ownership of media in smaller and poorer countries;
- How the growing importance of western-controlled technologies to media production and dissemination was making it difficult for others to keep up.

As the only UN body equipped to debate in a coherent manner the range of issues raised, the battle would primarily be staged at UNESCO, where it would stay for a decade. From 1973, the NAM was developing a much more sophisticated plan for a New World Information Order. At the 1976 UNESCO General Assembly, the wide gulf between NAM and western countries (USA, UK and others) became apparent. A showdown was avoided only by the creation of an International Commission for the Study of Communication Problems, generally called the MacBride Commission after its Chair, Seán MacBride. The MacBride Commission's report to the 1980 General Assembly, "Many Voices One World", bore the hallmarks of a fractious political process, fudging many issues and containing numerous caveats. But it was comprehensive (with a notable weakness in relation to gender) and wide-ranging, and came with concrete recommendations, including: "Communication needs in a democratic society should be met by the extension of specific rights such as the right to be informed, the right to inform, the right to privacy, the right to participate in public communication - all elements of a new concept, the right to communicate.

In developing what might be called a new era of social rights, we suggest all the implications of the right to communicate be further explored." For the first time, the NWICO had a general framework, a detailed justification, a set of proposals, and a unifying concept - the "right to communicate". Eventually the Commission's findings were endorsed-a defining moment for NWICO, but one which was short-lived. The veneer of agreement was thin; instead of bringing the sides together, the process merely exposed the gulf between them and entrenched the positions, especially of West governments mired within Cold War geo-politics. The USA led a "counter-offensive" on UNESCO, supported strongly by the private media industry and lobbies. The main charge was that less developed countries were attempting to impose government control of media, and to suppress freedom of the press - despite the fact that press freedom was strongly endorsed at every turn by NWICO. The US (in 1984) and UK (in 1985) eventually withdrew from UNESCO, partly due to NWICO.

While the newly politicised "information society" was becoming ascendant, NWICO in its original form had declined. It did manage to stay on the UNESCO agenda, though with little action, until 1987. With the "New Communication Strategy" under new UNESCO Director-General Federico

Mayor in 1989, it basically died out. Yet the arguments that animated the NWICO movement continued, and even in some respects became sharper. The arguments continued to surface in new calls-outside of governments this time - for "communication rights".

BEYOND NWICO: CIVIL SOCIETY ENGAGEMENTS

For many, the main session from NWICO was that the way forward would have to be through the democratization of media and communication, rather than through state - or industry - led efforts to create new global orders. In practice, a major shift was needed towards civil society, which had so far been largely excluded. Those that had been involved - mainly journalists' organizations and some academics - continued debating in the form of the MacBride Round Table, which met annually from 1989 to 1999, and brought new civil society actors into the discussion. A growing number of NGOs, some quite independent of previous debates and largely unaware of them (and often of each other), also began to question trends in media, knowledge, and communication.

These included community media associations, faith-based organizations, international trade unions, emerging Internet NGOs, and advocacy groups springing up to address diverse issues (*e.g.*, internet surveillance, concentration of media ownership, commercial censorship, copyright and patent excesses). These were now set alongside more traditional concerns of government censorship and controls. The growing significance of digital technologies and the emergence of the Internet also provided new arguments for democratization, as existing social contradictions manifested themselves in so-called "digital divides". New arenas opened up where traditional and emerging advocacies could converge. As was its strength, civil society let its praxis on the ground and advocacies on national and regional arenas dictate the discourse, although initiatives were not labelled "communication rights" work at the time. However, a history of the Communication Rights movement "from below", would probably include various threads of activism: the telecentre movement, Free/Open Source Software (FOSS) communities, independent media centres, gender-based organizations in communications, local content/local language advocates, nonprofit ISPs - all empowered by new networking tools and technologies. These formations - supported by sympathetic donor institutions and academics - evolved independently and sharpened critiques of new information/communication hierarchies.

By the 1990s, various coalitions were formed and initiatives taken to address the larger picture underlying many of these concerns, among them the People's Communication Charter and the Platform for Democratization of Communication. Many broad-based conferences and meetings were held to pull the threads together and exchange understanding internationally. Gradually a new civil society-based constituency was emerging, but now from a different perspective and benefiting from historical experience and on-the-ground praxis. Many of these coalesced in October 2001 into the Campaign for Communication Rights in the Information Society (CRIS Campaign), at the ¬onset of another global governance arena of struggle - the World Summit on the Information Society (WSIS).

THE "RIGHT TO COMMUNICATE" AND "COMMUNICATION RIGHTS"

The terms "right to communicate" and "communication rights" are not synonymous, and history, principle and tactics are bound in their usage by different groups. As we have seen, the term "right to communicate" became associated with a (mis)reading of the NWICO promoted by its opponents. Even today, in the context of the WSIS, some claim that attempts to promote a "right to communicate" are merely veiled efforts to revive the NWICO.

For these opponents, the idea of "communication rights" as distinct from a "right to communicate", is more difficult to criticize since it leaves behind the connotations of NWICO. At the political level, there also have been calls for the creation of a new right under international law. This would build on the existing international legal framework, establishing a "right to communicate" as an unambiguous right of all people. This position clearly recognizes that many existing human rights are key components of this, but that an explicit "right to communicate" would both bolster these, conceptually and on the ground. However, the specifics of this right, its precise wording, in what legal form it would be incorporated and so forth, have not been fully teased out.

On the other hand, the term "communication rights", in a plural form, implicitly points towards existing rights that relate to communication. The emphasis shifts subtly to realising the existing communication rights on the ground, not on establishing a new global covenant. Calling for the realisation of communication rights, and reaffirming that everyone has - or should have - a right to communicate, are entirely complementary.

The "right to communicate" can be used as an informal rallying cry for advocacy, while it can also be used in a formal legal sense, in which it should take its place alongside other fundamental rights enshrined in international law. "Communication rights" relates immediately to a set of existing human rights, that are denied many people, and whose full meaning can only be realised when they are considered together as an interrelated group. The CRIS Campaign is the most articulated global civil society alliance that seeks to promote the concept and praxis of communication rights. But beyond this formation, many others have adopted the term in various platforms.

A "right to communicate" was strongly endorsed at several points by influential actors during the WSIS process. The issue gained some prominence, although efforts to discredit it, and the fear of controversy, were probably responsible for its exclusion from the final text. UN Secretary-General Kofi Annan stated that: "millions of people in the poorest countries are still excluded from the "right to communicate", increasingly seen as a fundamental human right." And the European Commission noted: "The Summit should reinforce the right to communicate and to access information and knowledge." Other key NGOs not members of the CRIS Campaign have also endorsed it. Article 19, in its overview of the right to communicate, describes it as: "an umbrella term, encompassing within it a group of related, existing rights. This means that any elaboration of the right to communicate must take place within the framework of existing rights."

COMMUNICATION RIGHTS VIZ. "FREEDOM OF EXPRESSION"

"Freedom of expression" ranks among the sacrosanct foundations of all human rights. It is contained in numerous international Treaties and Conventions, and enshrined in varying formulations in virtually all national constitutions and legislation. The most frequently cited reference is to Article 19 of the UDHR:

- "Everyone has the right to freedom of opinion and expression; this right includes the freedom to hold opinions without interference and to seek, receive and impart information and ideas through any media and regardless of frontiers."

Is Freedom of Expression Enough?

The question facing communication rights advocates is why anything more than "freedom of expression" is needed. Furthermore, given that such a basic right is still denied to many in practice, surely our energies should focus on securing freedom of expression for all? Would securing freedom of expression in effect secure communication rights? The ideal from which freedom of expression draws its legitimacy assumes a group of communicating individuals, each with an equal right to conceive, impart and receive ideas from others, and thereby to rationally arrive at decisions of mutual benefit. The trouble with this is that we do not live as a group of equally empowered individuals.

We live in a society of hugely varying levels of access to power, a society in which most communication between people is heavily mediated and filtered - with mass media, governments, commercial corporations, special interest groups and many others all vying for attention, seeking to influence and control the content and flow of communications. An exclusive insistence on freedom of expression says nothing about the process by which society's means of expression - newspapers, television, radio, films, music and educational material - are controlled, and in whose interests they operate.

In this context, freedom of expression - in the sense of laws to prevent direct government interference and to defend free speech - can do little to prevent the domination of the loudest voices, *i.e.*, those who can most strongly influence the means of communication within society, whether they are the government, newspaper proprietors and media owners, or powerful interest groups. In this example, how real is the "freedom to receive and impart information" if one can hardly read nor write, or cannot speak the official language of the country? Or how real is freedom to "seek and receive information" if governments and corporations are not obliged to provide it? Or if you cannot afford to pay for educational materials, or access key means of communication such as telephony or (increasingly) the Internet? If you know your communications means are being spied on?

These are symptoms of unequal access to power, of a world in which communication is possible only increasingly through complex and contested media and mechanisms. Thus a key challenge for freedom of expression advocates is the conceptual shift from the idea of equal individuals, to a complex and variegated society with heavily mediated communication and various and differential configurations of power. Tackling this requires an additional set of concepts and instruments, which is at the core of "communication rights" discourse.

FRAMING "COMMUNICATION RIGHTS"

Communication rights can be seen as providing the conditions for the full exercise of freedom of expression in a complex and mediated society in which power and control of resources are distributed very unevenly. freedom of expression is indeed at the heart of Communication rights. However, the advocacy for Communication rights goes further in that it creates the environment in which freedom of expression may be fully consummated at the level of society. Communication rights are premised on communicating, the completion of an interaction between people; it maintains that freedom to interact with others is ultimately about generating a cycle of communication, from which learning, understanding and cooperation may ensue.

An initial approximation of the goal of Communication Rights is thus: to secure the generation of a considered, creative and respectful cycle of interaction between people and groups in society, that in practice endorses the right of all equally to have their ideas expressed, heard, listened to, considered and responded to.

ENABLING RIGHTS

Communication Rights draw on aspects of other key human rights - "flanking" or "enabling" rights - contained in the International Bill of Rights and supplementary treaties and legal documents.

For example:

- A right to participate in one's own culture, and use one's mother language, including ethnic, religious or linguistic minorities;
- A right to information regarding governance and matters of public interest (freedom of information);
- A right to information regarding governance and matters of public interest (freedom of information);
- A right to the protection of the moral and material interests of authorship;
- A right to one's honour and reputation, and to protection against attacks;
- A right to privacy;
- A right to peaceful assembly and association;
- A right to free primary education and progressive introduction of free secondary education.

A dimension of each of these bears strongly on the process

of communication in society (all could be suffixed with "in relation to media and communication"). These might be termed "top-level" communication rights. However, they are further specified and sometimes additional dimensions added. For example: the right to a diverse and independent media and to access to media, has been recognized in various fora as diverse as the European Court of Human Rights, Supreme Court of Sri Lanka, the German Federal Constitutional Court, UNESCO, and Resolutions of the Council of the European Union. The promotion of communication rights attempts to strip away layers of social, historical, economic, and psychological barriers to communication, to reinforce an environment of mutual respect, and to build the capacities of all in communication and interaction.

The Added Value of Communication Rights

This interpretation of communication rights has a number of implications. First, the whole set of communication rights yields something more than the sum of its parts. Communication rights bring together relevant dimensions from a set of component enabling rights, and can be realised only through them. However, Communication rights can also be seen as meta rights, which gives new and additional meaning to those enabling rights. Second, the emergence of communication rights in practice is the creation of a climate of mutual respect and tolerance not just between individuals which hold these rights, but between diverse communities and cultures, ethnic groups and nationalities.

Calling for communication rights at the same time endorses and supports the notion and value of diversity. Third, communication rights unavoidably implicate social processes and dynamics. Communication rights by their very nature question whether social structures differentially constrain and enable the capacity of different individuals and groups to communicate effectively within societies. The concept of communication rights forces us to engage much more comprehensively the spirit of "freedom of expression" towards the elimination of constraints on whole parts of society, and building the access and capacities of those who are excluded.

COMMUNICATION RIGHTS: WHY NOW?

Why is it that "communication rights" as a concept is especially relevant now more than it was in the past? What justifies a movement at this time to attempt to enforce and deepen our communication rights?

Communication rights have greatly grown in relevance in the last decades, due to a number of factors and trends in the sphere of global information and communications, including:

- Corporate media dominance and media concentration;
- Emergence of "copyright" regimes and the erosion of the public domain of global knowledge;
- Erosion of civil rights in the digital environment, especially post 9-11 (*e.g.*, stronger comprehensive and globally-framed and enforced frameworks for electronic surveillance).
- Limitations of market-driven initiatives in telecommunications and ICTs;
- Negative effects of media systems on identity/ies and culture/s;

All of these concerns can be analysed and understood, and integral solutions designed, using the concept of communication rights.

Together, these dynamics hugely influence each step of the communication process in society. These trends can fundamentally shape the outcomes of social communication and who benefits from it, through controlling the creation and ownership of knowledge, the processes and media of dissemination and communication, and its use to solve political, economic, and social goals.

The imminent danger is that each moment in the cycle is becoming harnessed to the needs of capital and the market. The ultimate danger is that the cycle of society's social communication process is interrupted, the process of social learning becomes ever more feeble, and in the end the process of creativity is transformed and reduced to short-term, unsustainable, generation of profits for a small minority. Society may find itself having virtually lost the capacity for creativity, for an inclusive and equitable sharing of knowledge, for democratic participation in political structures, for diverse cultural expression and expression of identity, even the capacity to learn from past and present generations. "Communication rights", as a concept and as praxis, potentially have the depth and breadth to analyse and understand these dangers, and design integral solutions designed to tackle them.

RIGHT TO COMMUNICATE VS. COMMUNICATION RIGHTS

A 'right to communicate' and 'communication rights' are closely related, but not identical, in their history and usage. In the Cold War tensions of the 1970s and 80s, the former became associated with the New World Information and Communication Order (NWICO) debate, thus, efforts within UNESCO to formulate such a right were abandoned. The latter emphasizes the fact that an array of international rights underpinning communication already exists, but many are too often ignored and require active mobilisation and assertion. While some, especially within the mass media sector, still see the right to communicate as a "code word" for state censorship, the technological innovations in interactive electronic, global communication of recent decades are seen by others as challenging the tradtional mass media structures and formulations of communication rights values arising from them, thereby renewing the need to re-consider the need for a right to communicate. These issues are explored more fully in Raboy's and Shtern,s Media Divides: Communication rights and the right to communicate in Canada (2010).

CONSUMER/SURVIVOR/EX-PATIENT MOVEMENT

The Consumer/Survivor/Ex-Patient Movement, also known as the User/Survivor Movement, is a diverse association of individuals (and organizations representing them) who are either currently "consumers" (clients) of mental health services, or who consider themselves survivors of psychiatry or mental health services, or who simply identify as "ex-patients" of mental health services. The movement typically campaigns for more choice and improved services, and/or empowerment and user-led alternatives, and against prejudice in society more generally. Common themes are "talking back to the power of psychiatry", rights protection and advocacy, and self-determination.

While activists in this movement may share a collective identity, individuals can be seen as enacting their concerns along a continuum from conservative to radical, just as to their position in relation to psychiatric treatment and their relative levels of resistance and patienthood. This can in turn relate to an individual's experiences of the mental health system, particularly if subject to forced detention and/or forced medication, electroshock or other practice. The modern self-help and advocacy movement in the field of mental health services developed in the 1970s, but former psychiatric patients have been campaigning for centuries to change laws, treatments, services and public policies.

"The most persistent critics of psychiatry have always been former mental hospital patients", although few were able to tell their stories publicly or to openly confront the psychiatric establishment, and those who did so were commonly considered so extreme in their charges that they could seldom gain credibility. In 1620 in England, patients of the notoriously harsh Bethlem Hospital banded together and sent a "Petition of the Poor Distracted People in the House of Bedlam (concerned with conditions for inmates)" to the House of Lords. A number of ex-patients published pamphlets against the system in the 18th century, such as Samuel Bruckshaw (1774), on the "iniquitous abuse of private madhouses", and William Belcher (1796) with his "Address to humanity, Containing a letter to Dr Munro, a receipt to make a lunatic, and a sketch of a true smiling hyena".

Such reformist efforts were generally opposed by madhouse keepers and medics. In the late 18th century, moral treatment reforms developed which were originally based in part on the approach of French ex-patient turned hospital-superintendent Jean-Baptiste Pussin and his wife Margueritte. From 1848 in England, the Alleged Lunatics' Friend Society campaigned for sweeping reforms to the asylum system and abuses of the moral treatment approach. In the United States, The Opal (1851-1860) was a ten volume Journal produced by patients of Utica State Lunatic Asylum in New York, which has been viewed in part as an early liberation movement. Beginning in 1868, Elizabeth Packard, founder of the Anti-Insane Asylum Society, published a series of books and pamphlets describing her experiences in the Illinois insane asylum to which her husband had had her committed.

A few decades later, another former psychiatric patient, Clifford W. Beers, founded the National Committee on Mental Hygiene, which eventually became the National Mental Health Association. Beers sought to improve the plight of individuals receiving public psychiatric care, particularly those committed to state institutions. His book, A Mind that Found Itself (1908), described his experience with mental illness and the treatment he encountered in mental hospitals.

Beers' work stimulated public interest in more responsible care and treatment. However, while Beers initially damned psychiatrists for tolerating mistreatment of patients, and envisioned more ex-patient involvement in the movement, he was influenced by Adolf Meyer and the psychiatric establishment, and toned down his hostility as he needed their support for reforms. His reliance on rich donors and his need for approval from experts led him to hand over to psychiatrists the organization he helped establish. In the UK, the National Society for Lunacy Law Reform was established in 1920 by angry ex-patients sick of their experiences and complaints being patronisingly discounted by the authorities who were using medical "window dressing" for essentially custodial and punitive practices.

In 1922, ex-patient Rachel Grant-Smith added to calls for reform of the system of neglect and abuse she had suffered by publishing "The Experiences of an Asylum Patient".We Are Not Alone (WANA) was founded by a group of patients at

Rockland State Hospital in New York in the mid to late 1940s, and continued to meet as an ex-patient group. Their goal was to provide support and advice and help others make the difficult transition from hospital to community. By the early 1950s WANA dissolved after it was taken over by mental health professionals who transformed it into Fountain House, a psychosocial rehabilitation service for people leaving state mental institutions.

The founders of WANA found themselves pushed aside by professionals with money and influence, who made them "members" of the new organization. During that period, people who received psychiatric treatment identified themselves as patients, and this term was generally unchallenged as a self-description until the 1970s. A perceived patronizing attitude by health care workers led to resentment among some current and former patients, which eventually found expression in more militant groups beginning in the early 1970s. Originated by crusaders in periods of liberal social change, and appealing not so much to other sufferers as to elite groups with power, when the early reformer's energy or influence waned, mental patients were again mostly friendless and forgotten.

The 1950s saw the advent and widespread use of lobotomy and shock therapy. These were associated with grave concerns and much opposition on grounds of basic morality, harmful effects, or misuse. Towards the 1960s, psychiatric medications came in to widespread use and also caused controversy relating to adverse effects and misuse. There were also associated moves away from large psychiatric institutions to community-based services (later to become a full-scale deinstitutionalization), which sometimes empowered service users, although community-based services were often deficient.

Coming to the fore in the 1960s, an anti-psychiatry movement vocally challenged the fundamental claims and practices of mainstream psychiatry. The ex-patient movement of this time contributed to, and derived much from, antipsychiatry ideology, but has also been described as having its own agenda, described as humanistic socialism. For a time, the movement shared aims and practices with "radical therapists", who tended to be Marxist and equally keen on challenging the social structures that kept people oppressed and boxed. However, the consumer/survivor/ex-patients gradually felt that the radical therapists did not necessarily share the same goals and were taking over, and they broke away from them in order to maintain independence. By the 1970s, the women's movement, gay rights movement, and disability rights movements had emerged.

It was in this context that former mental patients began to organize groups with the common goals of fighting for patients' rights and against forced treatment, stigma and discrimination, and often to promote peer-run services as an alternative to the traditional mental health system. Unlike professional mental health services, which were usually based on the medical model, peer-run services were based on the principle that individuals who have shared similar experiences can help themselves and each other through self-help and mutual support.

Many of the individuals who organized these early groups identified themselves as psychiatric survivors. Their groups had names such as Insane Liberation Front and the Network Against Psychiatric Assault. They saw the mental health system as destructive and disempowering. With more people out of mental hospitals, there was a larger number of people who could now make links with one another for progressive causes. Dorothy Weiner and about 10 others, including Tom Wittick, established the Insane Liberation Front in the spring of 1970 in Portland, Oregon.

Though it only lasted 6 months, it had a notable influence in the history of North American ex-patients groups. News that former inmates of mental institutions were organizing was carried to other parts of North America. Individuals such as Howard Geld, known as Howie the Harp for his harmonica playing, left Portland where he been involved in ILF to return to his native New York to help found the Mental Patients Liberation Project in 1971. During the early 1970s, groups spread to California, New York, and Boston, which were primarily antipsychiatry, opposed to forced treatment including forced drugging, shock treatment and involuntary committal. In 1972, the first organized group in Canada, the Mental Patients Association, started to publish In A Nutshell, while in the US the first edition of the first national publication by ex-mental patients, Madness Network News, was published in Oakland, continuing until 1986.

A well-known book of the time by an ex-patient was Judi Chamberlin's 1978 "On Our Own: Patient-Controlled Alternatives to the Mental Health System." Chamberlin publicized the concept of mentalism, a form of stereotyping and oppression of those associated with psychiatric treatment and diagnosis. The major spokespeople of the movement have been described in generalities as largely white, middle-class and well-educated. It has been suggested that other activists were often more anarchistic and anti-capitalist, felt more cut-off from society and more like a minority with more in common with the poor, ethnic minorities, feminists, prisoners and gay rights than with the white middle classes.

The leaders were sometimes considered to be merely reformist and, because of their "stratified position" within society, to be uncomprehending of the problems of the poor. The "radicals" saw no sense in seeking solutions within a capitalist system that creates mental problems. However, they were united in considering society and psychiatric domination to be the problem, rather than people designated mentally ill. Some activists condemned psychiatry under any conditions, voluntary or involuntary, while others, usually the more middle-class, conceded the right of people to undergo psychiatric treatment on a voluntary basis. Voluntary psychotherapy, at the time mainly psychoanalysis, did not therefore come under the same severe attack as the somatic therapies. But it was valued, if at all, only as a possibly helpful technique if applied by laypersons including ex-patients themselves.

The ex-patients emphasized individual support from other patients; they espoused assertiveness, liberation, and equality; and they advocated user-controlled services as part of a totally voluntary continuum. However, although the movement espoused egalitarianism and opposed the concept of leadership, it is said to have developed a cadre of known, articulate, and literate men and women who did the writing, talking, organizing, and contacting.

Very much the product of the rebellious, populist, anti-elitist mood of the 1960s, they strived above all for self-determination and self-reliance. In generally, the work of some psychiatrists, as well as the lack of criticism by the psychiatric establishment, was interpreted as an abandonment of a moral commitment to do no harm. There was a deep anger and resentment towards a profession that had the authority to label them as mentally disabled and was perceived as infantilizing them and disregarding their wishes.

By the 1980s, individuals who considered themselves "consumers" of mental health services rather than passive "patients" had begun to organize self-help/advocacy groups and peer-run services. While sharing some of the goals of the earlier movement, consumer groups did not seek to abolish the traditional mental health system, which they believed was necessary. Instead, they wanted to reform it and have more choice. Consumer groups encouraged their members to learn as much as possible about the mental health system so that they could gain access to the best services and treatments available.

In 1985, the National Mental Health Consumers' Association was formed in the United States. A 1986 report on developments in the United States noted that "there are now three national organizations... The 'conservatives' have created the National Mental Health Consumers' Association... The 'moderates' have formed the National Alliance of Mental Patients... The 'radical' group is called the Network to Abolish Psychiatry". Many, however, felt that they had survived the psychiatric system and its "treatments" and resented being called consumers. The National Association of Mental Patients in the United States became the National Association of Psychiatric Survivors. "Phoenix Rising: The Voice of the

Psychiatrized" was published by ex-inmates (of psychiatric hospitals) in Toronto from 1980 to 1990, known across Canada for its antipsychiatry stance. In late 1988, leaders from several of the main national and grassroots psychiatric survivor groups decided an independent coalition was needed, and Support Coalition International (SCI) was formed in 1988, later to become MindFreedom International.

In addition, the World Network of Users and Survivors of Psychiatry (WNUSP), was founded in 1991 as the World Federation of Psychiatric Users (WFPU), an international organisation of recipients of mental health services. An emphasis on voluntary involvement in services is said to have presented problems to the movement since, especially in the wake of deinstitutionalization, community services were fragmented and many individuals in distressed states of mind were being put in prisons or re-institutionalized in community services, or became homeless, often distrusting and resisting any help.

Patients rights groups have been speaking out against psychiatric abuses for decades but have been censored and denied by the psychiatric establishment. Reading about the experiences they suffered through has been described as comparable to reading the stories of Holocaust survivors. Recipients of mental health services demanded control over their own treatment and began to have an influence on the public mental health system. They often promoted a recovery model. Whether they considered themselves consumers or survivors, activists demanded a voice and a choice.

THE MOVEMENT TODAY

In the United States, the number of mental health mutual support groups (MSG), self-help organizations (SHO) (run by and for mental health consumers and/or family members) and consumer-operated services (COS) was recently estimated to be 7,467. The movement may express a preference for the "survivor" label over the "consumer" label, with more than 60 per cent of ex-patient groups reported to support anti-psychiatry beliefs and considering themselves to be "psychiatric survivors." There is some variation between the perspective on the consumer/survivor movement coming from psychiatry, anti-psychiatry or consumers/survivors themselves. The most common terms in Germany are "Psychiatrie-Betroffene" (people afflicted by/confronted with psychiatry) and "Psychiatrie-Erfahrene" (people who have experienced psychiatry). Sometimes the terms are considered as synonymous but sometimes the former emphasizes the violence and negative aspects of psychiatry.

The German national association of (ex-)users and survivors of psychiatry is called the Bundesverband Psychiatrie-Erfahrener (BPE). There are many grassroots self-help groups of consumers/survivors, local and national, all over the world, which are an important cornerstone of empowerment. A considerable obstacle to realising more consumer/survivor alternatives is lack of funding. Alternative consumer/survivor groups like the National Empowerment Centre in the US which receive public funds but question orthodox psychiatric treatment, have often come under attack for receiving public funding and been subject to funding cuts. As well as advocacy and reform campaigns, the development of self-help and user/survivor controlled services is a central issue. The Runaway-House in Berlin, Germany, is an example. Run by the Organisation for the Protection from Psychiatric Violence, it is an antipsychiatric crisis centre for homeless survivors of psychiatry where the residents can live for a limited amount of time and where half the staff members are survivors of psychiatry themselves.

In Helsingborg, Sweden, the Hotel Magnus Stenbock is run by a user/survivor organization "RSMH" that gives users/ survivors a possibility to live in their own apartments. It is financed by the Swedish government and run entirely by users. Voice of Soul is a user/survivor organization in Hungary. Creative Routes is a user/survivor organization in London, England, that among other support and advocacy activities puts on an annual "Bonkersfest".WNUSP is a consultant organization for the United Nations. After a "long and difficult discussion", ENUSP and WNUSP (European and World

Networks of Users and Survivors of Psychiatry) decided to employ the term (ex-)users and survivors of psychiatry in order to include the identities of the different groups and positions represented in these international NGOs. WNUSP contributed to the development of the UN's Convention on the Rights of Persons with Disabilities and produced a manual to help people use it called "Implementing the Disability Rights Treaty, for Users, Survivors of Psychiatry" and ENUSP is consulted by the European Union and World Health Organization. In 2007 at a Conference held in Dresden on "Coercive Treatment in Psychiatry: A Comprehensive Review", the president and other leaders of the World Psychiatric Association met, following a formal request from the World Health Organization, with four representatives from leading consumer/survivor groups.

The National Coalition of Mental Health Consumer/Survivor Organizations campaigns in the United States to ensure that consumer/survivors have a major voice in the development and implementation of health care, mental health, and social policies at the state and national levels, empowering people to recover and lead a full life in the community. The United States Massachusetts-based Freedom Centre provides and promotes alternative and holistic approaches and takes a stand for greater choice and options in treatments and care. The centre and the New York-based Icarus Project (which does not self-identify as a consumer/survivor organization but has participants that identify as such) have published a Harm Reduction Guide To Coming Off Psychiatric Drugs and were recently a featured charity in Forbes business magazine.

Mad pride events, organized by loosely connected groups in at least seven countries including Australia, South Africa, the United States, Canada, the United Kingdom and Ghana, draw thousands of participants. For some, the objective is to continue the destigmatization of mental illness. Another wing rejects the need to treat mental afflictions with psychotropic drugs and seeks alternatives to the "care" of the medical establishment. Many members of the movement say they are publicly discussing their own struggles to help those with similar conditions and to inform the general public. Survivor David Oakes, Director of MindFreedom, hosts a monthly radio show and the Freedom Centre initiated a weekly FM radio show now syndicated on the Pacifica Network, Madness Radio, hosted by Freedom Centre co-founder Will Hall. A new International Coalition of National Consumer/User Organizations was launched in Canada in 2007, called Interrelate.

IMPACT

There has been some substantial research into consumer/survivor initiatives (CSIs). Many of the studies have been cross-sectional or retrospective and have not used comparison groups, which limits the firm conclusions that can be drawn. However, the findings suggest that CSIs can help with social support, empowerment, mental wellbeing, self-management and reduced service use, identity transformation and enhanced quality of life. However, studies have focused on the support and self-help aspects of CSIs, neglecting that many organizations locate the causes of members' problems in political and social institutions and are involved in activities to address issues of social justice.

A recent series of studies in Canada compared individuals who participated in CSIs with those who did not. The two groups were comparable at baseline on a wide range of demographic variables, self-reported psychiatric diagnosis, service use, and outcome measures. After a year and a half, those who had participated in CSIs showed significant improvement in social support and quality of life (daily activities), less days of psychiatric hospitalization, and more were likely to have stayed in employment (paid or volunteer) and/or education.

There was no significant difference on measures of community integration and personal empowerment, however. There were some limitations to the findings; although the active and nonactive groups did not differ significantly at baseline on measures of distress or hospitalization, the active group did have a higher mean score and there may have been a natural pattern of recovery over time for that group (regression to the mean). The authors noted that the apparent positive impacts of consumer-run organizations were achieved at a fraction of the cost of professional community programmes. Further qualitative studies indicated that CSIs can provide: safe environments that are a positive, welcoming place to go; social arenas that provide opportunities to meet and talk with peers; an alternative worldview that provides opportunities for members to participate and contribute; and effective facilitators of community integration that provide opportunities to connect members to the community at large.

System-level activism was perceived to result in changes in perceptions by the public and mental health professionals (about mental health or mental illness, the lived experience of consumer/survivors, the legitimacy of their opinions, and the perceived value of CSIs) and in concrete changes in service delivery practice, service planning, public policy, or funding allocations. The authors noted that the evidence indicated that the work benefits other consumers/survivors (present and future), other service providers, the general public, and communities. They also noted that there were various barriers to this, most notably lack of funding, and also that the range of views represented by the CSIs appeared less narrow and more nuanced and complex than previously, and that perhaps the consumer/survivor social movement is at a different place than it was 25 years ago. There has also been criticism of the movement.

Well-positioned forces in the USA, led by figures such as psychiatrists E. Fuller Torrey and Sally Satel, and some leaders of the National Alliance for the Mentally Ill, have lobbied against the funding of consumer/survivor groups that promote antipsychiatry views or promote social and experiential recovery rather than a biomedical model, or who protest against outpatient commitment. Torrey has said the term "psychiatric survivor" used by ex-patients to describe themselves is just political correctness and has blamed them, along with civil rights lawyers, for the deaths of half a million people due to suicides and deaths on the street. Such claims have been controverted by recent publications such as U.S.A. Today which published an article indicating that the medical model and the way persons with mental illness are treated today cause people to die 25 years early on average. There is great need for further development of the recovery model whose outcome is to support people in regaining their wellness instead of a life sentence of psychiatry which has been found to cause early death.

His accusations have been described as inflammatory and completely unsubstantiated, however, and issues of self-determination and self-identity said to be more complex than that. More generally, organized psychiatry often views radical consumerist groups as extremist, as having little scientific foundation and no defined leadership, as trying to restrict "the work of psychiatrists and care for the seriously mentally ill", and as promoting disinformation on the use of involuntary commitment, electroconvulsive therapy, stimulants and antidepressants among children, and neuroleptics among adults.

EQUAL PAY FOR EQUAL WORK

Equal pay for equal work is the concept that individuals doing the same work should receive the same remuneration. It is most commonly used in a context of sexual discrimination, as equal pay for women.

Equal pay does not simply relate to basic salary but also to the full range of benefits, non salary payments, bonuses and allowances that are paid. The U.S. Democratic Party has historically supported legislating equal pay for equal work. Its 2008 party platform reads: "When women still earn 76 cents for every dollar that a man earns, it doesn't just hurt women; it hurts families and children.

As suggested, pass the 'Lilly Ledbetter' Act, which will make it easier to combat pay discrimination; as suggested, pass the Fair Pay Act; and as suggested, modernize the Equal Pay

Act." The Lilly Ledbetter Fair Pay Act was signed into law in January 2009. Free market supporters believe that government actions to correct gender pay disparity serve to interfere with the system of voluntary exchange. They see the fundamental issue is that the employer is the owner of the job, not the government or the employee. The employer negotiates the job and pays just as to performance, not just as to job duties. A private business would not want to lose its best performers by compensating them less and can ill afford paying its lower performers higher because the overall productivity will decline. There are also specific affirmative defences to the criticism above that government is forcing employers to pay less qualified workers the same as superior workers. The EPA's four affirmative defences allows unequal pay for equal work when the wages are set "pursuant to, a seniority system; a merit system; a system which measures earnings by quantity or quality of production; or ... any other factor other than sex" If an employer can prove that a pay differential exists because of one of these factors, there is no liability.

FETAL RIGHTS

Fetal rights are the legal or ethical rights of fetuses. The term is used most often in the context of the abortion debate, as the basis for an argument in support of the pro-life stance. Some laws seek to protect or otherwise recognize the fetus. Some of these grant recognition under specific conditions: the fetus can legally be a victim of a crime such as feticide, a beneficiary of insurance or social assistance, or an inheritor of property.

- The American Convention on Human Rights (1969) is a treaty signed by 24 Latin American countries, which states that from the moment of conception, human beings have rights.
- The Unborn Victims of Violence Act is a United States law which defines violent assault committed against pregnant women as being a crime against two victims: the woman and the fetus she carries. This law was passed in 2004 after the murder of Laci

Peterson and the fetus she was carrying.

- In 2002, U.S. President George W. Bush announced a plan to ensure health care coverage for fetuses under the State Children's Health Insurance Programme (SCHIP).
- Iranian law holds that anyone who brings about a miscarriage must pay a monetary fine, which varies depending upon the stage of development and/or sex of the fetus, in compensation.

Legislative measures sometimes seek to establish the right to life of the fetus from the moment of fertilization.

Such laws regard the fetus as a person whose legal status is on par with that of any other member of the species homo sapiens:

- The 1978 American Convention on Human Rights states, in Article 4.1, "Every person has the right to have his life respected. This right shall be protected by law and, in general, from the moment of conception." The Convention is considered binding only for the 24 of 35 member nations of the Organization of American States who ratified it.
- In 1983, the Eighth Amendment of the Constitution of Ireland, also known as the "Pro-Life Amendment," was added to the Constitution of The Republic of Ireland by popular referendum. It recognizes "the right to life of the unborn".
- In 1993, the Federal Constitutional Court of Germany held that the constitution guaranteed the right to life from conception, but that it is within the discretion of parliament not to punish abortion in the first trimester, providing that women agreed to undergo special counselling designed to discourage termination and "protect unborn life". The intermediate decision was the result of an attempt to join East Germany's abortion law to that of West Germany after reunification in 1990.

Other governments have laws in place that state that fetuses are not legally recognized persons:

- In Canadian law, under section 223 of the Criminal

Code of Canada, a fetus is a "human being... when it has completely proceeded, in a living state, from the body of its mother whether or not it has completely breathed, it has an independent circulation or the navel string is severed."

Much opposition to legal abortion in the West is based on a concern for fetal rights. Similarly many pro-choice groups oppose fetal rights, even when they do not impinge directly on the abortion issue, because they perceive this as a slippery slope strategy to restricting abortions. Various initiatives, prompted by concern for the ill effects which might be posed to the health or development of a fetus, seek to restrict or discourage women from engaging in certain behaviours while pregnant. Also, in some countries, laws have been passed to restrict the practice of abortion based upon the gender of the fetus.

- Many jurisdictions actively warn against the consumption of alcoholic beverages by pregnant women, recommending a maximum intake or total abstinence, due to its association with Fetal alcohol syndrome. Countries that encourage those who are pregnant to avoid alcohol either entirely or partially include Australia, Canada, France, Iceland, Israel, the Netherlands, Norway, New Zealand, Spain, the United Kingdom, and the United States.
- Many national and international agencies recommend dietary guidelines for pregnant women due to the health risks posed by the consumption of fish contaminated with methylmercury through industrial pollution. Studies have linked exposure to various levels of methylmercury in utero to neurological disorders in children.
- The use of tobacco products or exposure to secondhand smoke during pregnancy has been linked to low birth weight. Governor Mike Huckabee of Arkansas, citing studies which attribute 10% of infant deaths to tobacco-smoking mothers, considered adopting a smoking ban for pregnant women in 2006

with the aim of reducing infant mortality.

- No U.S. state has enacted a law which criminalizes specific behaviour during pregnancy, but, nonetheless, it has been estimated that at least 200 American women have been criminally prosecuted or arrested under existing child abuse statutes for allegedly bringing about harm in-utero through their conduct during pregnancy. Reasons for pressing charges included use of illicit drugs, consumption of alcohol, and failure to comply with a doctor's order of bedrest or caesarean part. Drug addicts have been accused of "supplying drugs to a minor" through unintentional chemical subjection via the umbilical cord. Others have been charged with assault with a deadly weapon with the "deadly weapon" in question being an illegal drug. Minnesota, Wisconsin and South Dakota allow women who continue to use substances while pregnant to be civilly committed. Some states require that medical providers report any infant who is born with a physical dependency, or who tests positive for residual traces of alcohol or drugs, to child welfare authorities.
- Cultural preferences for male children in some parts of Asia, such as Mainland China, India, South Korea, and Taiwan, have sometimes led to sex-selective abortion of female fetuses. This phenomenon might be partially responsible for the disparity between male-to-female birth rates which is observed in some places. India banned the practice of abortion for reasons of fetal sex in 1994.

CHILDREN'S RIGHTS

Children's rights are the human rights of children with particular attention to the rights of special protection and care afforded to the young, including their right to association with both biological parents, human identity as well as the basic needs for food, universal state-paid education, health care and criminal laws appropriate for the age and development of the child. Interpretations of children's rights range from allowing children the capacity for autonomous action to the enforcement of children being physically, mentally and emotionally free from abuse, though what constitutes "abuse" is a matter of debate. Other definitions include the rights to care and nurturing. "A child is any human being below the age of eighteen years, unless under the law applicable to the child, majority is attained earlier." Cornell University, a child is a person, not a subperson, and the parent has absolute interest and possession of the child, but this is very much an American view.

The term "child" does not necessarily mean minor but can include adult children as well as adult nondependent children. There are no definitions of other terms used to describe young people such as "adolescents", "teenagers," or "youth" in international law, but the children's rights movement is considered distinct from the youth rights movement. The field of children's rights spans the fields of law, politics, religion, and morality.

RATIONALE

As minors by law children do not have autonomy or the right to make decisions on their own for themselves in any known jurisdiction of the world. Instead their adult caregivers, including parents, social workers, teachers, youth workers and others, are vested with that authority, depending on the circumstances. Some believe that this state of affairs gives children insufficient control over their own lives and causes them to be vulnerable.

Louis Althusser has gone so far as describe this legal machinery, as it applies to children, as "repressive state apparatuses".Structures such as government policy have been held by some commentators to mask the ways adults abuse and exploit children, resulting in child poverty, lack of educational opportunities, and child labour. On this view, children are to be regarded as a minority group towards whom society needs to reconsider the way it behaves. However, there is no evidence that such views are widely shared in society.

Researchers have identified children as needing to be recognized as participants in society whose rights and responsibilities need to be recognized at all ages.

HISTORIC DEFINITIONS OF CHILDREN'S RIGHTS

Consensus on defining children's rights has become clearer in the last fifty years. A 1973 publication by Hillary Clinton stated that children's rights were a "slogan in need of a definition".

Some researchers, the notion of children's rights is still not well defined, with at least one proposing that there is no singularly accepted definition or theory of the rights held by children. Children's rights law is defined as the point where the law intersects with a child's life.

That includes juvenile delinquency, due process for children involved in the criminal justice system, appropriate representation, and effective rehabilitative services; care and protection for children in state care; ensuring education for all children regardless of their origin, race, gender, disabilities, or abilities, and; health care and advocacy.

TYPES OF RIGHTS

Children's rights are defined in numerous ways, including a wide spectrum of civil, cultural, economic, social and political rights. Rights tend to be of two general types: those advocating for children as autonomous persons under the law and those placing a claim on society for protection from harms perpetrated on children because of their dependency. These have been labeled as the right of *empowerment and as the right to protection.*

One Canadian organization categorizes children's rights into three categories:

- *Provision*: Children have the right to an adequate standard of living, health care, education and services, and to play. These include a balanced diet, a warm bed to sleep in, and access to schooling.
- *Protection*: Children have the right to protection from abuse, neglect, exploitation and discrimination. This

includes the right to safe places for children to play; constructive child rearing behaviour, and acknowledgment of the evolving capacities of children.

- *Participation*: Children have the right to participate in communities and have programmes and services for themselves. This includes children's involvement in libraries and community programmes, youth voice activities, and involving children as decision-makers.

In a similar fashion, the Child Rights Information Network, or CRIN for short, categorizes rights into two groups:

- Economic, social and cultural rights, related to the conditions necessary to meet basic human needs such as food, shelter, education, health care, and gainful employment. Included are rights to education, adequate housing, food, water, the highest attainable standard of health, the right to work and rights at work, as well as the cultural rights of minorities and indigenous peoples.
- Environmental, cultural and developmental rights, which are sometimes called "third generation rights," and including the right to live in safe and healthy environments and that groups of people have the right to cultural, political, and economic development.

Amnesty International openly advocates four particular children's rights, including the end to juvenile incarceration without parole, an end to the recruitment of military use of children, ending the death penalty for people under 21, and raising awareness of human rights in the classroom. Human Rights Watch, an international advocacy organization, includes child labour, juvenile justice, orphans and abandoned children, refugees, street children and corporal punishment. Scholarly study generally focuses children's rights by identifying individual rights.

The following rights "allow children to grow up healthy and free":

- Freedom of speech
- Freedom of thought

- Freedom from fear
- Freedom of choice and the right to make decisions
- Ownership over one's body

Other issues affecting children's rights include the sale of children, child prostitution and child pornography.

Difference Between Children's Rights and Youth Rights

"In the majority of jurisdictions, for instance, children are not allowed to vote, to marry, to buy alcohol, to have sex, or to engage in paid employment." Within the youth rights movement, it is believed that the key difference between children's rights and youth rights is that children's rights supporters generally advocate the establishment and enforcement of protection for children and youths, while youth rights generally advocates the expansion of freedom for children and/or youths and of rights such as suffrage. Also, many people who support youth rights, are concerned with adolescents and not children.

Parental Rights

Parents affect the lives of children in a unique way, and as such their role in children's rights has to be distinguished in a particular way. Particular issues in the child-parent relationship include child neglect, child abuse, freedom of choice, corporal punishment and child custody. There have been theories offered that provide parents with rights-based practices that resolve the tension between "commonsense parenting" and children's rights.

The issue is particularly relevant in legal proceedings that affect the potential emancipation of minors, and in cases where children sue their parents. A child's rights to a relationship with both their parents is increasingly recognized as an important factor for determining the best interests of the child in divorce and child custody proceedings. Some governments have enacted laws creating a rebuttable presumption that shared parenting is in the best interests of children.

MOVEMENT

The Children's Rights Movement is a historical and

modern movement committed to the acknowledgment, expansion, and/or regression of the rights of children around the world. While the historical definition of child has varied, the United Nations Convention on the Rights of the Child explains, "A child is any human being below the age of eighteen years, unless under the law applicable to the child, majority is attained earlier." There are no definitions of other terms used to describe young people such as "adolescents", "teenagers" or "youth" in international law. Thomas Spence's The Rights of Infants is an early English-language assertion of the natural rights of children.

In the USA, the Children's Rights Movement was born in the 1800s with the orphan train. In the big cities, when a child's parents died or were extremely poor, the child frequently had to go to work to support himself and/or his family. Boys generally became factory or coal workers, and girls became prostitutes or saloon girls, or else went to work in a sweat shop. All of these jobs paid only starvation wages.

In 1852, Massachusetts required children to attend school. In 1853, Charles Brace founded the Children's Aid Society, which worked hard to take street children in. The following year, the children were placed on a train headed for the West, where they were adopted, and often given work. By 1929, the orphan train stopped running altogether, but its principles lived on. The National Child Labour Committee, an organization dedicated to the abolition of all child labour, was formed in the 1890s. It managed to pass one law, which was struck down by the Supreme Court two years later for violating a child's right to contract his work. In 1924, Congress attempted to pass a constitutional amendment that would authorize a national child labour law.

This measure was blocked, and the bill was eventually dropped. It took the Great Depression to end child labour nationwide; adults had become so desperate for jobs that they would work for the same wage as children. In 1938, President Franklin D. Roosevelt signed the Fair Labour Standards Act which, amongst other things, placed limits on many forms of child labour. Now that child labour had been effectively eradicated in parts of the world, the movement turned to other things, but it again stalled when World War II broke out and children and women began to enter the work force once more. With millions of adults at war, the children were needed to help keep the country running. In Europe, children served as couriers, intelligence collectors, and other underground resistance workers in opposition to Hitler's regime. In the early twentieth century, moves began to promote the idea of children's rights as distinct from those of adults and as requiring explicit recognition.

The Polish educationalist Janusz Korczak wrote of the rights of children in his book How to Love a Child; a later book was entitled The Child's Right to Respect. In 1917, following the Russian Revolution, the Moscow branch of the organization Proletkult produced a Declaration of Children's Rights. However, the first effective attempt to promote children's rights was the Declaration of the Rights of the Child, drafted by Eglantyne Jebb in 1923 and adopted by the League of Nations in 1924.

This was accepted by the United Nations on its formation and updated in 1959, and replaced with a more extensive UN Convention on the Rights of the Child in 1989. From the formation of the United Nations in the 1940s and extending to present day, the Children's Rights Movement has become global in focus. While the situation of children in the United States has become grave, children around the world have increasingly become engaged in illegal, forced child labour, genital mutilation, military service, and sex trafficking. Several international organizations have rallied to the assistance of children.

They include Save the Children, Free the Children, and the Children's Defence Fund. The Child Rights Information Network, or CRIN, formed in 1983, is the group of 1,600 non-governmental organizations from around the world which advocate for the implementation of the Convention on the Rights of the Child. Organization's report on their countries' progress towards implementation, as do governments that have ratified the Convention. Every 5 years reporting to the

United Nations Committee on the Rights of the Child is required for governments. While there is a long history of children's rights in the U.S., scholars contend that there is no "golden age". Many children's rights advocates in the U.S. today advocate for a smaller agenda than their international peers. Groups predominately focus on child abuse and neglect, child fatalities, foster care, youth aging out of foster care, preventing foster care placement, and adoption. A long standing movement promoting youth rights in the United States has made substantial gains in the past.Anti-Children's Rights propagandists often raise the spectre of Rights without Responsibilities.

The Children's Rights Movement assert that it is rather the case that children have rights which adults, states and government have a responsibility to uphold. The UK maintains a position that UNCRC is not legally enforceable and is hence 'aspirational' only - albeit a 2003 ECHR ruling states: "The human rights of children and the standards to which all governments must aspire in realising these rights for all children are set out in the Convention on the Rights of the Child."

18 years after ratification, the four Children's Commissioners in the devolved administrations have united in calling for adoption of the Convention into domestic legislation, making children's rights legally enforceable. Several countries have created an institute of children's rights ombudsman, most notably Sweden, Finland and Ukraine, which is first country worldwide to install children at that post. In Ukraine Ivan Cherevko and Julia Kruk became first children's rights ombudsmen in late 2005

The United Nations Convention on the Rights of the Child has outlined a standard premise for the children's rights movement and has been ratified by all but two nations - the United States and Somalia. Somalia's inability to sign the Convention is attributed to their lack of governmental structure. The US administration under Bush has opposed ratifying the Convention because of "serious political and legal concerns that it conflicts with U.S. policies on the central role of parents, sovereignty, and state and local law." However, the new administration may be taking another look at it.

INTERNATIONAL LAW

The Universal Declaration of Human Rights is seen as a basis for all international legal standards for children's rights today. There are several conventions and laws that address children's rights around the world.

A number of current and historical documents affect those rights, including the 1923 Declaration of the Rights of the Child, drafted by Eglantyne Jebb and her sister Dorothy Buxton in London, England in 1919, endorsed by the League of Nations and adopted by the United Nations in 1946. It later served as the basis for the Convention on the Rights of the Child.

Convention on the Rights of the Child

The United Nations' 1989 Convention on the Rights of the Child, or CRC, is the first legally binding international instrument to incorporate the full range of human rights—civil, cultural, economic, political and social rights. Its implementation is monitored by the Committee on the Rights of the Child. National governments that ratify it commit themselves to protecting and ensuring children's rights, and agree to hold themselves accountable for this commitment before the international community.

The CRC is the most widely ratified human rights treaty with 190 ratifications. Somalia and USA are the only two countries which have not agreed to the CRC. The CRC is based on four core principles, namely the principle of non discrimination, the best interests of the child, the right to life, survival and development, and considering the views of the child in decisions which affect them.

The CRC, along with international criminal accountability mechanisms such as the International Criminal Court, the Yugoslavia and Rwanda Tribunals, and the Special Court for Sierra Leone, is said to have significantly increased the profile of children's rights worldwide.

Enforcement

A variety of enforcement organizations and mechanisms exist to ensure children's rights and the successful implementation of the Union. They include the Child Rights Caucus for the United Nations General Assembly Special Session on Children.

It was set up to promote full implementation and compliance with the Convention on the Rights of the Child, and to ensure that child rights were given priority during the UN General Assembly Special Session on Children and its Preparatory process. The United Nations Human Rights Council was created "with the hope that it could be more objective, credible and efficient in denouncing human rights violations worldwide than the highly politicised Commission on Human Rights."

The NGO Group for the Convention on the Rights of the Child is a coalition of international non-governmental organisations originally formed in 1983 to facilitate the implementation of the United Nations Convention on the Rights of the Child. Many countries around the world have children's rights ombudspeople or children's commissioners whose official, governmental duty is to represent the interests of the public by investigating and addressing complaints reported by individual citizens regarding children's rights. Children's ombudspeople can also work for a corporation, a newspaper, an NGO, or even for the general public.

United States Law

Children are generally afforded the basic rights embodied by the Constitution, as enshrined by the Fourteenth Amendment to the United States Constitution. The Equal Protection Clause of that amendment is to apply to children, born within a marriage or not, but excludes children not yet born. This was reinforced by the landmark US Supreme Court decision of In re Gault.

In this trial 15-year-old Gerald Gault of Arizona was taken into custody by local police after being accused of making an obscene telephone call. He was detained and committed to the

Arizona State Industrial School until he reached the age of 21 for making an obscene phone call to an adult neighbour. In an 8–1 decision, the Court ruled that in hearings which could result in commitment to an institution, people under the age of 18 have the right to notice and counsel, to question witnesses, and to protection against self-incrimination. The Court found that the procedures used in Gault's hearing met none of these requirements.

There are other concerns in the United States regarding children's rights. The American Academy of Adoption Attorneys is concerned with children's rights to a safe, supportive and stable family structure. Their position on children's rights in adoption cases states that, "children have a constitutionally based liberty interest in the protection of their established families, rights which are at least equal to, and we believe outweigh, the rights of others who would claim a 'possessory' interest in these children." Other issues raised in American children's rights advocacy include children's rights to inheritance in same-sex marriages and particular rights for youth.

CIVIL RIGHTS

In contemporary political thought, the term 'civil rights' is indissolubly linked to the struggle for equality of American blacks during the 1950s and 60s. The aim of that struggle was to secure the status of equal citizenship in a liberal democratic state. Civil rights are the basic legal rights a person must possess in order to have such a status. They are the rights that constitute free and equal citizenship and include personal, political, and economic rights. No contemporary thinker of significance holds that such rights can be legitimately denied to a person on the basis of race, colour, sex, religion, national origin, or disability.

Antidiscrimination principles are thus a common ground in contemporary political discussion. However, there is much disagreement in the scholarly literature over the basis and scope of these principles and the ways in which they ought to be implemented in law and policy. In addition, debate exists over the legitimacy of including sexual orientation among the other categories traditionally protected by civil rights law, and there is an emerging literature examining issues of how best to understand discrimination based on disability.

RIGHTS

The Civil-Political Distinction

Until the middle of the 20th century, civil rights were usually distinguished from 'political rights'. The former included the rights to own property, make and enforce contracts, receive due process of law, and worship one's religion. Civil rights also covered freedom of speech and the press. But they did not include the right to hold public office, vote, or to testify in court. The latter were political rights, reserved to adult males. The civil-political distinction was conceptually and morally unstable insofar as it was used to sort citizens into different categories.

It was part of an ideology that classified women as citizens who were entitled to certain rights but not to the full panoply to which men were entitled. As that ideology broke down, the civil-political distinction began to unravel. The idea that a certain segment of the adult citizenry could legitimately possess one bundle of rights, while another segment would have to make do with an inferior bundle, became increasingly implausible. In the end, the civil-political distinction could not survive the cogency of the principle that all citizens of a liberal democracy were entitled, in Rawls's words, to "a fully adequate scheme of equal basic liberties". It may be possible to retain the distinction strictly as one for sorting rights, rather than sorting citizens. But it is difficult to give a convincing account of the principles by which the sorting is done.

It seems neater and cleaner simply to think of civil rights as the general category of basic rights needed for free and equal citizenship. Yet, it remains a matter of contention which claims are properly conceived as belonging to the category of civil rights. Analysts have distinguished among "three generations" of civil rights claims and have argued over which claims ought to be treated as true matters of civil rights.

Three Generations of Rights

The claims for which the American civil rights movement initially fought belong to the first generation of civil rights claims. Those claims included the pre-20th century set of civil rights — such as the rights to receive due process and to make and enforce contracts — but covered political rights as well. However, many thinkers and activists argued that these first-generation claims were too narrow to define the scope of free and equal citizenship. They contended that such citizenship could be realised only by honouring an additional set of claims, including rights to food, shelter, medical care, and employment.

This second generation of economic "welfare rights," the argument went, helped to ensure that the political, economic, and legal rights belonging to the first generation could be made effective in protecting the vital interests of citizens and were not simply document guarantees. Yet, some scholars have argued that these second-generation rights should not be subsumed under the category of civil rights. Thus, Cranston writes, "The traditional 'political and civil rights' can...be readily secured by legislation.

Since the rights are for the most part rights against government interference...the legislation needed had to do no more than restrain the executive's own arm. This is no longer the case when we turn to the 'right to work', the 'right to social security' and so forth". However, Cranston fails to recognize that such first-generation rights as due process and the right to vote also require substantial government action and the investment of considerable public resources. Holmes and Sunstein have made the case that all of the first-generation civil rights require government to do more than simply "restrain the executive's own arm."

It seems problematic to think that a significant distinction can be drawn between first and second-generation rights on the ground that the former, but not the latter, simply require that government refrain from interfering with the actions of persons. Moreover, even if some viable distinction could be drawn along those lines, it would not follow that second-generation rights should be excluded from the category of civil rights. The reason is that the relevant standard for inclusion as a civil right is whether a claim is part of the package of rights constitutive of free and equal citizenship. There is no reason to think that only those claims that can be "readily secured by legislation" belong to that package. And the increasingly dominant view is that welfare rights are essential to adequately satisfying the conditions of free and equal citizenship. In the United States, however, the law does not treat issues of economic well-being *per se* as civil rights matters. Only insofar as economic inequality or deprivation is linked to race, gender or some other traditional category of antidiscrimination law is it considered to be a question of civil rights.

In legal terms, poverty is not a "suspect classification." On the other hand, welfare rights are protected as a matter of constitutional principle in other democracies. For example, section 75 of the Danish Constitution provides that "any person unable to support himself or his dependents shall, where no other person is responsible for his or their maintenance, be entitled to receive public assistance." And the International Covenant on Economic, Social, and Cultural Rights provides that the state parties to the agreement "recognize the right of everyone to an adequate standard of living for himself and his family, including adequate food, clothing and housing, and to the continuous improvement of living conditions." A third generation of claims has received considerable attention in recent years, what may be broadly termed "rights of cultural membership."

These include language rights for members of cultural minorities and the rights of indigenous peoples to preserve their cultural institutions and practices and to exercise some measure of political autonomy. There is some overlap with the first-generation rights, such as that of religious liberty, but rights of cultural membership are broader and more controversial. Article 27 of the International Covenant on Civil and Political Rights declares that third-generation rights ought to be protected: In those States in which ethnic, religious or linguistic minorities exist, persons belonging to such minorities shall not be denied the right, in community with the other members of their group, to enjoy their own culture, to profess and practice their own religion, or to use their own language. Similarly, the Canadian Charter of Rights and Freedoms protects the language rights of minorities and section 27 provides that "This Charter shall be interpreted in a manner consistent with the preservation and enhancement of the multicultural heritage of Canadians."

In the United States, there is no analogous protection of language rights or multiculturalism, although constitutional doctrine does recognize native Indian tribes as "domestic dependent nations" with some attributes of political self-rule, such as sovereign immunity. There is substantial philosophical controversy over the legitimacy and scope of rights of cultural membership. Kymlicka has argued that the liberal commitment to protect the equal rights of individuals requires society to protect such rights.

He argues that "granting special representational rights, land claims, or language rights to a minority....can be seen as putting the various groups on a more equal footing, by reducing the extent to which the smaller group is vulnerable to the larger". Such special rights do not amount to "group rights," in the sense of granting the group any power or priority over the individual. Rather, the rights "compensate for unequal circumstances which put the members of minority cultures at a systemic disadvantage in the cultural marketplace". Waldron criticizes Kymlicka for exaggerating the importance for the individual of membership in her particular culture and for underestimating the mutability and interpenetration of cultures.

Individual freedom requires some cultural context of choice, but it does not require the preservation of the particular context in which the individual finds herself. Liberal individuals must be free to evaluate their culture and to distance themselves from it. Kukathas criticizes Kymlicka for implying that the liberal commitment to the protection of individual rights is insufficient to treat the interests of minorities with equal consideration. Kukathas contends that "we need to reassert the importance of individual liberty or individual rights and question the idea that cultural minorities have collective rights". But the system of uniform legal rules that he endorses would keep the state from intervening even when a minority culture inflicts significant harm on its more vulnerable members, *e.g.*, when cultural norms strongly discourage females from seeking the same educational and career opportunities as males. Barry asserts that "there are certain rights against oppression, exploitation, and injury, to which every single human being is entitled to lay claim, and...appeals to cultural diversity and pluralism under no circumstances trump the value of basic liberal rights". The legal system should protect those rights by impartially imposing the same rules on all persons, regardless of their cultural or religious membership.

Barry allows for a few exceptions, such as the accommodation of a Sikh boy whose turban violated school dress regulations, but thinks that the conditions under which such exceptions will be justified "are rarely satisfied". Barry's position reflects and elaborates Gitlin's earlier condemnation of views advocating distinctive rights for cultural and ethnic minorities. Gitlin condemned such views on the ground that they represent a "swerve from civil rights, emphasizing a universal condition and universalizable rights, to cultural separatism, emphasizing difference and distinct needs". At the other end of the spectrum, Taylor argues for a form of communitarianism that attaches intrinsic importance to the survival of cultures. In his view, differential treatment under the law for certain practices is sometimes justifiable on the ground that such treatment is important for keeping a culture alive.

Taylor goes as far as to claim that cultural survival can sometimes trump basic individual rights, such as freedom of speech. Accordingly, he defends legal restrictions on the use of English in Quebec, invoking the survival of Quebec's French culture. However, it is unclear why intrinsic value should attach to cultural survival as such. Following John Dewey, Kymlicka rightly emphasizes that liberty would have little or no value to the individual apart from the life-options and meaningful choices provided by culture. But both thinkers also reasonably contend that human interests are ultimately the interests of individual human beings. In light of that contention, it would seem that a culture that could not gain the uncoerced and undeceived adherence of enough individuals to survive would have no moral claim to its continuation. Legal restrictions on basic liberties that are designed to perpetuate a given culture have the cart before the horse: persons should have their basic liberties protected first, as those protections serve the most important human interests. Only when those interests are protected can we then say that a culture should survive, not because the culture is intrinsically valuable, but rather because it has the uncoerced adherence of a sufficient number of persons.

Blacks and Native Americans

The treatment of blacks under slavery and Jim Crow presents a history of injustice and cultural annihilation that is similar in some respects to the treatment of Native Americans. However, civil rights principles played a very different role in the struggle of Native Americans against the injustices perpetrated against them by whites. Civil rights principles demand inclusion of the individuals from a disadvantaged group in the major institutions of society on an equal basis with the individuals who are already treated as full citizens. The principles do not require that the disadvantaged group be given a right to govern its own affairs.

A right of political self-determination, in contrast, demands that a group have the freedom to order its affairs at it sees fit and, to that extent, political self-determination has a separatist aspect, even if something less than complete sovereignty is involved. The pursuit of civil rights by American blacks overshadowed the pursuit of political self-determination.

The fact that American blacks lacked any territory of their own on which they could rule themselves favoured the civil rights strategy. Moreover, the civil war amendments, and the civil rights laws that accompanied them, were meant to incorporate black Americans into the body politic as free and equal citizens. Although this effort was defeated by Jim Crow, the principle of citizenship for blacks had been enshrined in law. And so, in their struggle to defeat Jim Crow, blacks could and did repeatedly demand that white Americans live up to their constitutional promise of equality. In contrast, for Native Americans, the pursuit of political-self-determination, in the form of tribal sovereignty, overshadowed the pursuit of civil rights. Even after the coerced tribal removals and federal efforts to impose regimes of individual land ownership, tribes still retained some territorial basis on which a measure of self-rule was possible.

Moreover, a line of Supreme Court decisions dating to the early 1800's held that Indian tribes possessed some — albeit very limited — inherent powers of sovereignty. Accordingly, pursuit of political self-determination rather than civil-rights protections seemed, in the eyes of many Indians, to be the most reasonable strategy for counteracting white oppression. During the civil rights movement of the 1950's and 60's, there was some tension between Native Americans and blacks due to their different attitudes towards self-determination and civil rights. Some Native Americans looked askance at the desire of blacks for inclusion and thought the desire hopelessly naïve. And activists emerged from the black power movement who had a similar view of the effort at racial inclusion and who called for a form of political self-determination. Such a call was part of a tradition of black nationalism that can still be found today in the United States.

Nonetheless, in the United States, unlike civil rights principles, black nationalist principles have not become part of the law. In 1968, Congress enacted an Indian Civil Rights Act. The act extended the reach of certain individual constitutional rights against government to intratribal affairs. Tribal governments would for the first time be bound by constitutional principles concerning free speech, due process, cruel and unusual punishment, and equal protection, among others. Freedom of religion was omitted from the law as a result of the protests of the Pueblo, whose political arrangements were theocratic, but the law was a major incursion on tribal self-determination, nonetheless. A married pueblo woman brought suit in federal court, claiming that the tribe's marriage ordinances constituted sex discrimination against her and other women of the tribe, thus violating the ICRA. The ordinances excluded from tribal membership the children of a Pueblo woman who married outside of the tribe, while the children of men who married outsiders were counted as members.

Martinez had initially sought relief in tribal forums, to no avail, before turning to the federal courts. The Supreme Court held that federal courts did not have jurisdiction to hear the case: the substantive provisions of the ICRA did apply to the Pueblo, but the inherent sovereign powers of the tribe meant that the tribal government had exclusive jurisdiction in the case. The ruling has been both questioned and defended by feminist legal scholars. In contrast to the United States, the Canadian Indian Act provides that men and women are to be treated equally when it comes to the band membership of their children.

This law and the Santa Clara case raise the general issue of whether and when it is justifiable for a liberal state to impose liberal principles on illiberal political communities that had been involuntary incorporated into the larger state. Addressing this issue, Kymlicka argues that "there is relatively little scope for legitimate coercive interference" because efforts to impose liberal principles tend to be counterproductive, provoking the charge that they amount to "paternalistic colonialism." Moreover, "liberal institutions can only really work if liberal beliefs have been internalized."

Kymlicka concludes, then, that liberals on the outside of an illiberal culture should support the efforts of those insiders who seek reform but should generally stop short of coercively imposing liberal principles. At the same time, Kymlicka acknowledges that there are cases in which a liberal state is clearly permitted to impose its laws, citing with approval the decision in a case that involved the application of Canadian law to a tribe that had kidnapped a member and forced him to undergo an initiation ceremony. Applying Kymlicka's general line of thinking might prove contentious in many cases. Consider Santa Clara. His arguments could be used to support the decision in that case: the exercise of jurisdiction might be deemed "paternalistic colonialism."

But one might argue, instead, that jurisdiction is needed to vindicate the basic liberal right of gender equality. However, it does seem that, if a wrong akin to kidnapping or worse is required before federal courts can legitimately step in, then the Santa Clara case falls short of meeting such a requirement. The argument might then shift to whether the requirement imposes an excessively high hurdle for the exercise of federal jurisdiction.

Accordingly, Kymlicka's approach might not settle the disagreement over Santa Clara, but it does provide a very reasonable normative framework in terms of which liberal thought can address the difficult issues presented by the case and, more generally, by the problem of extending liberal principles to Native American tribes.

FREE AND EQUAL CITIZENSHIP

Civil rights are those rights that constitute free and equal citizenship in a liberal democracy. Such citizenship has two main dimensions, both tied to the idea of autonomy. Accordingly, civil rights are essentially connected to securing the autonomy of the citizen.

Public and Private Autonomy

To be a free and equal citizen is, in part, to have those legal guarantees that are essential to fully adequate participation in public discussion and decisionmaking. A citizen has a right to an equal voice and an equal vote. In addition, she has the rights needed to protect her "moral independence," that is, her ability to decide for herself what gives meaning and value to her life and to take responsibility for living in conformity with her values. Accordingly, equal citizenship has two main dimensions: "public autonomy," *i.e.*, the individual's freedom to participate in the formation of public opinion and society's collective decisions; and "private autonomy," *i.e.*, the individual's freedom to decide what way of life is most worth pursuing. The importance of these two dimensions of citizenship stem from what Rawls calls the "two moral powers" of personhood: the capacity for a sense of justice and the capacity for a conception of the good. A person stands as an equal citizen when society and its political system give equal and due weight to the interest each citizen has in the development and exercise of those capacities.

Ancient and Modern Citizenship

The idea of equal citizenship can be traced back to Aristotle's political philosophy and his claim that true citizens take turns ruling and being ruled. In modern society, the idea has been transformed, in part by the development of representative government and its system of elections. For modern liberal thought, by contrast, citizenship is no longer a matter of having a direct and equal share in governance, but rather consists in a legal status that confers a certain package of rights that guarantee to an individual a voice, a vote, and a zone of private autonomy.

The other crucial differences between modern liberalism and earlier political theories concern the range of human beings who are regarded as having the capacity for citizenship and the scope of private autonomy to which each citizen is entitled as a matter of basic right. Modern liberal theory is more expansive on both counts than its ancient and medieval forerunners. It is true that racist and sexist assumptions plagued liberal theory well into the twentieth-century. However, two crucial liberal ideas have made possible an internal critique of racism, sexism, and other illegitimate forms of hierarchy.

The first is that society is constructed by humans, a product of human will, and not some preordained natural or God-given order. The second is that social arrangements need to be justified before the court of reason to each individual who lives under them and who is capable of reasoning. The conjunction of these ideas made possible an egalitarianism that was not available to ancient and medieval political thought, although this liberal egalitarianism emerged slowly out of the racist and sexist presuppositions that infused much liberal thinking until recent decades. Many contemporary theorists have argued that taking liberal egalitarianism to its logical conclusion requires the liberal state to pursue a programme of deliberately reconstructing informal social norms and cultural meanings.

They contend that social stigma and denigration still operate powerfully to deny equal citizenship to groups such as blacks, women, and gays. Accordingly, Kernohan has argued that "the egalitarian liberal state should play an activist role in cultural reform", and Koppelman has taken a similar position: "the antidiscrimination project seeks to reconstruct social reality to eliminate or marginalize the shared meanings, practices and institutions that unjustifiably single out certain groups of citizens for stigma and disadvantage".

This position is deeply at odds with at least some of the ideas that lie behind the advocacy of third-generation civil rights. Those rights ground claims of cultural survival, whether or not a culture's meanings, practices and institutions stigmatize and disadvantage the members of some ascriptively-defined group. The egalitarian proponents of cultural reconstruction can be understood as advocating a different kind of "third-generation" for the civil rights movement: one in which the state, having attacked legal, political and economic barriers to equal citizenship, now takes on cultural obstacles.

A cultural-reconstruction phase of the civil rights movement would run contrary to Kukathas's argument that it is too dangerous to license the state to intervene against cultures that engage in social tyranny. It also raises questions about whether state-supported cultural reconstruction would violate basic liberties, such as freedom of private association. The efforts of New Jersey to apply antidiscrimination law to the Boy Scouts, a group which discriminates against gays, shows the potential problems. The Supreme Court invalidated those efforts on grounds of free association. Nonetheless, it may be necessary to reconceive the scope and limits of some basic liberties if the principle of free and equal citizenship is followed through to its logical conclusions.

DISCRIMINATION

In liberal democracies, civil rights claims are typically conceptualized in terms of the idea of discrimination. Persons who make such claims assert that they are the victims of discrimination. In order to gain an understanding of current discussion and debate regarding civil rights, it is important to disentangle the various descriptive and normative senses of 'discrimination'.

The Idea of Discrimination

In one of its central descriptive senses, 'discrimination' means the differential treatment of persons, however justifiable or unjustifiable the treatment may be. In a distinct but still primarily descriptive sense, it means the disadvantageous treatment of some persons relative to others. This sense is not purely descriptive in that an evaluative judgment is involved in determining what counts as a disadvantage. But the sense is descriptive insofar as no evaluative judgment is made regarding the justifiability of the disadvantageous treatment. In addition to its descriptive senses, there are two normative senses of 'discrimination'.

In the first, it means any differential treatment of the individual that is morally objectionable. In the second sense, 'discrimination' means the wrongful denial or abridgement of the civil rights of some persons in a context where others enjoy their full set of rights. The two normative senses are distinct because there can be morally objectionable forms of differential treatment that do not involve the wrongful denial or abridgement of civil rights. If I treat one waiter rudely and another nicely, because one is a New York Yankees fan and the other is a Boston Red Sox fan, then we have acted in a morally objectionable way but have not violated anyone's civil rights. Discrimination that does deny civil rights is a double wrong against its victims. The denial of civil rights is by itself a wrong, whether or not others have such rights. When others do have such rights, the denial of civil rights to persons who are entitled to them involves the additional wrong of unjustified differential treatment. On the other hand, if everyone is denied his civil rights, then the idea of discrimination would be misapplied to the situation. A despot who oppresses everyone equally is not guilty of discrimination in any of its senses. In contrast, discrimination is a kind of wrong that is found in systems that are liberal democratic but imperfectly so: it is the characteristic injustice of liberal democracy.

The first civil rights law, enacted in 1866, embodied the idea of discrimination as wrongful denial of civil rights to some while others enjoyed their full set of rights. It declared that "all persons" in the United States were to have "the same right...to make and enforce contracts...and to the full and equal benefit of all laws...as is enjoyed by white citizens". The premise was that whites enjoyed a fully adequate scheme of civil rights and that everyone else who was entitled to citizenship was to be legally guaranteed that same set of rights. It is a notable feature of civil rights law that its prohibitions do not protect only citizens.

Any person within a given jurisdiction, citizen or not, can claim the protection of the law, at least within certain limits. Thus, noncitizens are protected by fair housing and equal employment statutes, among other antidiscrimination laws. Noncitizens can also claim the legal protections of due process if charged with a crime. Even illegal aliens have limited due process rights if they are within the legal jurisdiction of the country. On the other hand, noncitizens cannot claim under U.S. law that the denial of political rights amounts to wrongful discrimination.

Noncitizens can vote in local and regional elections in certain countries, but the denial of equal political rights would seem to be central to the very status of noncitizen. The application of much of civil rights law to noncitizens indicates that many of the rights in question are deeper than simply the rights that constitute citizenship. They are genuine human rights to which every person is entitled, whether she is in a location where she has a right to citizenship or not. And civil rights issues are, for that reason, regarded as broader in scope than issues regarding the treatment of citizens.

Why Discrimination is Unjust

Given the principle of equal citizenship, discrimination in the sense of the denial of civil rights is an injustice that denies certain citizens the rights to which they are entitled. But it is not obvious that the principle entails that discrimination in the sense of differential treatment is unjust, even if the differential treatment disadvantages persons based on their race, sex, or another paradigmatic civil rights category.

The common view is that such differential treatment is an injustice that violates the basic rights of the individual. In other words, the view is that it is a civil right to not be treated disadvantageously on account of one's race or sex. An argument for the soundness of the common view cannot simply invoke existing laws that ban discrimination based on race, sex, and similar categories.

The point of the common view is that the injustice of racial and gender discrimination explains why there ought to be those laws. What is required is an account that shows why such discrimination is an injustice. There are two main approaches to providing an account of the injustice of discrimination based on race and sex. The first is "individualistic" in that it seeks to explain the injustice in a way that abstracts from the broader social and political context in which the differential treatment occurs. The second is "systemic" in that it seeks to explain the injustice in a way that links the differential treatment to social patterns that reduce, or threaten to reduce, the members of certain groups to second-class citizenship.

Individualistic Accounts

Kahlenberg asserts the popular view that race discrimination is unjust because it treats a person on the basis of a characteristic that is immutable or beyond her control. But Boxill rejects such a view, arguing that there are many instances in which it is justifiable to treat persons based on features that are beyond their control. Denying blind people a driver's license or persons with little athletic ability a place on the basketball team is not an injustice to such individuals. Moreover, Boxill notes that, if scientists developed a drug that could change a person's skin colour, it would still be unjust to discriminate against people because of their skin colour. Flew argues that racism is unjust because it treats differently persons who "are *in all relevant respects* the same".

The defining characteristics of a race "are strictly superficial and properly irrelevant to all, or almost all, questions of social status and employability". But if 'relevant' means 'rationally related', then it does not appear to be a requirement of justice that a person always treat others only on the basis of relevant characteristics.

The idea that it is such a requirement rests on the false premise that all morally bad treatment is a violation of justice and rights. If I give a waiter a poor tip because he is not a fan of my favourite sports team, then we have behaved badly but have not violated the waiter's rights or committed an injustice against him. And it is unclear, on Flew's account, why giving a poor tip because of a waiter's race is any different than doing so because of his preferences in sports. Often people will insist that the injustice of racial or sex discrimination stems from the connection between those forms of discrimination and the reliance on stereotypes. It is not just that race is irrelevant but that those who act on race-based grounds are using inaccurate stereotypes instead of treating a person "as an individual," as the phrase goes.

However, if "being treated as an individual" means that others must take into account all of the potentially relevant information about the person in their behaviour towards her, then there is no plausibility to the claim that anyone has a right to such treatment. Life's scarcity of time and resources undermines the idea that there is such a right. Moreover, in some cases, stereotypical beliefs reflect reliable generalizations about a group. The term 'statistical discrimination' refers to the use of such reliable generalizations. Consider the case of a pregnant job applicant: as a statistical matter, there is a higher antecedent likelihood that she will take more sick days than a nonpregnant applicant during the first year of employment. Yet, an employer who relies on statistical discrimination in excluding the pregnant applicant is acting illegally under the Pregnancy Discrimination Act.

The act was passed because many people quite reasonably thought that it was unjust for a pregnant applicant to be treated in that way. But if the treatment is unjust, then one cannot explain why that is so by invoking the un reliability of the generalization on which the treatment is based. Garcia provides an account of racial discrimination that loosens the link between it and injustice, but still preserves some connection. On his account, such discrimination against others expresses a character defect, *viz.*, the failure to care enough, or in the right way, for their interests.

Accordingly, such discrimination is a matter of what is "in the heart" of the racist individual: "racially focused ill-will or disregard. This echoes the claim made by Gunnar Myrdal in his classic work, *An American Dilemma,* that "the American Negro problem is a problem in the heart of Americans". Garcia's account weakens the link between racial discrimination and injustice because not every act expressing racial ill-will or disregard will be an injustice.

Garcia writes that racial discrimination against a person "will often offend against justice," but he does not argue that it always so offends. He points out that discrimination against a person based on race may amount to a failure of benevolence, rather than a violation of rights. For example, racial disregard may lead a person to refuse to contribute to a charity organization that works with inner-city youth. In such a case, the person has failed to show benevolence for morally discreditable reasons, and so has behaved badly. But no injustice has been committed. On the other hand racial ill-will is often expressed in violations of the rights of persons: hate crimes that harm the property or person of an individual on account of race; efforts to prevent members of certain racial groups from voting; charging racial minorities higher prices for the same product than the prices charged to similarly situated whites; denying persons equality of opportunity in the job and housing markets on account of their race. Such actions would count as injustices, not simply failures of benevolence.

Thus, Garcia's approach preserves some link between discrimination and injustice, but it is much more attenuated than the link posited by the popular view that disadvantageous treatment on the basis of race is *ipso facto* an injustice to the person so treated.

Systemic Accounts

Many thinkers reject the idea that the injustice of discrimination stems fundamentally from what is in the mind or heart of the individual. Crespi criticized Myrdal on the ground that the latter's individualistic understanding of racial discrimination entailed that "ethical exhortation" was the remedy for racial injustice.

Crespi argued that what really needed remedy were the social and economic structures that advantage whites. More recently, Steinberg and Bonilla-Silva, among others, have argued that racial discrimination should not be understood as a "moral problem," *i.e.*, as a problem with individual attitudes or actions, but rather as a problem of persistent structural inequality.

And MacKinnon has made a parallel argument when it comes to sex discrimination. For example, she contends that pornography is "not a moral problem" but rather a political one, meaning that it does not pose a problem of the virtue and vice of individuals and their behaviour but rather one concerning relations of power that subordinate women to men. On the systemic account of racial and sex discrimination, the injustice of discriminatory acts lies in their connection to broader patterns in society that reduce the members of certain groups to second-class citizenship, or worse. Considered in abstraction from these broader patterns, refusing employment to someone on account of her race might be morally objectionable insofar as it treated a person arbitrarily when some important interest of hers was at stake. But the objectionable treatment amounts to an injustice because such acts are not sporadic but rather systemic and add up to a system in which persons have their entire lives substantially diminished on account of their race or sex. And such a system is what violates the right to equality — the basic civil right. Individual acts of racial or gender discrimination do so only derivatively, by reinforcing the systemic violation.

There are different ways in which a systemic account can be elaborated. For example, in MacKinnon's account of sex discrimination, the system of gender inequality revolves around the sexual subordination of women. Butler, Brown and other feminists provide accounts which do not share MacKinnon's focus on sexual subordination. On the matter of racial discrimination, Cox focuses on the ways in which racial conflict is rooted in class conflict, while Omi and Winant emphasize "the specificity of race as an autonomous field of social conflict, political organization, and cultural/ideological meaning".

In whatever way the details are elaborated, all systemic accounts rest on the premise that women, racial minorities, and other groups are second-class citizens and that they are so because of their group membership. The advocates of systemic accounts typically represent their views as incompatible with individualistic ones. They do so by insisting that discrimination is "not a moral problem" of the individual's heart or mind, but one concerning group power relations and social patterns of disadvantage. But their insistence rests on a false dichotomy. Discrimination based on race, sex and other categories can be a problem of the individual's heart and mind, as well as an issue that concerns systemic patterns of disadvantage in society.

As Wasserstrom pointed out, discrimination can operate at both the individual and systemic levels. It is not necessary to deny the existence of patterns of discriminatory treatment that reduce, or threaten to reduce, some persons to second-class citizenship in order to affirm that it is an injustice to deny a person a job because of her sex. And it is not necessary to deny that, apart from social patterns of disadvantage, the individual who is denied a job for such reasons has been treated in an unjust way, in order to affirm that there are such patterns that reduce some to second-class status.

Justifying Antidiscrimination Law

Antidiscrimination laws typically pick out certain categories such as race and sex for legal protection, define certain spheres such as employment and public accommodations in which discrimination based on the protected categories is prohibited, and establish special government agencies, such as the Equal Employment Opportunity Commission, to assist in the laws' enforcement.

There are many questions that can be raised concerning the justifiability of such laws. Some of the central philosophical questions derive from the fact that the laws restrict freedom of association, including the liberty of employers to decide whom they will hire. Some have argued that the liberal commitment to free association requires the rejection of antidiscrimination laws, including those that ban employment discrimination such as the Civil Rights Act of 1964. Most liberals thinkers reject this view, but any liberal defence of antidiscrimination laws must cite considerations sufficiently strong to override the infringements on freedom of association that the laws involve. There are two different approaches within liberal thought to the justification of antidiscrimination laws. Both approaches regard as very important the interests people have in the areas protected by the laws, such as employment and public accommodations.

And both approaches agree that the disadvantageous treatment of a person in those areas on the basis of race, sex, and the other traditional civil rights categories is morally arbitrary. However, on the first approach, the key to the justification of antidiscrimination laws rests squarely on the fact that the conduct prohibited by the laws is morally arbitrary. In contrast, the second approach holds that it is not the morally arbitrary conduct as such that justifies the laws but rather the fact that conduct based on those categories has had systemic effects reducing the members of certain groups to second-class citizenship. Thus, the difference between the two approaches tracks the distinction between the individualistic and systemic accounts of why discrimination is wrong. Although many legal theorists endorse the systemic approach to the justification of antidiscrimination law, the U.S. Supreme Court seems to have adopted the individualistic one.

The Existence of Discrimination

Many debates over civil rights issues turn on assumptions about the scope and effects of existing discrimination against particular groups. For example, some thinkers hold that systemic discrimination based on race and gender is largely a thing of the past in contemporary liberal democracies and that the current situation allows persons to participate in society as free and equal citizens, regardless of race or gender. Many others reject that view, arguing that white skin privilege and patriarchy persist and operate to substantially and unjustifiably diminish the life-prospects of nonwhites and women.

These differences drive debates over affirmative action, race-conscious electoral districting, and pornography, among other issues. Questions about the scope and effects of discrimination are largely but not entirely empirical in character. Such questions concern the degree to which participation in society as a free and equal citizen is hampered by one's race or sex. And addressing that concern presupposes some normative criteria for determining what is needed to possess the status of such a citizen.

Moreover, there are subtle aspects of discrimination that are not captured by thinking strictly in terms of categories such as race, sex, religion, sexual orientation, and so on. Piper analyses "higher-order" forms of discrimination in which certain traits, such as speaking style, come to be arbitrarily disvalued on account of their association with a disvalued race or sex. Determining the presence and effects of such forms of discrimination in society at large would be a very complicated conceptual and empirical task. Additional complications stem from the fact that different categories of discrimination might intersect in ways that produce distinctive forms of unjust disadvantage.

Thus, some thinkers have asserted that the intersection of race and sex creates a form of discrimination against black women which has not been adequately recognized or addressed by judges or liberal legal theorists. And other thinkers have begun to argue that our understanding of discrimination must be expanded beyond the white-black paradigm to include the distinctive ways in which Asian-Americans and other minority groups are subjected to discriminatory attitudes and treatment.

Among the most careful empirical studies of discrimination have been those conducted by Ayers. He found evidence of "pervasive discrimination" in several types of markets, including retail car sales, bail-bonding, and kidney-transplantation. Yet, his assessment is that "we still do not know the current ambit of race and gender discrimination in America".

SEXUAL ORIENTATION

Some civil rights laws in the United States include the category of sexual orientation, but many people contest the legitimacy of the laws. The state of Colorado went so far as to ratify an amendment to its constitution that would prohibit any jurisdiction within the state from enacting a civil rights law that would protect homosexuals. The amendment was eventually invalidated by the U.S. Supreme Court on the ground that it was the product of simple prejudice and served no legitimate state purpose, thus violating the Equal Protection Clause.

But federal courts have upheld the military's "don't ask, don't tell" policy and the U.S. Congress enacted the Defence of Marriage Act, which prohibits courts from ruling that same-sex marriages must be recognized on equal protection grounds. On the other hand, same-sex marriages are legally recognized in Massachusetts, though there are efforts to rescind the recognition, and marriage laws have also been extended to same-sex couples in the Netherlands, Belgium, Canada and Spain. In addition, several jurisdictions have recognized same-sex partnerships with many, though not all, of the legal rights of marriage. Opponents of same-sex marriage have claimed that it would weaken the commitment of heterosexuals to marriage, but some advocates have presented empirical data that appears to undercut any such claim. Much of the discussion of "gay rights" involves the question of whether sexual orientation is genetically determined, socially determined, or the product of individual choice.

However, it is not clear why the question is relevant. The discussion appears to assume that genetic determination would vindicate the civil rights claims of gays, because sexual orientation would then be like race or sex insofar as it would be biologically fixed and immutable. But it is a mistake to think that racial or sex discrimination is morally objectionable because of the biological fixity or unchosen nature of race and sex. It is objectionable because it expresses ill-will or indifference, and it is unjust because it treats an individual in a morally arbitrary manner and, under current conditions, reinforces social patterns of disadvantage that seriously diminish the life prospects of many persons.

The view that sexual orientation is like race or sex in a morally relevant way should focus on the analogous features of discrimination based on sexual orientation. Wintermute and Koppelman assert that discrimination based on sexual orientation is not just analogous to sex discrimination but that it is a form of sex discrimination.

If it is legally permissible for Jane to have sex with John, then banning Joe's having sex with John would seem to amount to discrimination against Joe on grounds of his sex. If Joe were a woman, his having sex with John would be permitted, so he is being treated differently because of his sex. However, Koppelman contends that this formal argument should be supplemented by more substantive ones referring to the systemic patterns of social disadvantage from which gays and lesbians suffer. In fact, one can argue that the treatment of gays and lesbians is an injustice to them as individuals and amounts to a systemic pattern of unjust disadvantage. The individual injustice arises from the arbitrary nature of denying persons valuable life-opportunities, such as employment and marriage, on the basis of their sexual orientation. The systemic injustice arises from the repeated and widespread acts of individual injustice. The most controversial civil rights issues regarding sexual orientation concern the principle of equal treatment for same-sex and heterosexual couples.

Most scholars endorse such a principle and argue that equal treatment requires that same-sex marriages be legalized. Moreover, it is often argued in the literature that a person's choice of sex partner is central to her life and protected under a right of privacy. In Bowers v. Hardwick, the United States Supreme Court rejected this argument, upholding the criminalization of homosexual sodomy. The decision was condemned by legal and political thinkers and was overturned by the Court in Lawrence v. Texas. The Court invoked the right of privacy in declaring the state's criminal ban on sodomy between same-sex partners.

Nonetheless, some scholars who argue for the equal legal treatment of same-sex relations contend that privacy-based arguments are inadequate. They point out that one can hold the view that adults have a right to engage in same-sex intimacies even as one contends that such intimacies are morally abominable and ought not to receive any encouragement from government. Such a view would reject equal legal treatment for those in intimate same-sex relationships.

Finnis takes such a view, arguing that same-sex relations are "manifestly unworthy of the human being and immoral" and should not be encouraged by the state, but finding that criminalizing same-sex relations violates rights of individual privacy. Lee and George also find such relations to be morally defective and unworthy of equal treatment by the state; though George does not think that any sound *a priori* principle prohibits criminalization. Finnis, Lee and George argue for their condemnation of same-sex relations on the ground of natural law theory. However, unlike traditional versions of natural law theory, their version does not rest on any explicit theological or metaphysical claims. Rather, it invokes independent principles of practical reasoning that articulate the basic reasons for action. Such reasons are the fundamental goods that action is capable of realising and, for Finnis, Lee and George, include "marriage, the *conjuntio* of man and woman". Homosexual conduct, masturbation, and all extra-marital sex aim strictly at "individual gratification" and can be no part of any "common good." Such actions "harm the character" of those voluntarily choosing them. In taking the actions, a person becomes a slave to his passions, allowing his reason to be overridden by his raw desire for sensuous pleasure.

On Finnis's account, when consensual sexual conduct is private, government may not outlaw it, but government "can rightly judge that it has a compelling interest in denying that 'gay lifestyles' are a valid and humanly acceptable choice and form of life". And for Finnis, Lee and George, equal treatment of same-sex and heterosexual relations is out of the question due to the morally defective character of same-sex relations. Macedo responds to Finnis by arguing that "all of the goods that can be shared by sterile heterosexual couples can also be shared by committed homosexual couples".

Macedo points out that Finnis does not condemn sexual intercourse by sterile heterosexual couples. But Finnis replies that there is a relevant difference between homosexual couples and sterile heterosexual ones: the latter but not the former are united "biologically" when they have intercourse. Lee and George make essentially the same point: only heterosexual couples can "truly become one body, one organism". But Macedo points out that, biologically, it is not the man and woman who unite but the sperm and the egg. It can be added that the "biological unity" argument seems to run contrary to Finnis's claim that his position "does not seek to infer normative conclusions from non-normative premises".

More importantly, Macedo and Koppelman make the key point that the human good possible through intimate relations is a function of "mutual commitment and stable engagement" and that same-sex couples can achieve "the precise kind of human good" that is available to heterosexual ones. Accordingly, equal treatment under the law for same-sex couples, including the recognition of same-sex marriage, would remove unjustifiable obstacles faced by same-sex couples to the achievement of that human good.

DISABILITY

During the 1970's and 80's, persons with disabilities increasingly argued that they were second-class citizens. They organized into a civil rights movement that pressed for legislation that would help secure for them the status of equal citizens.

Protection against discrimination based on disability was written into the Canadian Charter of Rights and Freedoms and The Charter of Fundamental Rights of the European Union. The disability rights movement in the U.S. culminated with the passage of the Americans With Disabilities Act of 1990. The ADA has served as a model for legislation in countries such as Australia, India and Israel

The Medical and Social Models

The traditional model for understanding disability is called the "medical model." It is reflected in many pre-ADA laws and in some philosophical discussions of disability which treat it as an issue of the just distribution of health care. The medical model, a disabled person is one who falls below some baseline level that defines normal human functioning. That level is a natural one, on this view, in that it is determined by biological facts about the human species.

Thus, the medical model supposes that the question of who counts as disabled can be answered in a way that is value-free and that abstracts from existing social practices and the physical environment those practices have constructed. It also gives the medical profession a privileged position in determining who is disabled, as the study and treatment of normal and subnormal human functioning is the specialty of that profession. The consensus among current disability theorists is that the medical model should be rejected. Any determination that a certain level of function is normal for the species will presuppose judgments that do not simply describe biological reality but impose on them some system of evaluation. Moreover, the level of functioning a person can achieve does not depend solely on her own individual abilities: it depends as well on the social practices and the physical environment those practices have shaped. Disability theorists thus posit an important analogy between the categories of 'race' and 'disability'.

As they understand it, neither category refers to any real distinctions in nature. Just as there is variation in skin colour, there is variation in acuity of vision, physical strength, ability to walk and run and so on. And just as there is no natural line dividing one "race" from another, there is no natural line dividing those who are functionally "abnormal" from those who are not so. The rejection of the medical model has led to a "social model," just as to which certain physical or biological properties are turned into dysfunctions by social practices and the socially-constructed physical environment. For example, lack of mobility for those who are unable to walk is not simply a function of their physical characteristics: it is also a function of building practices that employ stairs instead of ramps and by automotive design practices that require the use of one's legs to drive a car. There is nothing necessary about such practices. Accordingly, the social model conceives of disability as socially-imposed dysfunction.

The social model brings attention to how engineering and design practices can work to the disadvantage of persons with certain physical characteristics. And the idea of dysfunction is certainly a value-laden one. But it seems no more accurate to think that dysfunction is entirely imposed by society than it is to think that it is entirely the product of an individual's physical or mental characteristics. Individual characteristics in the context of the socially-constructed environment determine the level of functioning that a person can achieve. And some individual characteristics would impair a person's functioning under all or almost all practicable alternatives to current social practices. Moreover, despite the fact that "normal human functioning" is a value-laden concept, it does not follow that it is entirely subjective or that reasonable efforts to specify the elements of some morally acceptable level of human functioning are misguided.

Indeed, some defensible understanding of what counts as better or worse human functioning would seem to be necessary to determine when some social practice has turned a physical characteristic into a significant disadvantage for a person. In addition, the social model's conception of what it is to be a disabled person seems overbroad. The social practice of requiring students to pass courses in order to receive a degree creates a barrier that some persons cannot surmount. It does not seem that such people are, *ipso facto*, disabled. Such examples of "exclusionary" social practices could be multiplied indefinitely.

Some thinkers may not be troubled by the implication that everyone is disabled in every respect in which she is excluded or otherwise disadvantaged by some social practice. But it is difficult to see how the idea of disability would then be of much use.

Race, Disability, and Discrimination

The disability rights movement began with the idea that discrimination on the basis of disability was not different in any morally important way from discrimination based on race. The aim of the movement was to enshrine in law the same kind of antidiscrimination principle that protected persons based on their race. But some theorists have questioned how well the analogy holds. They point out that applying the antidiscrimination norm to disability requires taking account of physical or mental differences among people. This seems to be treatment based on a person's physical features, apparently the exact opposite of the ideal of "colour blindness" behind the traditional antidiscrimination principle.

Even race-based affirmative action does not really seem to be parallel to antidiscrimination policies that take account of disability. Advocates of affirmative action assert that the social ideal is for persons not to be treated on the basis of their race or colour at all. Race-conscious policies are seen as instruments that will move society towards that ideal. In contrast, policies designed to counter discrimination based on disability are not sensibly understood as temporary measures or steps towards a goal in which people are not treated based on their disabilities. The policies permanently enshrine the idea that in designing buildings or buses or constructing some other aspect of our physical-social environment, we must be responsive to the disabilities people have in order for the disabled to have "fair equality of opportunity". The need for a permanent "accommodation" of persons with disabilities seems to mark an important difference in how the antidiscrimination norm should be understood in the context of disability, as opposed to the context of race.

However, it is important to recognize that, at the level of fundamental principle, the reasons why disability-based discrimination is morally objectionable and even unjust are essentially the same as the reasons why racial discrimination is so. At the individual level, disadvantageous treatment of the disabled is often rooted in ill-will, disregard, and moral arbitrariness. At the systemic level, such treatment creates a social pattern of disadvantage that reduces the disabled to second-class status. In those two respects, the grounds of civil rights law are no different when it comes to the disabled.

Another way in which disability is thought to be fundamentally different from race concerns the special needs that the disabled often have that make life more costly for them. These extra costs would exist even if the socially-constructed physical environment were built to provide the disabled with fair equality of opportunity and their basic civil and political liberties were secured. In order to function effectively, disabled persons may need to buy medications or therapies or other forms of assistance that the able-bodied do not need for their functioning. And there does not seem to be any parallel in matters of race to the special needs of some of those who are disabled. The driving idea of the civil rights movement was that blacks did not have any special needs: all they needed was to have the burdens of racism lifted from them and, once that was accomplished, they would flourish or fail like everyone else in society. However, Silvers argues that the parallel between race and disability still holds: all the disabled may claim from society as a matter of justice is that they have fair equality of opportunity and the same basic civil rights as everyone else. Any special needs that the disabled may have do not provide the grounds of any legitimate claims of justice. On the other hand, Kittay argues that the special needs of the disabled are a matter of basic justice. She focuses on the severely mentally disabled, for whom fair opportunity in the labour markets and political rights in the public sphere will have no significance, and on the families which have the responsibility of caring for the severely disabled.

Pogge also questions Silvers' view, suggesting that it is implausible to deny that justice requires that society provide resources for meeting the needs of the severely disabled. Still, it may be the case that some version of Silvers' approach may be justifiable when it comes to disabled persons who have the capacity "to participate fully in the political and civic institutions of the society and, more broadly, in its public life". In the case of such persons, the basic civil right to equal citizenship would require that they have the equal opportunity to participate in such institutions, regardless of their disability. Although there may be some aspects of the racial model that cannot be applied to persons with severe forms of mental disability, the principles behind the American civil rights struggles of the 1950's and 60's remain crucial normative resources for understanding and combating forms of unjust discrimination that have only more recently been addressed by philosophers and by society more broadly.

Contractarianism and the Disabled

The emergence of the issue of disability rights has posed an important challenge for versions of liberalism inspired by the social contract tradition. One of the putative advantages of such forms of liberalism is that they better reflect strong and widely held intuitions about justice and individual rights than does utilitarianism. As Rawls famously wrote, "Each person possesses an inviolability founded on justice that even the welfare of society as a whole cannot override".

However, several thinkers have argued that Rawls's own contractarian theory does not make adequate room for the severely disabled. These arguments are not about the rights of the severely disabled, but rather begin from the assumption that those who are so disabled do have robust moral rights and then proceed to the question whether contractarianism can account for those rights.

The problem for Rawls derives from the conception of personhood that accompanies his idea that society should be conceived as a fair system of cooperation among free and equal persons, extending over generations. On that conception, "a person is someone who can be a citizen, that is, a normal and fully cooperating member of society over a complete life." Additionally, persons are represented as having two "moral powers," the capacities for a sense of justice and for a conception of the good. The parties to Rawls's original position choose principles of justice with such a conception of the person in mind. Critics have argued that Rawls's principles of justice fail to take adequate account of the legitimate claims of the severely disabled and that the heart of the problem is Rawls's contractarianism.

Nussbaum claims that Rawls goes astray in following traditional contractarianism and conceiving of society as a scheme of cooperation for mutual advantage. Yet, Becker defends mutual-advantage theories, arguing that they can incorporate a conception of reciprocity sufficiently rich to underwrite principles that truly do justice to the disabled. Stark and Brighouse argue that Rawls's theory, in particular, can be extended or modified to take account of disabled, without repudiating its contractarian core. Kittay agrees with the liberal idea that justice must not be sacrificed for other values, but she doubts that any form of liberalism can make adequate room for the claims of justice made on behalf of the severely disabled. In contrast, Silvers and Francis defend a form of contract theory in which the parties seek to build mutual trust. They argue that the interests of disabled would not be discounted in such a contract.

LEGAL CASES AND STATUTES

- Americans With Disabilities Act. 42 U.S.C. §§12101-12213.
- Bowers v. Hardwick 478 U.S. 186.
- Boy Scouts v. Dale, No. 99-699.
- Civil Rights Act of 1866. 42 U.S.C §1981.
- Civil Rights Act of 1964. 42 U.S.C. §§2000e et seq.
- Defence of Marriage Act 28 U.S.C. §1738c.
- Ex Parte Crow Dog 109 U.S. 556.
- Indian Civil Rights Act of 1968. 28 U.S.C. §§1301-1303.
- Oklahoma Tax Commission v. Citizen Band, Potawatomi Indian Tribe 498 U.S. 505.
- Pregnancy Discrimination Act 42 U.S.C. §2000 (e)(k).
- Romer v. Evans 517 U.S. 620.
- Santa Clara Pueblo v. Martinez 436 U.S. 49.
- Thomasson v. Perry 80 F.3d 915

BUSINESS AND HUMAN RIGHTS

Non-state actors, particularly multinational or trans-national corporations have become important players throughout the world. As the influence and reach of corporations has grown as a result of globalization and other global developments, there is an increasing debate about the roles and responsibilities of corporate actors with regard to human rights.

International human rights standards have traditionally been the responsibility of governments, aimed at regulating relations between the state and individuals/groups. In view of the increased role played by corporate actors at both the national and international level, the United Nations human rights machinery is considering the scope of business' human rights responsibilities and exploring ways for corporate actors to be accountable for the impact of their activities on human rights. However, the practical meaning of the link between business and human rights remains unclear for many and substantial debates over which human rights can and should apply to business, and in what way are ongoing.

OHCHR's work on the issue of business and human rights is focused on three areas:

- Advocacy by the High Commissioner;
- Support to the Special Representative of the Secretary-General on the issue of transnational corporations and other business enterprises;
- Active involvement in the United Nations Global Compact;

The High Commissioners has expressed support for the development of human right standards applicable to the business sector, while at the same time advocating the implementation of voluntary initiatives towards corporate social responsibility.

OHCHR is providing ongoing support and advice to the work of the Special Representative of the Secretary-General on the issue of transnational corporations and other business enterprises with regard to human rights. The mandate was established by the United Nations Commission on Human Rights in 2005 by resolution 2005/69 and was extended by the Human Rights Council.

In resolution 2005/69, the Commission on Human Rights mandated the High Commissioner, in collaboration with the SRSG, to convene annually a consultation with executives from a particular business sector to discuss the human rights challenges faced by that sector.

In November 2005, the High Commissioner convened a consultation with representatives from the extractive sector. In January 2007, the High Commissioner convened a consultation with representatives from the finance sector. The UN Global Compact is certainly the most prominent voluntary initiative in the field of business and human rights. It is a personal initiative of the United Nations Secretary-General dating from 2000, aimed at getting business leaders to voluntarily promote and apply within their corporate domains 10 principles relating to human rights, labour standards, the environment, and anti-corruption. At present, thousands of companies, many of them large transnational companies, from all continents have signed on to the Global Compact. OHCHR is one of now 6 UN agencies which work in partnership with the Secretary-General's Global Compact office. Since the launch of the Global Compact, OHCHR has been requested by the United Nations Secretary-General to serve as "guardian" of the human rights principles and to contribute to efforts made to encourage companies to implement these principles in their core operations and business model.

OHCHR activities have been grouped around the themes of learning and dialogue. OHCHR is involved in Global Compact governance through its membership of the Global Compact Inter-Agency Team which is responsible for ensuring coherent support for the internalization of the principles within the United Nations and among all participants.

OHCHR has joined the Global Compact Office and other partners in publishing tools for companies participating in the Global Compact on how to understand and implement the human rights principles of the Global Compact. The 18th of June 2008 the Human Rights Council was unanimous in "welcoming" the policy framework for business and human rights the SRSG proposed in his final report under the 2005 mandate.

The policy framework comprises three core principles: the State duty to protect against human rights abuses by third parties, including business; the corporate responsibility to respect human rights; and the need for greater access by victims to effective remedies. The Human Rights Council has renewed the mandate for a period of 3 years with the new resolution A/HRC/8/L.8 that requests the Special Representative of the Secretarv General to operationalize the framework elaborated and specifically:

- To provide views and recommendations on ways to strengthen the fulfillment of the duty of the State to protect all human rights from abuses by transnational corporations and other business enterprises, including through international cooperation;

- To elaborate further on the scope and content of the corporate responsibility to respect all human rights and to provide concrete guidance to business and other stakeholders;
- To explore options and make recommendations, at the national, regional and international levels, for enhancing access to effective remedies available to those whose human rights are impacted by corporate activities;
- To integrate a gender perspective throughout his work and to give special attention to persons belonging to vulnerable groups, in particular children;
- To liaise closely with the efforts of the human rights working group of the Global Compact in order to identify, exchange and promote best practices and sessions learned on the issue of transnational corporations and other business enterprises;
- To work in close coordination with United Nations and other relevant international bodies, offices, departments and specialized agencies, and in particular with other special procedures of the Council;
- To continue to consult on the issues covered by the mandate on an ongoing basis with all stakeholders, including States, national human rights institutions, international and regional organizations, transnational corporations and other business enterprises, and civil society, including academics, employers' organizations, workers' organizations, indigenous and other affected communities and non-governmental organizations, including through joint meetings;
- To report annually to the Council and the General Assembly;

In Resolution 2005/69 The Commission on Human Rights requested the Secretary-General to appoint a special representative on the issue of human rights and transnational corporations and other business enterprises, for an initial period of two years, with the following mandate:

- To identify and clarify standards of corporate responsibility and accountability for transnational corporations and other business enterprises with regard to human rights;
- To elaborate on the role of States in effectively regulating and adjudicating the role of transnational corporations and other business enterprises with regard to human rights, including through international cooperation;
- To research and clarify the implications for transnational corporations and other business enterprises of concepts such as "complicity" and "sphere of influence";
- To develop materials and methodologies for undertaking human rights impact assessments of the activities of transnational corporations and other business enterprises;
- To compile a compendium of best practices of States and transnational corporations and other business enterprises.

FREEDOM OF RELIGION OR BELIEF

DEFINING RELIGION OR BELIEF

The word "religion," meaning to bind fast, comes from the Western Latin word religare. It is commonly, but not always, associated with traditional majority, minority or new religious beliefs in a transcendent deity or deities. In human rights discourse, however, the use of the term usually also includes support for the right to non-religious beliefs. In 1993 the Human Rights Committee, an independent body of 18 experts selected through a UN process, described religion or belief as "theistic, non-theistic and atheistic beliefs, as well as the right not to profess any religion or belief." Religions and other beliefs bring hope and consolation to billions of people, and hold great potential for peace and reconciliation. They have also, however, been the source of tension and conflict. This complexity, and the difficulty of defining "religion" and "belief," are showed by the still developing history of the protection of freedom of religion or belief in the context of international human rights.

A Complex and Contentious Issue

The struggle for religious liberty has been ongoing for centuries, and has led to innumerable, tragic conflicts. The twentieth century has seen the codification of common values related to freedom of religion and belief, though the struggle has not abated. The United Nations recognized the importance of freedom of religion or belief in the 1948 Universal Declaration of Human Rights, in which Article 18 states that "Everyone shall have the right to freedom of thought, conscience and religion. This right shall include freedom to have a religion or whatever belief of his choice."

Since the Universal Declaration, the attempt to develop an enforceable human rights instrument related to freedom of religion and belief has been unsuccessful. In 1966 the UN passed the International Covenant on Civil and Political Rights, expanding its prior statement to address the manifestation of religion or belief.

Article 18 of this Covenant includes four paragraphs related to this issue:

- Everyone shall have the right to freedom of thought, conscience and religion. This right shall include freedom to have or to adopt a religion or belief of his choice, and freedom either individually or in community with others and in public or private, to manifest his religion or belief in worship, observance, practice and teaching.
- No one shall be subject to coercion which would impair his freedom to have or to adopt a religion or belief of his choice.
- Freedom to manifest one's religion or belief may be subject only to such limitations as are prescribed by

law and are necessary to protect public safety, order, health, morals or the fundamental rights and freedoms of others.

- The States Parties to the present Covenant undertake to have respect for the liberty of parents and, when applicable, legal guardians, to ensure the religious and moral education of their children in conformity with their own convictions.

Some of the articles of the Covenant on Civil and Political Rights regarding fundamental freedoms have become international conventions, which are legally binding treaties. In contrast, however, because of the complexity of the topic and the political issues involved, Article 18 of the Covenant on Civil and Political Rights has not been elaborated and codified in the same way that more detailed treaties have codified prohibitions against torture, discrimination against women, and race discrimination.

After twenty years of debate, intense struggle and hard work, the General Assembly in 1981 adopted without a vote the Declaration on the Elimination of All Forms of Intolerance and of Discrimination Based on Religion or Belief. While the 1981 Declaration lacks any enforcement procedures, it remains the most important contemporary codification of the principle of freedom of religion and belief.

RIGHTS AT STAKE

The 1981 UN Declaration on the Elimination of All Forms of Intolerance and of Discrimination Based on Religion or Belief contains eight articles, three of which define specific rights. The remaining articles act in a supportive role by outlining measures to promote tolerance or prevent discrimination.

Taken together, the eight articles constitute a paradigm, an overall concept, to advocate for tolerance and to prevent discrimination based on religion or belief. While human rights are individual rights, the 1981 UN Declaration also identifies certain rights related to states, religious institutions, parents, legal guardians, children, and groups of persons.

Article 1: *Legal Definition.*

This article repeats several rights from the Covenant on Civil and Political Rights's Article 18:

- Right to thought, conscience, and religion or belief;
- Right to have a religion or whatever belief of your choice;
- Right either individually or in community with others, in private or public, to manifest a religion or belief through worship, observance, practice and teaching;
- Right not to suffer coercion that impairs the freedom to choose a religion or belief;
- Right of the State to limit the manifestation of a religion or belief if based in law, and only as necessary to protect public safety, order, health, morals and the fundamental rights and freedoms of others.

Article 2: *Classification of Discrimination.*

This article identifies categories of potential discriminators, affirming the right not to be subject to discrimination on the grounds of religion or belief by:

- States;
- Institutions;
- Groups of persons;
- Persons.

Article 3: *Link to Other Rights.*

This article links the 1981 UN Declaration to other international documents. Article 3 declares that discrimination based on religion or belief constitutes an affront to human dignity and a disavowal of the principles of the Charter of the United Nations, and shall be condemned as a violation of the human rights and fundamental freedoms proclaimed in the Universal Declaration of Human Rights, and enunciated in detail in:

- The International Covenant on Civil and Political Rights;
- The International Covenant on Economic, Social and Cultural Rights.

Article 4: *Possible Solutions.*

Article 4 declares that all States [including all sectors of civil society] shall take effective measures to prevent and eliminate discrimination based on religion or belief through:

- Actions in all fields of civil, economic, political, social, cultural life;
- Enacting or rescinding legislation where necessary to prohibit such discrimination;
- Taking all appropriate measures to combat intolerance based on religion or belief.

Article 5: *Parents, Guardians, Children.*

At stake in the implementation of this article are the following rights:

- Right of parents or legal guardians to bring the child up in their religion or belief;
- Right of the child to education in religion or belief, in accordance with the wishes of parents, and the right not to be compelled to receive education against their wishes;
- Right of the child to protection from discrimination and to education for tolerance;
- Right of the child's wishes when not under the care of parents or legal guardians;
- Right of the State to limit practices injurious to child's development or health.

Article 6: *Manifesting Religion or Belief.*

At stake in the implementation of this article are the following rights:

- Right to worship and assemble, and to establish and maintain places of worship;
- Right to establish and maintain appropriate charitable or humanitarian institutions;
- Right to make, acquire and use materials related to rites and customs;
- Right to write, issue and disseminate relevant publications in these areas;
- Right to teach a religion or belief in places suitable for these purposes;

- Right to solicit and receive voluntary financial and other contributions;
- Right to train, appoint, elect or designate appropriate leaders;
- Right to observe days of rest and celebrate holidays and ceremonies;
- Right to establish and maintain communication with individuals and communities at national and international levels.

Article 7: *National Legislation.*

This article declares that all of the rights at stake in the 1981 UN Declaration need to be accorded in national legislation in such a manner that everyone shall be able to avail themselves of such rights and freedoms in practice.

Article 8: *Existing Protections.*

This article specifies that the 1981 UN Declaration is non-binding on States so as to ensure that the Declaration does not negate existing legal protections on freedom of religion or belief.

Article 8 states that nothing in the Declaration shall be construed as restricting or negating any right defined in the Universal Declaration of Human Rights and International Covenants on Human Rights. The 1981 UN Declaration is a compromise between states after twenty years of complex discussion and debate, and after final passage by the General Assembly.

Several sensitive issues are still in need of further clarification, including:

- Religious or national law versus international law,
- Proselytism,
- Conscientious objection to military service,
- Status of women in religion or belief,
- Claims of superiority or inferiority of religions and beliefs,
- Choosing and changing a religious commitment,
- Religious registration and association laws,
- Public media and religion or belief, and the relationship of religion or belief to the state.

INTERNATIONAL AND REGIONAL INSTRUMENTS OF PROTECTION

International legal instruments take the form of a treaty which may be binding on the contracting states. When negotiations are completed, the text of a treaty is established as authentic and definitive and is signed by the representatives of states.

There are various means by which a state expresses its consent to be bound by a treaty, with the most common being ratification or accession. A new treaty is ratified by those states that have negotiated the instrument, while a state that has not participated in the negotiations may, at a later stage, accede to the treaty.

The treaty enters into force when a pre-determined number of states have ratified or acceded to the treaty. When a state ratifies or accedes to a treaty, that state may make reservations to one or more articles of the treaty, unless the treaty prohibits this actions. Reservations are exceptions that a state makes to a treaty-provisions that it does not agree to follow-and may normally be withdrawn at any time. In some countries, international treaties take precedence over national law. In others, a specific law may be required to give an international treaty, although ratified or acceded to, the force of law.

Almost all states that have ratified or acceded to an international treaty may issue decrees, amend existing laws or introduce new legislation in order for the treaty to be fully effective on the national territory. While the 1981 Declaration was adopted as a non-binding human rights instrument, several states had reservations.

Romania, Poland, Bulgaria, Czechoslovakia and the then U.S.S.R. said that the 1981 UN Declaration did not take sufficient account of atheistic beliefs. Romania, Syria, Czechoslovakia, and the U.S.S.R. made a general reservation regarding provisions not in accordance with their national legislation.

Iraq entered a collective reservation on behalf of the Organization of the Islamic Conference as to the applicability of any provision or wording in the Declaration which might be contrary to Shari'a law or to legislation or acts based on Islamic law, and Syria and Iran endorsed this reservation.

Monitoring Freedom of Religion or Belief

Many international treaties have a mechanism to monitor their implementation. As part of the Covenant on Civil and Political Rights, Article 18 is legally-binding and is monitored by the Human Rights Committee. As of 2002, there were 149 States Parties to this Covenant.

Under an Optional Protocol, 102 States Parties recognize the authority of the Human Rights Committee to consider confidential communications from individuals claiming to be victims of violations of any rights proclaimed under the treaty. The 1981 UN Declaration on the Elimination of All Forms of Intolerance and of Discrimination Based on Religion or Belief is a non-binding declaration, and does not, therefore, have a treaty mechanism. Instead, in what is called an extra-conventional mechanism, the UN Commission on Human Rights appointed a Special Rapporteur for the 1981 UN Declaration. The Special Rapporteur is mandated to report annually to the Commission on the status of freedom of religion or belief worldwide.

8

Passing Legislation for Human Rights

INTRODUCTION

As the law-makers of a country, it is parliaments that ensure international human rights standards are met through domestic legislation. Bringing domestic laws in line with the standards required by treaty commitments usually requires parliament to pass legislation that specifically incorporates treaty provisions into domestic law.

This part also discusses a constitutional Bill of Rights with key human rights protections, and explains that all laws should accord with international law. The importance of prioritising key human rights issues such as poverty alleviation and justice sector reform, in budget allocations by providing substantial funds to support the work of national human rights institutions, and guaranteeing a transparent, participatory budget process is also discussed.

It concludes by highlighting ways the legislature can support the judiciary to protect human rights, as well as the responsibility of the judiciary to consistently maintain a human rights approach in its decision-making process.

BILL OF RIGHTS: ENSHRINING HUMAN RIGHTS IN THE CONSTITUTION

Subject-specific domestic legislation is one way to protect and promote rights. One of the most effective national efforts is through a constitutional Bill of Rights. The national

Constitution is the highest law of a country and overrides all other laws. Enshrining human rights in the Constitution, therefore, gives them enormous legal weight –all other laws must be in consonance with the standards set out in the Constitution.

Most Commonwealth countries have a constitutional Bill of Rights. New Zealand and the UK are examples of countries that have relied upon common law traditions for safeguarding rights but in the modern context have legislated for specific protection of rights.

Most Bills of Rights enshrine core values such as respect for human dignity; equality and non-discrimination; and the opportunity to realise one's potential through the exercise of fundamental freedoms. While many focus on civil and political rights, some notable examples, like the Bill of Rights in the South African Constitution, also include economic and social rights. Constitutions should ideally also enshrine the establishment of an independent human rights institution.

PASSING COMPLEMENTARY LEGISLATION

Ratification of treaties requires that all domestic laws be brought up to the standards of the international commitment and be in harmony with it. In some countries, such as the United States, this is a simple matter because when a treaty is ratified, it is "self-executing" so the provisions in the treaty automatically become part of domestic law, such that the public can take the Federal government to court if it has failed to implement the treaty.

In Commonwealth countries though, even where a treaty has been ratified, this does not necessarily mean that the commitments in it can be automatically enforced in domestic courts. This is because while the executive might have the constitutional power to bind the State at international law, only the parliament has the power to change domestic law.

As such, parliament must pass legislation to specifically 'incorporate' the treaty provisions into domestic law. One recent example of this was the United Kingdom's enactment of the Human Rights Act 1998, which was specifically enacted to make the rights contained in the European Convention on Human Rights enforceable in UK courts. Likewise, Fiji's Human Rights Commission Act, 1999 for the purposes of the Fiji Human Rights Commission describes human rights as rights embodied in the United Nations Covenants and Conventions on Human Rights and includes the rights and freedoms set out in the Bill of Rights.

Despite the obligation to pass laws that are consonant with treaty obligations many domestic considerations prevent or slow their passing. The conflict between personal laws, customary law and prevailing culture has been cited by some countries in explanation as to why they haven't passed laws that conform to treaty standards, although other countries have managed to do so.

ENSURING ALL OTHER LEGISLATION MEETS HUMAN RIGHTS STANDARDS

In addition to legislation that specifically domesticates international treaties, all laws which parliament passes should be in accordance with international human rights standards. This requirement also applies to the constitutional Bill of Rights, if one exists.

Specific human rights oversight committees set up to review legislation ensure it conforms to human rights standards. These committees are bolstered by legislation that specifically requires that all legislation meet minimum human rights standards.

In the State of Queensland, in Australia, for example, the Legislative Standards Act 1992 enshrines fundamental legislative principles that "must be considered when legislation is drafted so that it does not infringe individual liberties".

These principles include whether the legislation is consistent with the principles of natural justice and if it has sufficient regard for aboriginal traditions and customs, or provides for protection against selfincrimination. In the United Kingdom, the Human Rights Act 1998 specifically requires that all UK legislation should, if possible, fit with the European

Convention on Human Rights. Because the UK does not permit judicial review of legislation, the courts cannot strike down inconsistent legislation, but if a court finds that a law is incompatible with the Convention, it can make a "declaration of incompatibility" and parliament must decide what action to take.

An example is when Section 23 of the Anti-Terrorism Crime and Security Act 2001, was ruled incompatible with the Human Rights Act 1998 and the European Convention on Human Rights, by the highest court in the country. This part allowed indefinite detention without trial, of foreign nationals suspected of involvement in international terrorism.

The Act makes it clear that parliamentarians have a key role to play in ensuring that all legislation is in line with universal standards. The Act also makes it unlawful for a public authority to violate Convention rights, unless it had no choice due to an Act of Parliament.

This explicit extension of the duty to respect human rights on to the bureaucracy is a major step forward in creating a domestic environment genuinely respectful of and committed to human rights.

PROMOTING PRO-HUMAN RIGHTS BUDGETS

Allocations made in budgets show where a country's priorities lie. Optimum budget allocations towards poverty alleviation, human rights education, justice sector reforms, and socio-economic areas reflect the State's commitment to these areas and determine whether human rights can be truly upheld.

Budget allocations also indicate the relative importance given to institutions such as human rights commissions, minority commissions, women's commissions, police complaints commissions, human rights courts and ombudsmen – both to be established and to be maintained with sufficient resources to properly discharge their duties. Despite a strong mandate and excellent networks, human rights institutions are often unable to function to their true potential due to lack of funds. The difference between tokenism and true commitment of a government to human rights can often be seen through the funds available to these institutions. These priorities will be brought to the forefront through genuine consultation and participation of the people. By providing space for such participation and making sure that these views are incorporated into the budget, governments show their commitment to ensuring that both the process and final document are human-rights friendly. NGOs are increasingly engaging with the process through submissions, as well as analysing the final budget for adherence to human rights and social justice norms.

One example is an initiative in Tanzania that has led to budget guidelines for government departments that now require that budget submissions be prepared with a gender focus. Since 1996, the Commonwealth Secretariat has also supported gender budget initiatives. In the pilot phase of their project, technical assistance was provided to Barbados, Fiji, St Kitts and Nevis, South Africa and Sri Lanka, for projects with the joint support of the Ministry for Finance and Ministry for Women's Affairs.

It must be recognized though that it is not just the community within the country that will influence the budget process, but also international bodies. Donors, for instance, whether through bi-lateral or multi-lateral agreements wield increasing leverage in setting the budgetary agenda in beneficiary countries.

The process of developing Poverty Reduction Strategy Papers (PRSPs), for instance, involves not just national stakeholders, but external development partners as well, particularly the IMF and World Bank. PRSPs aim to bring about a comprehensive national strategy for poverty reduction and describe the macroeconomic, structural and social policies and programmes that a country will pursue over several years, as well as external financing needs and the associated sources of financing.

These provide an opportunity for all stakeholders to ensure that poverty reduction is designed and implemented through a human rights framework and that explicit human rights activities are prioritized. A country's commitment to human rights is also gauged by willingness to contribute to international development agencies that promote human rights, democracy and good governance. Countries quite often make statements committing funds to international agencies but delay in releasing the money.

Many crucial bodies such as the Office for the High Commissioner on Human Rights receive some general UN money but require voluntary contributions to function as designed. Financial contributions included in the budget reflect a State's commitment to international human rights.

Bibliography

Abdullahi, A.: *Human Rights in Cross-cultural Perspectives: A Quest for Consensus*, Philadelphia, PA: University of Pennsylvania Press, 1998.

Adrienne, Stone: *Protecting Human Rights: Instruments and Institutions*, New York: Oxford University Press, 2003.

Agosin, Marjorie: *Women, Gender, and Human Rights: A Global Perspective*, New Brunswick, NJ: Rutgers University Press, 2001.

Allen, Robin: *Employment Law and Human Rights*, New York: Oxford University Press, 2002.

Alston: *Children, Rights and the Law*, New York: Oxford University Press, 2003.

Anaya, S.: *Indigenous Peoples in International Law*, New York: Oxford University Press, 2001.

Andreassen: *Development as a Human Right: Legal, Political and Economic Dimensions*, London: Harvard University Press, 2006.

Baderin: *International Human Rights and Islamic Law*, New York: Oxford University Press, 2003.

Bailey, Sydney D.: *The UN Security Council and Human Rights*, New York: St. Martin's Press, 2003.

Banda, Fareda: *Women, Law and Human Rights: An African Perspective*, UK: Oxford, 2005.

Bard, A.: *Development as a Human Right: Legal, Political and Economic Dimensions*, London: Harvard University Press, 2006.

Bartlett, Peter: *Mental Disability and the European Convention on Human Rights*, Leiden: E. J. Brill, 2006.

Bayefsky, Anne F.: *The UN Human Rights Treaty System*, New York: Transnational Publication, 2001.

Chatterjee, S.: *Ethics and Foreign Intervention*, UK: Cambridge University Press, 2003.

Chesterman: *Just War or Just Peace? Humanitarian Intervention and International Law*, New York: Oxford University Press, 2001.

Clapham, Andrew: *Human Rights in the Private Sphere*, New York: Oxford University Press, 2005.

Clapham, Andrew: *Human Rights Obligations of Non-State Actors*, New York: Oxford University Press, 2006.

Donnelly, Jack: *International Human Rights*, Boulder, CO: Westview Press, 2006.

Drzemczewski: *European Human Rights Convention in Domestic Law: A Comparative Study*, New York: Oxford University Press, 2000.

Dunne: *Human Rights in Global Politics*, UK: Cambridge University Press, 1999.

Eldridge, Phil.: *Politics of Human Rights in Southeast Asia*, London: Routledge, 2002.

Elisabeth Burgi: *Human Rights and International Trade*, New York: Oxford University Press, 2005.

Emberland, Marius: *The Human Rights of Companies: Exploring the Structure of ECHR Protection*, New York: Oxford University Press, 2006.

Franklin, Bob: *The New Handbook of Children's Rights: Comparative Policy and Practice*, London: Routledge, 2002.

Frost, Mervyn: *Constituting Human Rights: Global Civil Society and the Society of Democratic States*, London: Routledge, 2002.

Gearty, Conor: *Principles of Human Rights Adjudication*, New York: Oxford University Press, 2004.

George, J.: *American Bioethics: Crossing Human Rights and Health Law Boundaries*, New York: Oxford University Press, 2005.

Gewirth, Alan: *Human Rights*, Chicago: University of Chicago Press, 2002.

Henkin, Louis: *The Age of Rights,* New York: Columbia University Press, 2005.

Ignatieff, Michael: *Human Rights as Politics and Idolatry,* Princeton, NJ: Princeton University Press, 2001.

Janis: *European Human Rights Law: Texts and Materials,* New York: Oxford University Press, 2001.

Klein, B.: *Dignity and Human Rights: The Implementation of Economic, Social and Cultural Rights,* New York: Transnational Publication, 2002.

Korey, William: *NGOs and the Universal Declaration of Human Rights: 'A Curious Grapevine,'* New York: St. Martin's Press, 2003.

Lillich, Richard B.: *International Human Rights: Problems of Law, Policy, and Practice,* New York: Aspen, 2006.

Index

A

Acceptability 192
Accommodation 196, 239, 253, 276
Accountability 1, 19, 21, 31, 98, 108, 167, 174, 179, 182, 183, 186, 189, 191, 235, 272
ACP 137
Adaptability 192
Antidiscrimination 234, 237, 245, 246, 247, 253, 254, 261, 262
Archaeological 159
Archbishops 70
Atrocities 19, 20
Availability 192

B

Babylonians 55, 81
Benevolence 250, 251
Benimpuhwe 25
BPE 216, 231
Breadwinners 8

C

CDHRI 48, 49, 50, 51
CEDAW 6, 17, 23, 25, 26
Colonialism 45, 49, 242, 243
Complementarity 163
Conceptualizations 162, 172, 175
Contextualization 99
Contractarianism 263, 264

D

Deinstitutionalization 211, 215
Disability 132, 212, 217, 234, 235, 259, 260, 261, 262, 263
Disproportionate 5, 6, 7, 8

E

Economicover 116
ECOSOC 17, 63
Egalitarianism 172, 214, 245
Emphasis 12, 97, 100, 103, 111, 132, 143, 145, 147, 165, 171, 203, 216
Employability 249
Empowerment 93, 95, 96, 98, 101, 102, 103, 104, 105, 106, 107, 109, 110, 111, 167, 181, 185, 186, 209, 216, 218, 226
EUMC 128, 132

F

FOSS 201

H

HDR 139
Homophobia 75, 158

I

ICCPR 4, 17, 117, 120, 121, 122, 123, 172, 175
ICESCR 4, 17
Implementation 4, 17, 20, 21, 23, 25, 45, 64, 88, 103, 104, 105, 110, 111, 112, 121, 125, 126, 132, 144, 148, 163, 166, 171, 172, 194, 217, 230, 231, 232, 233, 266, 273, 276
Institutionalized 153, 157, 215
Interdependencies 93, 98
Internalized 153, 154, 180, 242
Internalizing 160

J

Judiciary 20, 26, 52, 147, 166, 179, 180, 181, 182, 189, 277
Justifiability 246, 253

L

Legislation 5, 9, 16, 20, 24, 26, 37, 47, 79, 128, 159, 193, 196, 203, 231, 236, 237, 259, 273, 274, 275, 276, 277, 278, 279, 280
Legitimacy 52, 55, 108, 154, 174, 177, 180, 182, 183, 203, 219, 235, 238, 255

M

Marginalized 160, 163, 172, 185
Misconceptions 155, 161
MSG 215

N

NGOs 15, 16, 17, 21, 23, 25, 54, 89, 95, 132, 134, 135, 136, 137, 184, 192, 200, 203, 217, 281
NWICO 198, 199, 200, 201, 208

O

OAS 18, 133
OSCE 126, 128, 129, 130

P

Participatory 98, 101, 103, 110, 111, 162, 186, 187, 277
Polarization 179
Politicization 178
Pornography 228, 251, 254
POWS 10
Predominantly 32, 48, 75
Prohibited 28, 49, 253, 254
Prohibitions 5, 9, 27, 247, 271
PRSPs 281
Psychiatric 209, 210, 211, 212, 213, 214, 215, 216, 217, 218, 220

R

Rationale 108, 225
Reconceptualised 90
Rehabilitative 226

S

SAPs 143
Separationist 170, 171

SHO 215
Sovereignty 46, 61, 118, 119, 174, 198, 232, 240, 241
Stability 97, 98, 131, 169
Sustainability 97, 98, 103, 110, 146

U

UDHR 3, 4, 41, 43, 44, 48, 51, 63, 131, 137, 172, 175, 182, 197, 198, 203
UNDP 139, 143, 144
UNESCO 190, 191, 198, 199, 200, 206, 208
Universalism 172
Utilitarianism 264

V

Violations 1, 2, 5, 6, 12, 13, 14, 15, 16, 17, 18, 20, 21, 27, 97, 116, 125, 134, 135, 136, 169, 174, 182, 183, 187, 233, 251, 276
Vulnerabilities 101, 102, 103, 104, 105, 106, 107, 109

W

WFPU 215
WNUSP 215, 216, 217
WSIS 201, 202